To John + Mary

Enjoy!

THE NEW YORK YANKEES ALL-TIME ALL-STARS

THE BEST PLAYERS AT EACH POSITION FOR THE BRONX BOMBERS

JIM GRIFFIN

LYONS
PRESS

Guilford, Connecticut

An imprint of The Rowman & Littlefield Publishing Group, Inc.
4501 Forbes Blvd., Ste. 200
Lanham, MD 20706
www.rowman.com

Distributed by NATIONAL BOOK NETWORK

British Library Cataloguing in Publication Information available

Library of Congress Cataloging-in-Publication Data available

ISBN 978-1-4930-3817-6 (paperback)
ISBN 978-1-4930-3818-3 (e-book)

∞™ The paper used in this publication meets the minimum requirements of American National Standard for Information Sciences—Permanence of Paper for Printed Library Materials, ANSI/NISO Z39.48-1992.

Printed in the United States of America

For Richard J. Griffin, who would have had an awful *lot to say about all this*

CONTENTS

Preface vii

Introduction: Setting the Stage ix

CHAPTER I: Catchers 1
    Yogi Berra 1
    Bill Dickey. 8
    Thurman Munson 12
    Jorge Posada 16

CHAPTER II: First Basemen 23
    Lou Gehrig 23
    Don Mattingly. 30

CHAPTER III: Second Basemen 37
    Willie Randolph 37
    Joe Gordon 42
    Robinson Canó 46

CHAPTER IV: Third Basemen 53
    Graig Nettles 53
    Alex Rodriguez 58

CHAPTER V: Shortstops 65
    Derek Jeter. 65
    Phil Rizzuto 73

CHAPTER VI: Outfielders 79
    Babe Ruth 79
    Mickey Mantle 87

Joe DiMaggio 96
Charlie Keller 104
Bernie Williams 110
Roy White 116
Earle Combs 122
Tommy Henrich 126
Reggie Jackson 130

CHAPTER VII: Pitchers 137
Whitey Ford 137
Ron Guidry 145
Lefty Gomez 152
Andy Pettitte 158
Red Ruffing 165
Waite Hoyt 171
Mel Stottlemyre 177
David Cone 183
Mike Mussina 189
Mariano Rivera 196
Dave Righetti 204
Goose Gossage 210

CHAPTER VIII: Manager 215
Joe McCarthy 215

CHAPTER IX: Optimization of Batting Order 219

CHAPTER X: Honorable Mentions 225

Acknowledgments 235

Appendix I: Statistics and Supplemental Factors Used
    for Rankings 237

Appendix II: Detailed Rankings 243

Bibliography 257

PREFACE

Let's say you're the manager of the most successful professional baseball team in history, with every past and current player available on your bench. Game time is approaching and the ump needs your lineup card. Who's your starting pitcher? The Chairman of the Board Whitey Ford or the Louisiana Lightning Man Ron Guidry? Is the cantankerous Thurman Munson behind the plate or the eccentric Yogi Berra? Who'll bat cleanup? Who's your DH? Combining statistical analysis, common sense, and a host of intangibles, I took a stab at answering these questions back in 2014 while writing for *Pinstripe Alley*, a blog dedicated to the Yankees on the SB Nation sports news website. What started out as a fun idea for a brief article leading into that year's All-Star Game will be expounded upon fully in the pages to follow.

Even after a deep dive into the numbers and history of each Yankee great, the choices made in this book are largely the same as the ones made for the original article. Here, though, you'll get an in-depth look into each player's Yankee career, highlighting key accomplishments, clutch moments, and anecdotes that make them stand out among their peers. For those that didn't make the cut, there are blurbs summarizing the careers of many very good, if not all-time great Yankees. As an added bonus, there's a section on how to optimize this Yankees All-Star lineup using the principles set forth in *The Book: Playing the*

Percentages in Baseball, a must read for any baseball fan fasci-
nated by the numbers behind the game.

Just as in the original article, the rules for constructing this
all-time All-Star team follow those that have been in place for
the Major League Baseball All-Star Game since 2010. That
means the roster will contain 34 total players. The starting nine
will include a designated hitter and the outfield spots will be
generic in that the top three outfielders will be chosen to start
regardless of specific position. The remaining 25 spots on the
roster will be filled with 13 bench players and 12 pitchers. No
strict guideline was set as far as the breakdown between starters and relievers on the pitching staff, just as there's no such
requirement for the MLB All-Star Game.

To fill the roster spots, I ranked players within each position based solely on their Yankee résumé, named starters by
taking the top ranked at each position, and stocked the bench
with the best of the rest. The appendix defines the context-
neutral metrics that were the primary ranking criteria as well
as the supplemental factors considered, such as end of season
awards and World Series play. Note that there was some sub-
jectivity involved too, as close calls had to be made with such a
deep pool of players to choose from. The Honorable Mentions
section covers all of those close calls, since those players deserve
at least a token shout-out.

My hope here is that every Yankee fan from the most
casual to the most die-hard can learn a thing or two about, or
at least look back fondly on, the great Yankee figures throughout history when reading these pages. Better yet, you can read,
disagree with the results, and be inspired to create your own
Yankees all-time All-Star team.

INTRODUCTION

Setting the Stage

During the course of baseball's great rollercoaster ride, one team has remained at the forefront, evoking strong feelings, for better or worse, from fans of every era. In 1913, the middling franchise formerly known as the New York Highlanders officially renamed themselves the New York Yankees, which soon became a household name. Babe Ruth's sale from the Boston Red Sox to the Yankees in 1920 sent shockwaves throughout the baseball world that are still felt nearly 100 years later. Baseball's biggest stage now featured its biggest star, who put on a show for the ages over the next decade, both on and off the field. As Ruth piled up home runs along with his young partner in crime Lou Gehrig, the Yankees started to win World Series championships and by 1937 their six World Series wins was a major-league record. At the same time, the Red Sox became perennial cellar dwellers and the Curse of the Bambino was born.

The Yankees' winning ways continued into the 1940s thanks to Joe DiMaggio, a graceful and charismatic center fielder who quickly asserted himself as the game's next superstar. He was the most prominent player to step away from the game to serve in the military during World War II. Accordingly, he was one of the biggest reasons for baseball's spike in popularity after the war years as he was named American League MVP and put the Yankees back on top with a World Series win in 1947.

The franchise somehow found another gear heading into the 1950s. Powered by Mickey Mantle, who was second only to Ruth in notoriety, and the unassuming Yogi Berra, the Yankees capped off their fifth straight World Series win in 1953. After near annual trips back to the World Series, their run of dominance came to a halt in the early 1960s. Berra found a new job with the crosstown Mets in 1965, and when Mantle retired in 1968, the team found itself off the baseball grid.

That all changed when a bombastic businessman named George Steinbrenner bought a controlling interest in the franchise in 1973. Ever the opportunist, Steinbrenner made sure his new team aggressively pursued Jim "Catfish" Hunter when he became baseball's first free agent prior to the 1975 season, just as the team's young core was beginning to gel. Similar moves over the next few years paid off as the Yankees returned to the World Series four times between 1976 and 1981, taking home the championship twice.

Steinbrenner's aggressiveness would prove to be his undoing. His erratic style—which included overpaying for stars well past their prime, defaming his actual star players, and an unhealthy obsession with hiring, firing, and then re-hiring Billy Martin as manager—resulted in competitive teams that never found success throughout the 1980s. Despite the lack of success, the Yankees remained a team that every baseball fan had an opinion on, usually a poor one, thanks to George's antics.

Heading into the 1990s, Steinbrenner's underhanded ways inspired Major League Baseball to suspend him. Without his interference, the Yankees patiently built a winning team by avoiding expensive free agents and found themselves in pole position for the American League pennant before the 1994–95 players' strike ended the party prematurely. The heartbreak didn't last long. In 1995 the Yankees returned to the playoffs for the first time in 14 years and although they exited early, it was clear they were one of the best young teams in the major leagues.

From 1996 through 2001, the Yankees dominated baseball in a way that hadn't been seen since their last extended run in the 1950s. They won four of their five World Series appearances and in 1998 they won a then–American League record 114 regular-season games on their way to the championship. With their captain Derek Jeter at the helm, the Yankees remained among the best teams in baseball for the next decade. However, they had only one World Series win in 2009 to show for it. In their infinite pursuit of the next ring, the team started to feel the effects again of overspending for aging players. In 2013 and 2014 they missed the playoffs in back-to-back seasons for the first time in 20 years.

The team quietly began a roster transformation in 2015 by significantly cutting back on free agent spending and making smart trades for young players with potential. On the strength of homegrown players, they made a deep run to the seventh game of the American League Championship Series in 2017 and lost to the Red Sox in the Division Series in 2018. They appear poised to remain a contender for years to come. The poster boy of this resurgence, Aaron Judge, is arguably the largest man to ever play major-league baseball. The hulking slugger was the American League home-run king in 2017, took home Rookie of the Year honors, and was runner-up in the MVP vote. Before long, he'll likely make the case for earning a spot on this all-time Yankee All-Star roster.

As any Yankee fan will be quick to remind you, and any non-Yankee fan will begrudgingly concede, the franchise is without a doubt the most prominent, successful one in baseball history. With 40 World Series appearances and 27 wins, 16 more than the second-place St. Louis Cardinals, they have the hardware to prove it. So what is it about the Yankees that has made them so successful? Why do they always seem to be at the heart of the baseball conversation in America? How is it that the Yankees can be the most loved *and* most hated team in baseball at the same time?

The answers lie within the characters that have donned the Yankee pinstripes over the last 115 years. They include some of the greatest players to have ever played the game, some who were extremely flawed human beings, some who were underappreciated in their time, and others who were as goodhearted off the field as they were talented on it. Here's a peek into the soul of the Yankees.

Chapter I

CATCHERS

Starting Catcher—Yogi Berra

You can't think and hit at the same time.

—*Yogi Berra*

For a man whose trademark was saying outlandish, nonsensical things, it's amazing how accurately this quote sums up Yogi Berra's career. His hitting style was anything but calculated. It didn't matter if a pitch was up in his eyes, skimming his shoe tops, or anything in between. If he could reach it, he was swinging. Thinking wasn't even secondary; it simply never happened during a Yogi Berra at-bat.

Such an unorthodox approach at the plate was made all the more peculiar by his short stature and awkward appearance. At just 5'7" with a face, body type, and gait that inspired childhood friends to nickname him after a praying Hindu yogi, intimidation wasn't an option for Berra. Despite, or perhaps even because of, his homely appearance, Yogi persevered his way to baseball's pinnacle, playing for the most World Series–winning teams (10) in Major League Baseball history. He also established himself as one of baseball's most irresistible personalities and remained in the spotlight well past his playing days.

1

Yogi Berra is considered one of the greatest catchers in baseball history.
BOWMAN GUM/WIKIMEDIA COMMONS/PUBLIC DOMAIN

A baseball career seemed like an unlikely path for Lawrence Peter Berra, born to Italian immigrants in 1925 in St. Louis, Missouri. His father didn't even know what baseball was. However, he grew up in a neighborhood obsessed with the game that also produced future fellow major-league catcher and Hall of Fame broadcaster Joe Garagiola. In fact, the childhood friends were both offered contracts after a tryout in 1942 with their hometown St. Louis Cardinals. Berra turned his offer down for lack of a bonus.

The Cardinals' loss turned out to be the Yankees' gain later that year when they signed Berra for a modest salary but included the bonus he desired. After a year in the minor leagues, Yogi spent the next two seasons serving in the Navy during World War II. His service overseas included being a part of the D-Day invasion of Normandy, and he returned home a hero. In 1946 he was called up for a brief stint with the Yankees to close out the year. He stuck around for good in 1947, splitting time between catcher and outfield for the World Series winners. Yogi made history in Game 3 by hitting the first ever pinch-hit home run in the World Series. Both the volume and quality of play increased for Berra in 1948, but his first of 15 straight All-Star selections was soured by the fact that the Yankees failed to return to the World Series.

Although he was a capable hitter to this point in his career, Yogi had a deserved reputation for being marginal at best behind the plate. That changed when Casey Stengel was named to replace Bucky Harris as Yankee manager prior to the 1949 season. The only man in Yankee history that would give Yogi a run for his money when it came to goofy looks and colorful personality had a plan for the young, struggling catcher.

Maybe it was because he could relate to the eccentric young star, but Stengel instilled confidence in him right away by making him the full-time catcher. He helped his case by also employing the services of Yankee great Bill Dickey to improve his play behind the mask, or as Yogi put it, "he's learning me all of his experience." Berra instantly improved to an above average catcher, and combined with his already potent bat, he helped the Yankees return to the World Series where they defeated the Brooklyn Dodgers.

That was the beginning of an unprecedented run of success for both Yogi and the Yankees. He remained in pinstripes as a player until 1963 and served as the team's manager in 1964. In the 16 years between 1949 and 1964, the Yankees brought home the AL pennant 14 times, winning the World Series nine times. That included a record five straight World Series wins between 1949 and 1953. All of this success was due in no small part to the wildly effective bat and surprisingly smooth play of Berra in the field.

During this period, Yogi reached the 20-home-run plateau 10 years straight from 1949 to 1958 on his way to establishing the career record for home runs by a catcher. The real highlight for Berra, though, was the three American League MVP awards he earned in the 1950s. In 1951 the 26-year-old Berra was the best player on a 98-win Yankee team and earned his first MVP by a slim margin. Since he didn't look the part of a baseball superstar, Yogi developed the reputation of being an overachiever and was admired for it. He finished in the top five of the MVP vote for the next five seasons, winning the award again in 1954 and 1955 amidst high praise from contemporary sportswriters. *Sports Illustrated* noted that, "Berra is the best catcher in the league," and Frank Graham of the *New York*

Journal-American wrote, "Everybody loves Yogi ... the best, the most consistent, [and] the hardest working player on the club."

Berra's durability and consistent production was often pointed to by writers as the reason that he was the key to the Yankees' success over young slugger Mickey Mantle. In their account of Mantle's Triple Crown season in 1956, authors Randy Roberts and Johnny Smith drive this point home, writing, "before 1956 the Yankees were really Yogi Berra's team. He was the club's most important player." Truly, though, the Yankees enjoyed so much success because they were both superstars playing at a superstar level. As the *Sporting News* noted of the dynamic duo, they were the "greatest one-two punch the Bombers have boasted since Babe Ruth and Lou Gehrig."

Berra continued to be a great teammate and manager's best friend during his waning years as a player. When the Yankees needed him to move to the outfield in the early 1960s to make room for the younger Elston Howard behind the plate, Yogi moved willingly. There he navigated the notoriously spacious left field in Yankee Stadium well enough to be considered average and saw no significant dropoff in offensive production. No matter the circumstances, Berra could seemingly do no wrong in a Yankee uniform. Casey Stengel once aptly summed this up by saying, "He'd fall in a sewer and come up with a gold watch." The crowning achievement for Berra as a player came during a game in which he was conspicuously quiet, yet it sealed the legacy of his Midas touch.

In 1956 the Yankees took on the Brooklyn Dodgers in the World Series. The series was tied at two heading into Game 5 at Yankee Stadium with young journeyman Don Larsen due to start for New York. With the series hanging in the balance and Yogi Berra behind the plate, Larsen for one day became the greatest pitcher in baseball history. At least part of his brilliance was due to the faith he had in his veteran catcher. More than 50 years after the game, Yogi clearly recalled, "He didn't shake me off once. He was throwing pretty hard and had a good breaking ball that day. Everything was working for him." After Larsen retired the first 26 Dodgers in order, he faced pinch-hitter Dale Mitchell and put the exclamation point on his perfect game by striking him out. An overjoyed Berra was the first to greet him by leaping into his arms and wrapping all four limbs around the lanky pitcher. Of course, the Yankees went on to win the series and his celebration with Larsen remains an indelible image for Yankee fans to this day.

Despite managing the Yankees to a 99-win season and a tough seven-game loss in the 1964 World Series during his first year on the job, Berra was unceremoniously fired. He was probably better off. As the Yankees spiraled to the bottom of the American League in the late 1960s and early 1970s, Berra found a new job across town with the up and coming New York Mets. By the late 1970s he came back to the Yankees as Billy Martin's bench coach as they won back-to-back World Series championships in 1977 and 1978. In 1984 he was promoted to manager, 20 years after his first stab at it with the Yankees.

The Yankees won only 87 games in 1984. However, he was well liked by his players, especially their budding star and American League batting champion, Don Mattingly. Given George Steinbrenner's assurance that his job would be safe from his infamously quick trigger finger in 1985, Berra agreed to return. That promise lasted just 16 games. With the Yankees' record sitting at 6-10, Steinbrenner gave Yogi the axe in favor of re-hiring Billy Martin for the fourth time since 1975. The heartbroken Berra was understandably angry, especially because the news was broken to him via messenger rather than in person. Berra vowed to cut all ties to the Yankees as long as Steinbrenner owned the team.

That unfortunate incident did nothing to tarnish Berra's legacy. When Yogi retired there was little doubt that he was the greatest catcher in baseball history, a claim that can still arguably be made today. Furthermore, he had the reputation of being impossible to get out, especially in high-pressure situations, due to his unparalleled ability to hit "bad" balls out of the strike zone. The only player since to rival him in this regard is recent Hall of Fame inductee Vladimir Guerrero, who is about twice the size and twice as athletic as Berra.

What has come to define Yogi, though, are the insane yet insightful things that would fly out of his mouth with ease. Whether it was about baseball ("Baseball is 90 percent mental. The other half is physical."), or life in general ("Always go to other people's funerals. Otherwise, they won't come to yours."), his one-liners inspired equal parts awe, laughter, and confusion from listeners. There have been entire books dedicated to Yogi quotes and some have a firm place in baseball's lexicon. The best of them came in response to the notoriety of his Yogi-isms: "I really didn't say everything I said."

Given Yogi's long run of success with the Yankees, it would have been unfortunate for his time in New York to have ended bitterly. Luckily, by 1999 Steinbrenner agreed, setting up a pleasant coda for Yogi's Yankee legacy. Prior to that season, Steinbrenner personally visited Berra at his home to apologize for his prior misdeeds. Berra accepted and the Yankees deemed a July 18 game at Yankee Stadium against the Montreal Expos as Yogi Berra Day. That day Yogi relived his greatest moment as a player when his old buddy Don Larsen delivered the ceremonial first pitch to him. From there it was déjà vu all over again. David Cone started for the Yankees and put together one of the greatest pitching performances in baseball history. He retired the first 26 Expos he faced and then induced a popup from Orlando Cabrera to third base to put the stamp on his masterpiece and Yogi's story with the Yankees. Perfect.

Reserve Catcher—Bill Dickey

I always say I owe everything I did in baseball to Bill Dickey. He was a great man.

—Yogi Berra

Before gaining the reputation of being a great catching instructor, Bill Dickey was a hell of a catcher himself. In the early years of the Yankee franchise, they had their share of star power, but the catcher position was a revolving door. When Dickey entered his prime in the early 1930s, he put an end to that, becoming the first legitimate star behind the plate in the franchise's history. Just like his protégé Yogi Berra, he did this by combining a potent bat, spectacular play as a backstop, and a masterful knack for getting the most out of his pitchers.

Born in northern Louisiana to a large family, Dickey had a baseball pedigree. His father and older brother played semipro ball while his younger brother George, also a catcher, spent six seasons in the major leagues. He started his baseball career bouncing around minor-league affiliates of the Chicago White Sox before being purchased by the Yankees prior to the 1928 season. That year he earned a brief callup and looked on as the Yankees sealed the second of back-to-back World Series championships. In 1929 he broke camp with the big-league club and played his way into the starting lineup. At just 22 years old he hit .324 to go along with 10 home runs and 65 runs driven in, proving his bat belonged in the vaunted Yankee lineup led by Ruth and Gehrig.

While Dickey was personally successful early on, his team found themselves as bridesmaids during his first three full seasons. From 1929 through 1931 the Yankees finished second or third in the American League behind the Philadelphia Athletics, who won over 100 games each year. Things started to turn around in 1932 under second year manager Joe McCarthy. The key to success was a vastly improved pitching staff. As Dickey honed his craft as a game manager, his pitchers reaped the rewards and the Yankees cruised to the fourth World Series title in team history. For his efforts, Dickey earned MVP votes for the first time. Better yet, an altercation he had during a game with the Washington Senators that July helped him to earn the respect of his teammates. With a running history of bad blood between the clubs, Washington right fielder Carl Edwards plowed through Dickey during a play at the plate, causing him to drop the ball. Edwards returned to the plate to make sure he touched it, only to be met with Dickey's fist in his face, breaking his jaw in two places. A contrite Dickey would say, "I never was so sorry about a thing in my life" and earned a lengthy suspension. Regardless, the scuffle stood as a testament to the catcher's willingness to fight for his team.

With continued improvement both as a hitter and catcher, Dickey was named an All-Star in 1933 and 1934. However, the Yankees returned to second fiddle status for three straight years following their World Series win. In 1936 Dickey kicked his bat into high gear, establishing then career highs in every meaningful offensive category. That was the start of a four-year run in which he averaged 26 home runs, 115 RBIs, a .326 batting average, and a 144 OPS+. The Yankees won the World Series in each of those four seasons as their pitching staff also continued to flourish under Dickey's leadership.

Starting in 1940, Dickey was pretty much done as a star player. As a left-handed batter, he was always more effective against right-handed pitching and he began to settle into a platoon role, sitting against lefties. After adding two more World Series rings to his collection in 1941 and 1943, Dickey left professional baseball for military service in 1944 and 1945. When he returned in 1946, the Yankees were a team in transition as ownership had just changed hands. When McCarthy stepped down as manager just 35 games into the season, the well-respected Dickey was appointed player-manager for the balance of the season. He didn't even last that long. The team stumbled to a third-place finish and a remorseful Dickey resigned as manager with 14 games left in the season, his last as a player.

As a hitter, Dickey has a case for the best offensive catcher in Yankee history. Using the Batting Runs Above Average statistic, he was a little over 30 runs better than the prolific Yogi Berra, albeit with less of a reputation in the clutch and in the World Series. As a backstop, he had the deserved reputation of being among the best fielders of his era and it was his favorite aspect of baseball. "I loved to make a great defensive play, I'd rather do that than hit a home run," he once said. What may be most impressive about Dickey's body of work, though, is the clear impact he had on the effectiveness of the pitchers he caught.

Oral Hildebrand was a major-league pitcher for eight years prior to being traded to the Yankees in 1938. In those eight years he was mildly effective, posting a 72-73 record with a 4.52 ERA, which was good for a 105 ERA+. He then spent the last two years of his career in New York, splitting time as a starter and reliever. In those two years he was a superb 11-5 with a 2.90 ERA (149 ERA+) and earned the only World Series ring of his career.

Prior to the 1936 season, the Yankees traded for Indians starting pitcher Monte Pearson, who was solid but unspectacular, with a 36-31 record, 4.21 ERA, and 107 ERA+. Working with Bill Dickey as his catcher for the next five years he improved to 63-27 with a 3.82 ERA, which gave his ERA+ a 10-point bump. On top of that, he made one start each in the Yankees' four straight World Series wins from 1936 through 1939, earning the win in each game and going the distance in three of them. He also made his only two All-Star appearances as a Yankee.

Last but not least is Red Ruffing, who was dealt to the Yankees from the Red Sox midseason in 1930. Ruffing's seven years in Boston can simply be described as bad, going 39-96 with a below average ERA+ of 92. He spent the next 15 seasons in New York, nearly all of them overlapping with Dickey's career, and became a Hall of Fame pitcher. During his career, he once alluded to Dickey's positive impact, saying "Dickey never has bothered me, never has shaken me off. He just lets me pitch my game." His 231-124 record while pitching to Dickey in pinstripes came with a 119 ERA+ and a spot on this All-Star roster. Bill Dickey was much more than a catcher who could hit. He was a magician behind the plate who could turn rags into riches.

Reserve Catcher—Thurman Munson

He has just the right cockiness, he's a born leader.

—Billy Martin

Heading into the early 1970s the Yankees were a once-proud franchise in desperate need of some cockiness and a heavy dose of leadership. In the 29-year period between 1936 and 1964, they appeared in a remarkable 22 World Series, winning 16 of them. However, for five straight years between 1965 and 1969 they found themselves no better than 20 games out of first place in the American League. Just as all hope seemed lost in the Bronx, the help they needed came in the form of a crotchety young backstop who would will the Yankees back to relevance by the middle of the decade.

The son of a sweetheart of a mother and a father who was probably the largest contributor to the sizable chip on his shoulder, Thurman Munson hailed from Akron, Ohio. A three-sport athlete in high school, he settled on baseball prior to attending college locally at Kent State University. By his junior year he was ready to play professional ball and was chosen by the Yankees as their first pick, fourth overall, in the 1968 draft. After spending less than 100 games in the high levels of the Yankees' farm system, Munson was called up to the majors for the final month of the 1969 season as their new starting catcher.

Although the franchise was struggling, there were some quality young players on that team including Mel Stottlemyre and Roy White, both members of this all-time All-Star team. Together with their new catcher, they offered a glimmer of hope in 1970. Munson hit .302, established what would be a career high in walks and on-base percentage, and was among the best fielding catchers in the league according to advanced defensive metrics. He was a near unanimous selection for Rookie of the Year as he helped the Yankees to 93 wins and a second-place finish in the American League East.

The good times would be short-lived as the not quite ready for prime time Yankees would fail to reach the 90-win plateau for each of the next five seasons. Still, Munson cemented his place as one of baseball's true stars during these years. He was named an All-Star four times, including three straight from 1973 through 1975, which coincided with receiving three straight Gold Glove Awards as the American League's best catcher. Heading into the 1976 season, a very much still in his prime Munson was just the man to usher his team into the "Bronx Zoo" era.

Sporting a badass, no-nonsense moustache to match his no-nonsense style, Munson officially became the face of the Yankees when new manager Billy Martin named him team captain in 1976. Being named the first Yankee captain since Lou Gehrig would have been too burdensome for most, but the fiery, zealous manager recognized the same traits in his star catcher and the move got the desired result. Commanding the respect of young talented players and hardened veterans alike, Munson led the Yankees to a first-place finish in their division and their first World Series appearance in 12 years. Along the way he drove in a career-high 105 runs and was named the American League's MVP.

Despite getting swept by the Cincinnati Reds in the Fall Classic, he went blow for blow with Hall of Fame catcher Johnny Bench, batting .529 for the series to Bench's .533 MVP performance. After the series, Reds manager Sparky Anderson rubbed Munson the wrong way when speaking to reporters as he said, "Thurman is an outstanding hitter . . . but don't ask me to compare Johnny Bench with any other catcher, don't embarrass anyone." Once hearing of Munson's displeasure, Anderson issued a public letter of apology. The curmudgeonly catcher grudgingly accepted.

Ever the competitor, the Yankee captain was hell bent on returning to the World Series the following year, but his leadership skills would be put to the test when George Steinbrenner brought the brash Reggie Jackson to New York on the team's richest contract. During spring training in 1977 the outspoken Jackson began a series of verbal jabs in the press with Munson, questioning his ability to effectively lead his team to a World Series title after their sweep at the hands of the Reds. He was later quoted in *SPORT* magazine as saying, "I'm the straw that stirs the drink. It all comes back to me. Maybe I should say me and Munson but really he doesn't enter into it . . . Munson thinks he can be the straw that stirs the drink but he can only stir it bad." Naturally, Munson took umbrage with the comments, but their tumultuous relationship off the field had no impact on the team's on-field performance. The Yankees won 100 games for the first time since 1963, and cruised to a World Series victory in six games over the Los Angeles Dodgers. Jackson's record-setting performance in the series earned him MVP honors, but Munson remained the unquestioned leader in the clubhouse.

The 1978 season saw Munson and the Yankees return to the World Series. Although his relationship with Jackson warmed after their successful 1977 campaign, the road back to the series was a tough one and Munson was clutch in getting them back there. Despite being 14 games back of the first-place

Red Sox in mid-July, the Yankees stormed their way back to tie them at 99 wins at the end of the regular season. That necessitated a 163rd game played at Fenway Park to break the tie. Bucky Dent's infamous home run gave the Yankees a 3–2 lead in the seventh inning, but two batters later Munson doubled home Mickey Rivers for an insurance run that was crucial in a 5–4 Yankees victory.

Four days later the Yankees hosted the Kansas City Royals for a pivotal Game 3 of the then five-game American League Championship Series. The two teams exchanged haymakers all game and in the bottom of the eighth Munson stepped to the plate down 5–4 with a runner on. Though not known for his home-run prowess, Munson belted a mammoth shot to the deepest part of Yankee Stadium near the left field bleachers, providing a lasting memory in Yankee postseason lore. That was the turning point of the series as the Yankees moved on for a repeat World Series matchup with the Dodgers, which they won again in six games thanks in part to Munson's seven RBIs.

Tragically, those would be the last great moments in Thurman Munson's far too short career. As gruff as he appeared to be in the baseball world, Munson was truly a family man who wanted to spend as much time as he could with his wife and children, even during the season. For that reason, he purchased a private jet and had eyes on learning to fly it so he could return home to Ohio often. The 1979 season found the Yankees listless and out of contention. That August Munson decided to take advantage of an off day by practicing landing his jet at a local Ohio airport. Inexperienced as he was, his third landing was botched, veering off into nearby trees. The impact of the crash caused the small plane to combust and in a flash Munson lost his life, sending shockwaves through the baseball world.

His Yankee family was hit the hardest. To this day the team grieves over the heartbreaking loss of their captain by leaving his locker untouched, even going so far as moving it into the new Yankee Stadium when it opened in 2009.

What stands as the most impressive tribute to the respect that Thurman Munson commanded, though, is the reaction of his fiercest rival to his passing. As the starting catcher for the Boston Red Sox opposite Munson for the entirety of his career, Carlton Fisk had his share of run-ins with the man. These did not end well, as bench-clearing brawls instigated by one or the other were a common occurrence between the hated rivals during their era. However, he was effusive in his praise of Munson when asked by reporters shortly after his death. "If we were the worst or best of enemies, it was because we had the highest amount of respect for one another. We both thought we were the best catcher in the league and we tried to prove it to one another that each of us was better than the other," Fisk said. "I respect the man so much . . . I really miss him. There was no such thing as hatred between us. I really had the utmost respect for him as a person." Thurman Munson was such an effective leader that even his worst enemy confessed that he loved him when it was all said and done.

RESERVE CATCHER—JORGE POSADA

He's the fiery guy. . . . When guys need a little kick, Jorge is always there for them.

—*Joe Girardi*

Lauded as a member of the Core Four Yankees who helped revitalize the franchise in the late 1990s, Jorge Posada was the

Jorge Posada congratulates Mariano Rivera after sealing a victory.
KEITH ALLISON/WIKIMEDIA COMMONS

one thing not like the others. Mariano Rivera, Derek Jeter, and Andy Pettitte were all known for their icy reserve, especially when tensions were at their highest. That stood in stark contrast to Posada, who wore his heart on his sleeve and was an agitator in crunch time. He was more than just an effective bad cop in the clubhouse though. Thanks to his remarkable durability and capacity to flat-out hit, Posada was a valuable asset to some all-time great Yankee teams. Along the way he carved a place for himself among the catching elite in major-league history when it came to hitting.

Drafted as a middle infielder out of a small Alabama college in 1990, the native Puerto Rican Posada had a steep hill to climb on his way to the big show. Never considered fleet afoot even as a young man, the Yankees decided to move Posada from second base to catcher against his will after just one minor-league season. Despite his displeasure, he developed his skills behind the plate and methodically worked his way through each level of the Yankees' system from 1991 through 1994. He spent the majority of the next two seasons at Triple-A Columbus while the other three-quarters of the Core Four became overnight stars for a Yankee team that won the 1996 World Series.

Posada broke camp with the Yankees in 1997, and for the next three seasons was deployed in a platoon with his future manager Joe Girardi. Although still unpolished as a backstop, Posada's offensive contributions as a switch-hitting catcher left the Yankees with no choice but to skew the playing time in his favor over time. Coming off back-to-back World Series championships, the Yankees cut ties with Girardi prior to the 2000 season, making Posada the full-time starter.

For the next four seasons, Posada earned All-Star honors and Silver Slugger Awards as the American League's best-hitting catcher each year. Uncoincidentally, the Yankees' run of success continued. After winning the 26th World Series title in franchise history, they returned to the World Series in 2001 and 2003, losing seven-game heartbreakers to the Arizona Diamondbacks and Florida Marlins. That 2003 season was a career year for Posada. He put up career highs in nearly every meaningful category, joined Yogi Berra as the only other Yankee catcher to hit 30 home runs in a season, and finished third in the American League MVP vote.

To top things off, Posada even flashed some of his trademark temper during a particular testy Game 3 of the American League Championship Series with the Red Sox. After the teams had traded beanballs earlier in the game, a fight erupted later between some brave Red Sox fans and Yankee right fielder Karim Garcia that spilled over to the Yankee bullpen. Posada sprinted all the way from home plate to join the fracas, showing his teammates he had their backs no matter how far away from the action he was.

While the Yankees faltered in the postseason for each of the next five years, Posada remained one of baseball's most productive catchers. This was particularly true in 2007 when he hit .338, by far a career high, was selected as an All-Star, earned his fifth Silver Slugger Award, and finished sixth in the MVP vote. That was a remarkable achievement for a 35-year-old catcher, but age caught up with him the following season. He made his first ever trip to the disabled list and appeared in just 51 games after shoulder surgery ended his season. The fiercely competitive Posada returned in 2009 at age 37 to belt 22 home runs for the World Series champions and added a fourth ring to his collection.

A few years later Posada's tenuous relationship with former teammate turned manager Joe Girardi nearly came to a head. Posada's reverence for former manager Joe Torre and philosophical differences with Girardi put them at odds, but the breaking point was Girardi informing him he would be a full-time designated hitter in 2011. With his career as a catcher over, the prideful Posada was devastated and later noted in his memoir, "When you take me out from behind the plate, you're taking my heart and my passion." Insult was added to injury when Girardi moved the slumping Posada to ninth in the batting order that May. In retaliation, he asked to be removed from the lineup entirely. Luckily, he soon apologized and returned to the team after his temper cooled. That October, he would put up a heroic effort, hitting .429 in a Division Series loss to the Detroit Tigers. Despite the rocky road they traversed, Girardi had nothing but respect for Posada afterwards, saying, "I don't think there is a prouder moment that I've had for Jorge."

First and foremost, Posada's legacy is tied to his ability to stay healthy and produce offensively. Unlike most catchers, he was able to play full seasons behind the plate without breaking down physically. Better yet he was a switch-hitter that could get on base and hit for power with equal effectiveness on either side of the plate. Per Baseball Reference's Batting Runs Above Average, he is eighth best among all catchers in major-league history. That's ahead of Hall of Famers Carlton Fisk, Gary Carter, and Roy Campanella. However, he had an unflattering reputation when it came to fielding his position. The numbers back this up as advanced defensive metrics rate him as nearly 60 runs below average for his career. Despite that poor rating, the pitchers he worked with spoke highly of the intangible effect he could have. Hall of Fame pitcher Mike Mussina spent eight years pitching to Posada and once said of him, "It's a lot more for him than just sitting behind the plate and catching, you have to talk to us (pitchers), you have to relate to them, you have to know what buttons to push. I think the success of this team shows how well he does because it does turn over quite a bit."

Speaking of pushing buttons, one can't describe Jorge Posada's legacy without mentioning his ability to get under his opponents' skin. Just as any Yankee lifer, Posada endured many battles with the Red Sox, especially with Pedro Martinez. Shortly after being elected to the Hall of Fame, Martinez was asked in an interview which Yankee he liked to hit the most. Without hesitation, he answered, "Jorge Posada . . . he always seemed to have a bad attitude towards me . . . he was always mad at me for some reason." Yankee fans everywhere smiled proudly.

Chapter II

FIRST BASEMEN

Starting First Baseman—Lou Gehrig

Gehrig never learned that a ballplayer couldn't be good every day.

—*Hank Gowdy*

No baseball player in history combined greatness and durability quite like Lou Gehrig did. As a hitter, he's surely in any conversation on the greatest all-time. As an Iron Man, he established the record for consecutive games played that stood for 56 years. As a character in the Yankee story, though, he was the diametric opposite of Babe Ruth. Each day he went about his business with a quiet, steadfast dedication atypical of someone with the immense talent he possessed. He was a hero the common man could relate to, which made it all the more difficult for the baseball world when an extremely rare neurological disease ended his career and life. Even with all of his achievements, his grace in the face of such adversity remains his greatest victory.

The sole survivor of four children born to poor German immigrants, Gehrig came from humble beginnings on the

Lou Gehrig paired with Babe Ruth to be an unstoppable force.

Upper East Side of Manhattan. He caught the baseball bug at a young age and visited the Polo Grounds often to see his hometown New York Giants play. In high school he was a two-sport star and then attended nearby Columbia University on a football scholarship. Despite being there to play football, Gehrig became the Babe Ruth of college baseball, a lights-out pitcher who could also hit. During his sophomore year a Yankee scout was convinced he was the second coming of The Babe after seeing him play just twice. A day later, general manager Ed Barrow offered Gehrig a deal to leave college for the Yankees. Eager to provide for his struggling family, he jumped at the chance.

For most of 1923 and 1924, Gehrig played in the minor leagues as the Yankees already had Wally Pipp, a two-time home-run champ, playing first base. Still, Gehrig was called up for two brief stints and impressed in his limited opportunities, hitting .447 with a home run and 13 RBIs across 23 games. The real highlight, though, was a run-in with the notorious Ty Cobb at the end of the 1924 season in Detroit.

After driving in two runs with a single, Gehrig got caught in a pickle between first and second. Cobb darted in from center field to tag him out, and finished the play with some four-letter words directed at the young slugger. Normally shy and reserved, Gehrig retaliated with his own verbal venom and continued yelling at Cobb from the Yankee dugout. He was tossed from the game, but that didn't stop him from intercepting Cobb on his way to the clubhouse once it ended. Not known for swinging and missing too often, Gehrig threw a punch intended for Cobb's face that found nothing but air. To make matters worse, his momentum took him headfirst into the concrete floor where he remained unconscious for a while.

When he came to, he at least had a sense of humor about the situation, simply saying, "Did I win?"

Gehrig started the 1925 season on the Yankee bench until a roster shake-up on June 2. Legend has it that manager Miller Huggins started Gehrig at first base that day because Wally Pipp had a headache possibly caused by a batting practice fastball to the temple. Those stories have proven to be unfounded. Truth is, Pipp was severely underperforming and with the Yankees out of contention, Huggins had nothing to lose by seeing what his new first baseman was made of. Gehrig went 3-for-5 that day and Huggins gave him a vote of confidence, saying "You're my first baseman, today and from now on. Now don't get rattled. If you muff a few, nobody's going to shoot you." For the balance of the season, Gehrig dwarfed Pipp's production.

Gehrig's bat improved further in his first full season as a starter, and with a healthy Babe Ruth back in the fold, the Yankees returned to the World Series in 1926. Gehrig performed admirably in the series, but the Yankees lost in crushing fashion as it went the distance. While he led the American League in triples, he hit only 16 home runs during the regular season. Huggins griped that as a lefty he wasn't pulling the ball enough to take advantage of Yankee Stadium's dimensions. The humble, yet hungry Gehrig took the criticism to heart. In 1927 he and Ruth went blow for blow in the first great home-run chase in major-league history. Serving as motivation for each other, they both had over 40 home runs by the end of August. Ruth caught fire in September and broke his own record with 60 longballs for the season whereas Gehrig settled for just 47. Even if he wasn't as loud and ostentatious as his partner in crime, Gehrig had sent a clear message with his bat. He was already among the best sluggers in baseball history.

With two all-time great hitters and a host of other quality bats in the lineup, the Yankees were dubbed Murderers' Row and coasted to an easy World Series win over Pittsburgh in 1927. Gehrig was named MVP as Ruth was ineligible per the odd rules at the time. His hot hitting was no fluke as from 1927 to 1933, an average Gehrig season included a .350/.452/.659 slash line with a 191 OPS+, 37 home runs, and 156 RBIs. There are Hall of Famers that haven't come close to that for even one season, yet Gehrig consistently did it for seven years. Ruth was similarly brilliant as the Yankees earned two more World Series rings in 1928 and 1932. Despite each slugger's importance to the Yankee cause, they got more bang for their buck from Gehrig. The brash Ruth negotiated hard for a salary that reached as high as $80,000 in 1930. Meanwhile, Gehrig never negotiated a raise once his salary hit $25,000 in 1928.

Salary gaps notwithstanding, Ruth forged an unlikely friendship with Gehrig. What started out as a tumultuous relationship due to their polar opposite personalities eventually warmed. Success on the field helped that, but Gehrig's mother was also key. Estranged from his mother at a young age, Ruth warmed up to Mrs. Gehrig, who often welcomed him into the close-knit Gehrig home for dinner. For Lou, a friendship with Ruth was also beneficial to his bank account. During the offseason he would take part in The Babe's barnstorming tours, significantly boosting his income.

In 1933 Gehrig made national news by playing in his 1,308th consecutive game, breaking Everett Scott's record for baseball's longest consecutive games streak. After the game

Gehrig wasn't impressed with himself as he mentioned he worked only eight months a year and said, "I think it's a real stunt, but I don't think anybody else will try it again." By 1934 a 39-year-old Babe Ruth was in decline and Gehrig, by then known as "The Iron Horse," became the main attraction at Yankee Stadium. That season he set a career high with 49 home runs, hit .363, and drove in 166 runs. He led the major leagues in all three categories, becoming just the third player in baseball history to win the major-league Triple Crown. Despite his continued personal success, the Yankees were second-place finishers in both 1934 and 1935, a disappointment for a player who always put the team first.

During the 1935 season, Gehrig's manager Joe McCarthy officially gave him the title of Yankee captain. He reluctantly accepted the role, but he was precisely what the Yankees needed in a leader as they embarked on an unprecedented championship run. In 1936 he had another monumental season, matching his career high with 49 home runs and taking home his second MVP Award. The Yankees won over 100 games, beat the New York Giants in the World Series, and introduced a much-hyped rookie named Joe DiMaggio. Gehrig heaped praise upon the headline-stealing center fielder, saying "I envy this kid. He has the whole world before him. He has everything, including the mental stability, to be a great one." That mentality ensured a smooth transition of power as for the next three years DiMaggio became the next great Yankee superstar while Gehrig's play declined. The Yankees were World Series winners all three years.

By the end of 1938, Gehrig's quality of play was in free fall. Some, even Gehrig himself, chalked it up to the fact that he hadn't taken a day off in nearly 14 years. However, keen observers feared that something more serious was brewing. His longtime teammate Lefty Gomez said, "To see that big guy coming back to the dugout after striking out with the bases loaded would make your heart bleed. He couldn't understand what was wrong." Leading up to the 1939 season, Gehrig severely underperformed in spring training and was reported as collapsing on occasion without explanation. Just eight games into the season he couldn't stand hurting the team any further and pulled himself from the lineup, ending his consecutive streak at 2,130 games. He would never play baseball again.

A month later Gehrig sought help at the Mayo Clinic, where he received the crushing diagnosis of amyotrophic lateral sclerosis (ALS). Slowly but surely his body would be robbed of the muscles and nerves that made him one of the greatest baseball players in history. Paralysis and death were inevitable, and sooner rather than later. It's a disease so rare that it has since become synonymous with his name. Such news would break lesser men, but Gehrig's spirit remained strong as ever. On July 4, 1939, the Yankees celebrated the life of their ailing captain at Yankee Stadium. With old pals Babe Ruth, Wally Pipp, and a host of others in attendance, an emotional Gehrig addressed the crowd by saying, "Fans, for the past two weeks you have been reading about a bad break I got. Yet today, I consider myself the luckiest man on the face of the earth." He went on to praise both his immediate and extended Yankee family. He finished with, "So, I close in saying that I might have been given a tough break, but I've got an awful lot to live for."

Less than two years later a 37-year-old Lou Gehrig lost his battle with ALS. He's still lauded as an all-time great hitter, yet his uplifting farewell speech in the face of his tragic diagnosis is what stands as a testament to the truly great man that Gehrig was. His words inspired 42,000 fans at Yankee Stadium that day, but have continued to inspire millions more every day since.

RESERVE FIRST BASEMAN—DON MATTINGLY

100% ballplayer. 0% bullshit.

—*Bill James*

At a time when the volume of bullshit within the Yankee organization was at an all-time high, Don Mattingly ingratiated himself with a rabid, angry fan base that still loves him to this day. That's no small feat considering that the entirety of his career spanned the longest World Series drought in Yankee history. With a thick moustache, copious eye black, and a smooth left-handed swing, he looked like a textbook baseball player. He lived up to that reputation on the field and was considered by some to be the best player in baseball during his prime. More than anything, what made him such a fan favorite was his unparalleled work ethic and discreet, yet maniacal pursuit of mastering his craft. While other stars of his era were beginning to get paid like rock stars and acted the part, Mattingly was a class act who still garners the utmost respect.

Growing up in Evansville, Indiana, Don Mattingly began to hone his hitting skills and competitive spirit by playing Wiffle ball in his backyard with his four older siblings. The unique dimensions of the yard rewarded opposite field hits from left-handers, a practice that Mattingly would continue in the major leagues. As a junior in high school, he was a key contributor to his baseball team's 59-game winning streak and gained attention from collegiate scouts regularly. With his heart seemingly set on playing baseball in college, the Yankees gambled with

Despite being a Yankee fan favorite, Don Mattingly never played in a World Series.   JIM ACCORDINO/WIKIMEDIA COMMONS

their 19th round pick in 1979, and it paid off when they convinced Mattingly to start playing professionally.

Over the first three years spent in the lower levels of the Yankees' minor-league system, Mattingly displayed that he had great command of the strike zone. Despite not showing much home-run power, he earned his first trip to the big leagues in 1982. In 1983 he was named to the Yankee roster coming out of spring training but found playing time hard to come by in his usual corner outfield and first base spots. Luckily for him, Bobby Murcer's retirement cleared enough roster space to get him in the lineup regularly in the second half of the season. At just 22, Mattingly hit .283 for the season and proved that he could hold his own as a major leaguer.

New Yankee manager Yogi Berra made it clear during spring training of that year that Mattingly would have a reserve role in 1984. The ultra-competitive youngster made it a personal mission to convince his manager otherwise. In March he told the *New York Times*, "This is kind of hard to swallow without getting any kind of chance at all and there's no way I can accept that. There's no way I can say, OK, sit back, relax and do that. I feel I can change their mind or at least make it a very tough decision to sit me down." Mattingly played so well for the balance of the spring that Berra had no choice but to name him his starting first baseman.

Thanks to new hitting coach Lou Piniella, Mattingly was able to add some power to his bat by shifting his weight better. By the All-Star break he was hitting .330 with a career-high 12 home runs. He made his first of what would be six straight All-Star appearances, but the highlight of his season would come down to its last day. Mattingly was tied with teammate

Dave Winfield for the American League batting title. At home against Detroit to finish the season, he had a monster game going 4-for-5 to edge out Winfield for the title with a .343 average. The Yankee Stadium faithful showered him with praise, christening him the next great Yankee.

Never one to rest on his laurels, Mattingly improved on that season over the next two years. He hit a career-high 35 home runs in 1985 to go with a .324 batting average and flashed enough leather at first base to earn his first Gold Glove. The Yankees' acquisition of Rickey Henderson that year meant he also had the greatest leadoff hitter of all time in front of him in the lineup. As a result, he led the major leagues in RBIs with 145 and took home American League MVP honors. In 1986 he may have had the best year of his career, hitting .352 with 31 home runs and a whopping 238 hits including 53 doubles, both of which led the major leagues.

By the end of the 1986 season, the 25-year-old Mattingly had gained nationwide recognition as baseball's next superstar, and for good reason. Even the advanced metrics back up his gaudy conventional stats during this time. Between 1984 and 1986 he led the majors with an OPS+ of 161. He also was fourth in the majors in WAR, just a few wins shy of first-ballot Hall of Famers Wade Boggs, Henderson, and Cal Ripken. Given that Mattingly gets the stiffest positional penalty among that group, that is quite an accomplishment. His greatness was also validated by his teammates. Dave Righetti, former Yankee closer and member of this all-time team, was able to observe Mattingly day in and day out and once said "he was the best player I ever played with and ever saw over a long period of time . . . [he] was the x factor." Perhaps his best endorsement came from inner-circle Hall of Famer Stan Musial who simply said, "He reminds me of myself." Unfortunately, Mattingly's stay on top of the game wouldn't last long.

His 1987 season was for the most part on par with his previous three-year stretch. He even made his way into the record books, setting the single-season record for grand slams in a season with six. During a remarkable stretch in July he also tied Dale Long for most consecutive games hitting a home run by going deep 10 times in eight games. Despite those accolades, he suffered his first career injury due to a congenital disk deformity in his lower back, which caused the chronic pain that would plague him for the rest of his career. In 1988 and 1989 he made his final two All-Star appearances, hit over .300, and earned two more Gold Gloves, but his power numbers declined thanks to his back issues. What made the end of his six-year All-Star run even more painful was the lack of success the Yankees had during it. Even after averaging 87 wins over that stretch, they had no playoff appearances to show for it.

Heading into the 1990 season Mattingly was the highest paid player in baseball, but his career would soon hit rock bottom. In a season where his back pain would reach a tipping point, he hit just .256 with five home runs as the Yankees finished dead last in the American League. He worked harder than ever that offseason to regain his form and was also named Yankee captain just prior to the 1991 season, a job he didn't take lightly. However, both he and the team improved only marginally. The only notable event of these years for Mattingly was a rather ridiculous public feud with Yankee brass over the length of his hair, which was lampooned in a classic episode of *The Simpsons*.

By 1993, the Yankees had shed their roster of overpriced has-beens who had been holding the team back for over a decade. They couldn't have hand-picked a better leader for a group of young, hungry players than Don Mattingly. He led by example, showing players the effort it took to be successful, and also provided sage advice for handling everyday life in the spotlight of New York City. Bernie Williams would later note, "As a young player, you get a chance to be a sponge and absorb everything around here. You take the good and make use of it and take the bad and discard it. Obviously, [Mattingly's] influence was a very good influence." The Yankees rode that good influence to an 88-win season, their first winning season in five years, and a second-place finish in the American League East.

Things were looking even better the following year as the Yankees took hold of first place in their division by early May and never looked back. Alas, the 1994 players' strike ended the season in early August and cancelled that year's World Series. The news was devastating for Yankee fans, who saw Mattingly's best chance for a ring slip away. The Yankees remained among the best teams in the American League when play resumed in 1995 and ended the season on a tear. They won 25 of their last 31 games to edge out the California Angels for the new wild card spot by one game. After they clinched, manager Buck Showalter said, "There is a silent torch that we have all carried for Donnie." Even the self-centered George Steinbrenner was pulling for Mattingly over anything else as he noted, "It's more important for Mattingly than for me . . . I think the guys rallied for him. I really do."

In his first ever playoff series, the Yankee captain didn't disappoint. He went 2-for-4 with an RBI in a thrilling win over the Seattle Mariners in Game 1 at Yankee Stadium, and stepped to the plate in the bottom of the sixth inning in Game 2 with a chance to break a 2–2 tie. Mattingly drilled a 1-0 pitch into the right field bleachers, breaking the tie and working the Yankee Stadium crowd into a frenzy of epic proportions. Lou Piniella, the Mariners manager at the time, even pulled his team off the field until it died down. The Yankees would go on to win, but found no luck in Seattle where they lost three straight, ending the series and Mattingly's World Series hopes. Ever the competitor, he took the loss hard. He hit .417 for the series, but his performance, cathartic as it was, provided only a small consolation. He would never play another game, but watched the team he mentored fulfill their World Series potential just one year later.

In 1997, the Yankees sealed Mattingly's Yankee legacy by retiring his number 23 and dedicating a plaque in his honor in Monument Park. In the ensuing years he served on the Yankees' coaching staff from 2004 through 2007, part of another World Series drought for the franchise. Still, he would always get the loudest ovation from the crowd while sharing the stage with far more decorated players on Old-Timers' Day. Since then he has moved on from the Yankees to manage both the Los Angeles Dodgers and Miami Marlins in his seemingly endless pursuit of baseball's Holy Grail. Yankee fans are conspicuously hoping that he'll fulfill that quest in pinstripes one day.

CHAPTER III

SECOND BASEMEN

STARTING SECOND BASEMAN—WILLIE RANDOLPH

You could see there was more there, though. This was when all sorts of crazy stuff was going on there—with Reggie [Jackson], with Thurman Munson. But Willie, with all the turmoil in those years, he was the professional.

—Fran Healy

Reggie Jackson made it clear when signing with the Yankees that he would be the straw that stirs the drink in New York. If that was true, then Willie Randolph was the ice, keeping everything cool no matter how crazy the concoction got. Randolph spent 13 seasons as the Yankees' everyday second baseman and at a very young age he showed extreme poise in a hostile situation. His quiet leadership also served the team well throughout some rough years in the 1980s as he was eventually named Yankee captain. What gets lost in the shuffle, though, is how great a player Randolph was for the Yankees. Contributing in ways that weren't fully appreciated, he consistently churned out valuable seasons and is in the discussion for best all-around player in franchise history.

A direct descendant of slaves from South Carolina, Willie Randolph was born to sharecroppers who sought better work in the Brownsville section of Brooklyn after his birth. The conditions in Brownsville would be no better for the Randolphs. It was one of the most notorious sections of New York City to the point that gang activity and drug trafficking were commonplace in the housing projects that Willie grew up in. Luckily, baseball was his refuge. Looking back on his youth, Randolph would later say, "I was totally zeroed in. . . . I was so focused on wanting to play major-league baseball that I had this mentality, this military mentality, even at a very early age." He even credited the poor field conditions for sharpening his skills as a fielder. After starting his professional career with the Pittsburgh Pirates, a fortuitous trade in the winter of 1975 sent the 21-year-old Randolph back to the city he hailed from.

In the late 1970s the Bronx resembled the Brownsville neighborhood that Randolph knew 20 years prior. Living conditions were poor, public funding was increasingly unavailable, and arson was common. As Howard Cosell famously put it during a live broadcast of a Yankee game, "Ladies and gentlemen, the Bronx is burning." Randolph didn't need to adjust to his new setting, and he became a key catalyst on an up and coming Yankee team. He was one of six Yankees selected to represent the American League in the 1976 All-Star Game as they returned to the World Series, but were swept by the Cincinnati Reds. Randolph's .267 batting average, one home run, and 40 RBIs didn't impress on the surface, but he was actually above average offensively thanks to his ability to draw walks and 37 stolen bases in 49 attempts. To boot, he was fantastic with the glove. His 19 Fielding Runs Above Average was by far the best mark among major-league second basemen that year.

The following year Randolph was an All-Star again and the Yankees fulfilled their championship potential. As their success on the field grew, so did the controversy off of it, but Randolph was never a part of that circus. He simply played at a high level every day and steered clear of the nonsense his teammates took part in and the temptations New York City offered him as a successful young man. Behind another strong year from Randolph, the Yankees looked to earn back-to-back World Series wins after a thrilling pennant race with the Boston Red Sox in 1978. Alas, he injured his hamstring at the close of the regular season and had to watch from the dugout. His replacement, Brian Doyle, became the Cinderella story of another successful World Series run for the Yankees.

Randolph continued his stellar play in 1979, but the sudden loss of captain Thurman Munson proved too much for the Yankees as they missed the playoffs. Powered by a career year from Randolph, the Yankees won 103 games in 1980. For the season, he hit .294 with a career-high seven home runs, stole 30 bases, and led the major leagues with an astounding 119 walks. Walk totals like that are typically reserved for sluggers who pose a serious home-run threat. Randolph was no such threat. What's more, he struck out just 45 times. His 1980 season stands as a testament to his razor-sharp batting eye, which remains underrated to this day. His bat stayed hot in the American League Championship Series against the Kansas City Royals where he hit .375 in a losing effort.

In what was a down year for Randolph, he went back to the World Series one last time with the Yankees after the strike-shortened 1981 season. He put up another heroic effort in a losing cause as he hit two home runs, drew nine walks, and never struck out against the Los Angeles Dodgers in the tough, six-game series. Still at just 27 years old, Randolph was probably the best second baseman in the major leagues despite flying under the radar. From 1976 to 1981, his 29.8 WAR at second base was more than three wins better than runner-up Bobby Grich. More than that, though, he was a leader whose winning attitude infected his teammates. Former Yankee pitcher George Frazier once said of him, "I just think Willie as a teammate was all about winning. . . . We didn't care about how much money people made or anything else. . . . And Willie was probably the king leader of that kind of stuff . . . he was also a very good leader in the locker room. A quiet leader. He was good at what he did." His partner on the right side of the Yankee infield during the early 1980s, Bob Watson, added "He was one heck of a player—not only a player, but he was a leader. He showed up every day, he gave you everything he's got."

The lack of postseason success the Yankees had throughout the rest of the 1980s was no fault of Randolph. From 1982 through 1987 he averaged nearly four WAR per season for Yankee teams that averaged 89 wins. He also mentored an up and coming Don Mattingly, whose leadership style would mirror Randolph's years later. For his efforts as a leader, and as a reward for his decade of service, he was named co-captain along with Ron Guidry prior to the 1986 season. This honor notwithstanding, when Randolph had the worst season of his career in 1988, the Yankees chose not to re-sign the 34-year-old in favor of Steve Sax who was fresh off a World Series win with the Dodgers. Randolph spent the rest of his career as a journeyman, albeit an effective one, before retiring in 1992.

The Yankees soon brought Randolph back into the fold when Buck Showalter named him the team's third base coach in 1994. Also serving as the infield coach, he maintained his position when Joe Torre took over as manager and through their dominance in the late 1990s and early 2000s. He left the Yankees in 2005 to take over as manager of the Mets, but by then his Yankee legacy was set in stone. In 24 years as a player or coach with the Yankees, he significantly contributed to winning a combined 10 American League pennants and six World Series.

In spite of those accomplishments, Willie Randolph remains a criminally underrated player, even among Yankee fans. He didn't have a single, great skill that made him stand out. Rather, he had a diverse set of above average skills that combined made him great. Those skills didn't result in the numbers or awards that were used to determine greatness during his era. As a batter he never hit for a high average, but was an above average producer thanks to impeccable plate discipline that kept his on-base percentage high. As a baserunner he never put up gaudy stolen base totals, in fact he never stole more than 16 in a season after age 25, but he was effective into his later years thanks to his ability to take extra bases on his teammates' hits. As a fielder, he never won a Gold Glove despite being among the best glovemen of his generation. This was due to his gift of grace that made difficult plays look easy, effortless even. Bob Watson would later say, "I called him 'Houdini at Second Base,' because playing first base, you see guys coming down on him as he's turning the double play, and very rarely did he get hit. He was up in the air, he did a sidestep."

Perhaps the best way to sum up Randolph's greatness is to quantify his skills as a batter, baserunner, and fielder via the components that make up WAR. In the history of the New York Yankees, only two players have been calculated as being at least 35 runs above average in all three categories. One is Rickey Henderson, undoubtedly the greatest leadoff hitter that ever lived and a first ballot Hall of Famer, but more mercenary than hero for the Yankees in his five seasons. The other is Randolph, who quietly showed up every day and played with a subtle grace that got him mostly unnoticed. Albert Einstein once said that the definition of genius is taking the complicated and making it simple. That's exactly how Willie Randolph played baseball.

RESERVE SECOND BASEMAN—JOE GORDON

The greatest all-around player I ever saw, and I don't bar any of them, was Joe Gordon.

—*Joe McCarthy*

In the late 1930s and heading into the 1940s the Yankees transitioned from one all-time superstar in Lou Gehrig to another in Joe DiMaggio. During that transition they continued to win the World Series on a near yearly basis, but in baseball, championships are never won on the strength of one player alone. Every Batman needs a Robin, so to speak. For the first half of his immortal career, Joe DiMaggio's Robin was Joe Gordon. Even as a rookie, Gordon played like a seasoned veteran. A virtuoso fielder at second base, he also hit with extraordinary power for the position. In his seven years in pinstripes, he was among the most valuable players on four World Series winning teams. It's hard to imagine the Yankees being as successful during that period with a lesser player at the keystone.

Born in Los Angeles, California, Joe Gordon's family eventually settled in Portland, Oregon, where he established himself as a talented, if unconventional, triple threat in high school. He was a star center fielder for his baseball team and a dynamic halfback in football, as one might expect. However, he was also a proficient violinist who was part of the symphony orchestra in Portland, a skill that no doubt helped his rhythm and timing when he was converted to a middle infielder on the baseball field. He attended college at the University of Oregon where he played shortstop for back-to-back conference champions and was also a member of the gymnastics team, further contributing to his skill as a fielder. In 1936 he signed with the Yankees and stayed on the West Coast to play for the Oakland Oaks of the Pacific Coast League, a Yankee affiliate at the time, where he impressed as their regular shortstop.

Gordon was major-league-ready heading into 1937, but seasoned veterans Frank Crosetti and Tony Lazzeri were ensconced as the Yankees starting shortstop and second baseman, respectively. Instead, Gordon spent that year with the Newark Bears where he was the best player on one of the greatest teams in minor-league history. Newark won 109 games and the Junior World Series. Meanwhile in the Bronx, Tony Lazzeri had the worst season of his career and was cut loose to make way for Gordon at second base in 1938. He didn't disappoint in his rookie season, clubbing 25 home runs with 97 RBIs and forming the best double play combination in the American League with Crosetti. In a World Series sweep of the Chicago Cubs, he hit .400 with a home run and six RBIs. The deadly Yankees had another lethal weapon at their disposal.

In 1939 Gordon improved to 28 home runs and 111 RBIs with a .284 batting average while making his first of five straight All-Star teams. The Yankees won 106 games and swept their way to another World Series win. Their streak of four straight World Series appearances ended in 1940, but that year Gordon reached the 30-home-run plateau for the first time in his career and continued to dazzle at second base. That made a decision by Joe McCarthy heading into the 1941 season all the more peculiar. Unhappy with Babe Dahlgren, the man who replaced Lou Gehrig at first base, McCarthy installed Gordon as his new everyday first baseman.

It only took 30 games for McCarthy to recognize his error and Gordon returned to second base that May, where his brilliance in the field wasn't wasted. There he formed another dynamic duo with rookie shortstop Phil Rizzuto and the Yankees made a triumphant return to the World Series. Contemporary accounts confirm that Gordon's move back to second base was a needed adjustment. *Chicago Tribune* columnist Irving Vaughan made the point in September of 1941: "Sending Gordon back to second . . . worked an overnight miracle. [Rizzuto] was a different player than when yanked along with Priddy [Gordon's replacement at second base] back in May. What made him a different player? It was the presence at his side of the peerless, experienced Gordon." Esteemed sportswriter Grantland Rice also offered a favorable comparison with their counterparts on the Brooklyn Dodgers: "Billy Herman and Pee Wee Reese around the highly important keystone spot don't measure up, over a season anyway, with Joe Gordon and Phil Rizzuto, a pair of light-footed, quick-handed operatives who can turn seeming base hits into double plays often enough to save many a close scrap."

Gordon had a career year in 1942. He combined his usual stellar glove with a .322 batting average and .409 on-base percentage, by far career highs. Despite hitting just 18 home runs, a career low to that point, his performance earned him MVP honors in the American League as the Yankees won 103 games. He narrowly won the award over Ted Williams, who earned the major-league Triple Crown that year and whose WAR was more than two full wins better. Even in defeat, the outspoken young slugger openly praised the Yankee second baseman for his victory, saying "I was glad Gordon got it. I really think he kept the Yankees up there." Things fell apart in the World Series as Gordon reached base just twice in 21 plate appearances during a five-game loss to the St. Louis Cardinals.

By 1943 US involvement in World War II was in full swing and Joe DiMaggio had put his career on hiatus to serve in the war effort. That left Gordon as the best player on the team and a de facto leader. His numbers on the season weren't impressive as he hit .249 with 17 home runs and 69 RBIs. However, he did draw a career-high 98 walks and led the Yankees to a third straight trip to the World Series. In a repeat matchup with the Cardinals, Gordon exorcised his demons from the previous year, hitting a home run in a Game 1 victory as the Yankees took the series in five games.

Gordon served his country in the Air Force for the next two years. He returned to the Yankees in 1946 but had a disastrous season thanks mainly to a variety of injuries. The team finished well out of contention even though they fielded a team full of championship-caliber players. To make matters worse, while Gordon was away the Yankees were sold to a new ownership team that had little use for aging, underperforming veterans. Co-owner and general manager Larry MacPhail publicly disliked Gordon in particular and sent him to Cleveland for pitcher Allie Reynolds. Just like that, his Yankee career was over. He remained in professional baseball for another 23 years as player, manager, or scout, but was never again employed by the Yankees.

Even if Gordon's Yankee career ended on a sour note, he cemented himself as one of the most productive players in franchise history. During his six-year run with the Yankees from 1938 to 1943, the only major leaguer more productive in terms of WAR was Joe DiMaggio. His home-run power notwithstanding, what truly made Gordon stand out was his sublime fielding ability. The advanced fielding metrics now available substantiate claims of contemporary sportswriters that he was peerless. Per Fielding Runs Above Average, Gordon saved 91 runs as a Yankee. That was tops in the majors, six more than runner-up and Cincinnati Reds second baseman Lonny Frey, and a monstrous 43 runs better than third-place Lou Boudreau, shortstop for the Cleveland Indians. What Joe Gordon lacked in longevity with the Yankees he made up for with an all-time great six-year sprint in pinstripes. He may have done it in the shadow of a Yankee legend, but he was lightning in a bottle nonetheless.

RESERVE SECOND BASEMAN—ROBINSON CANÓ

What does he look like? To me he looks like one of the best players to ever play the game. That's what he looks like.

—Bobby Valentine

During the mid-2000s the Yankees tried desperately to rekindle the magic that had sparked a prolonged championship run just a few years earlier. Their annual trip to the postseason was resulting in a first round exit more often than not. That meant no prospect was safe as the trigger happy George Steinbrenner demanded that the best major leaguers available be acquired at any and all cost in a futile effort to get back to the World Series.

Robinson Canó showing off his smooth lefty swing.
KEITH ALLISON/WIKIMEDIA COMMONS

Amid the madness, the lone Yankee prospect not flipped for a quick fix was Robinson Canó. Not trading Canó might have been the best move the team made during this era. He started out as a much needed breath of fresh air as a rookie, became a key contributor to the team's 27th World Series championship, and continued to play at a Hall of Fame level, nearly single-handedly keeping the Yankees competitive as they said goodbye to legends Mariano Rivera and Derek Jeter.

The Dominican-born Robinson Canó was destined to become a baseball player. His father, Jose Canó, was signed as an amateur free agent pitcher by the Yankees in 1980. Jose was a minor-league journeyman for over a decade. During that journey he named his son after groundbreaking Hall of Fame second baseman Jackie Robinson. Robinson spent his adolescence in Newark, New Jersey, with his mother, where he admired an up and coming Yankees team in the midst of a championship run. He took a particular liking to Derek Jeter and while watching a game on TV with his cousin once remarked, "You'll see, I'm going to be turning double plays with that guy someday." At his father's behest, Robinson spent his high school years back in the Dominican Republic where the Yankees signed him as a free agent at 18 years old in 2001. He was living out his dream, but his prediction as a teenager would be jeopardized frequently during his minor-league career.

Even with his major-league pedigree, Canó was never a top prospect within the Yankee organization. He started out as a light hitter and inconsistent fielder, but plodded his way up the ranks, steadily improving at the plate. At just 21 years old he was promoted to Triple-A in the middle of the 2004 season. However, that year he was mentioned in nearly every trade rumor that involved the Yankees. The Texas Rangers could have included him in the Alex Rodriguez deal but declined. Canó was also mentioned in two potential blockbusters near the trade deadline as the Yankees were deep into negotiations for the services of Carlos Beltrán and Randy Johnson. Both deals fell through thanks in part to Canó's lackluster ranking as a prospect.

Not convinced that Canó was major-league-ready yet, the Yankees signed Tony Womack to play second base prior to the 2005 season. Just a month into the season the Yankees were already five games under .500 and the aging Womack was an unmitigated disaster. With nothing to lose, they called up Canó and installed him as Womack's replacement. Still raw in the field, Canó was a major upgrade offensively. With him in the lineup, the Yankees went on a tear and he soon earned the respect of his new teammates. Less than a month after being called up, the Yankees opened a pivotal weekend series against the Boston Red Sox and trailed 3–1 going into the bottom of the sixth inning. With a runner on, Canó tied the game with a blast to right-center off of knuckleballer Tim Wakefield. The Yankees would win 6–3 and Canó's clutch performance instilled further confidence in his coaching staff. By August he was regularly hitting second in the order for a team that would win the division for the eighth year in a row. Even with his struggles in the field, third base coach Luis Sojo cited his poise and professionalism as the reason for sticking with him, saying "It was the attitude of the kid. I was a rookie before, and you get frustrated. But instead of getting frustrated, he said, 'O.K., I'm going to hit.'"

In typical frustrating fashion, the Yankees lost a close American League Divisional Series against Anaheim, though Canó did drive in five runs in five games. He kept that momentum going into the 2006 season where he hit .342, smacked more than 40 doubles, and was named to his first All-Star team. It was clear the Yankees had a potential superstar on their hands, even if the season ended in another first-round exit. In 2007 he hit over .300 and established new career highs in home runs, RBIs, and runs scored with 19, 97, and 93, respectively. Better yet, he drastically improved in the field as his 23 Defensive Runs Above Average led all second basemen. His improvement was thanks to better footwork and increased range, although he still had his fair share of mental lapses. This was backed up by Yankees third base coach Larry Bowa after a rough, three-error game for Canó against the Mets that May. The former Gold Glove shortstop said, "The one that bothered me was the one right at him, but he's getting to a lot of balls other guys don't get to."

For all the strides Canó made to improve his game, he took a step backwards in 2008. His batting average dipped down to .271 as his offensive production was well below average. He also let those struggles affect his glove, which fell below average again. Things got so bad that new manager Joe Girardi pulled him from a September game against the Tampa Bay Rays for failing to chase down a deflected ball in the outfield. He sat out the next game too, after which Girardi said, "I think it's important that everyone knows there are consequences when you don't do things the right way. We've all been taught that since we were kids. My intention was to make sure that Robby knows what we expect from him." The Yankees failed to make the playoffs for the first time in 13 seasons and Canó was at a career crossroad. Was he a flash in the pan whose best days were behind him at just 25 years old, or was his 2008 season an aberration?

In 2009 Canó proved that his early career success was no fluke. He racked up over 200 hits and scored over 100 runs for the first time in his career and hit a career-high 25 home runs. More importantly for Yankee fans, he accounted for one-quarter of one of the greatest infields in major-league history as they made a triumphant return to the World Series, their first in nine years. All of his struggles clearly behind him, Canó was ready to fulfill his superstar potential.

Between 2010 and 2013 Canó averaged 29 home runs and 107 RBIs, hit more than 40 doubles each year, and slashed .312/.373./.533, good for a 142 OPS+. He also steadied his previously inconsistent glove as he earned two Gold Gloves and was worth nearly 40 Defensive Runs Above Average. The baseball community recognized that Canó was the total package as he was an All-Star and finished in the top six in MVP voting each year. In terms of WAR, he was the most productive position player in the majors over this time period, edging two-time MVP Miguel Cabrera by more than a full win. Even with all of those accomplishments, the most special moment for Canó was during a game that didn't count at all. In 2011 he participated in the annual Home Run Derby during the All-Star festivities in Phoenix. He crushed 32 taters to take home the crown in front of a packed house, but he might as well have been in his backyard. His father Jose served up those batting practice fastballs and watched gleefully as they left the park. Big smiles and huge hugs were abundant and the Canós, at least for one night, reminded the baseball world how simple and fun the game can be.

Despite the extraordinary play of Canó during this time, the Yankees didn't return to the World Series. As the team around him got older and less productive, the burden of winning fell more heavily on his shoulders, yet he always put the team first. He said as much in 2013 when the Yankees dealt with a slew of injuries, telling reporters "That's what you want, especially when you don't have the main guys here. With most of the guys out, you want to do what you can to help us win games." After that season, the combination of a 10-year mega-contract offer from Seattle and a suddenly thrifty Steinbrenner family meant Canó would leave the only professional organization he had called home. He continued his great play in Seattle and was well on his way to the Hall of Fame until a 2018 suspension for steroid use undoubtedly soured his career in the eyes of voters. However, that should do nothing to tarnish his Yankee career, the entirety of which took place during formal steroid testing in Major League Baseball. For nine years as a Yankee, Robinson Canó played second base at a level among the all-time greats, and for that he should be celebrated.

Chapter IV

THIRD BASEMEN

Starting Third Baseman—Graig Nettles

I wouldn't trade him for any other third baseman in the majors. In fact, I wouldn't trade him for any other player in the majors.

—*Sparky Lyle*

Any pitcher who had the privilege of playing with Graig Nettles at the hot corner probably felt the same as Sparky Lyle did in the late 1970s. One of the best fielding third basemen baseball has ever seen, Nettles had a knack for making his most spectacular plays in clutch situations. It didn't hurt that he had the power and plate discipline to occupy the middle of a potent lineup. In the clubhouse he was always quick with a joke, but would just as quickly start throwing haymakers in defense of his teammates. As the grizzled elder statesman among a team full of stars, he was often an afterthought on the Bronx Zoo Yankees that won back-to-back championships. He didn't have Reggie Jackson's bravado or the leadership qualities of Thurman Munson, but he was just as important to that championship run.

Graig Nettles was born and raised in San Diego, California, where in high school he was a basketball star who happened to play baseball. He earned a basketball scholarship at San Diego State University where he also played baseball in the spring. By the time he graduated he no longer had the speed for basketball, but was a serious home-run threat on the baseball diamond. The Minnesota Twins made him their fourth round draft pick in 1965, and he spent five seasons with the Twins organization. In 1968 he played mainly for the Denver Bears, the Twins' Triple-A affiliate who were managed by Billy Martin. When Minnesota named Martin their big-league manager a season later, Nettles was a key reserve at left field and third base as the Twins took home the division crown. Looking back on that time, Nettles would say of his abrasive skipper, "The first month or so, I didn't like Billy. To be more precise; I hated him." After their success in Minnesota, though, they earned a healthy respect for each other.

With no starting role for Nettles, Minnesota shipped him to Cleveland that winter. There, Nettles was given the everyday job at third base and was a durable, high-quality player for some bad Indians teams. In 1972 he was sent packing again, this time to New York, and he couldn't have been happier about it. As a left-handed slugger he was a perfect fit for Yankee Stadium and after the trade he prophetically said, "If I could have picked the spot I wanted to go, it would have been the Yankees . . . I hope I'll satisfy the team and be here for ten years or so." At 28 years old Nettles was still in his prime and ready to join a young team whose future looked bright. In 1973 and 1974 Nettles hit 22 home runs each year, drove in at least 75 runs, was a human vacuum at third base, and played in all but nine of his team's games. With the Yankees finishing around .500 each year, a notable event for Nettles happened in September of 1974 when a broken bat single revealed six superballs lodged in it. He claimed that the bat was given to him by a fan. Luckily, better times weren't too far ahead.

Nettles put up another representative season in 1975 with the added bonus of hitting .267 and driving in 91 runs, both career highs to that point. He was also named an All-Star for the first time, but the Yankees were still hovering around .500. Manager Bill Virdon was fired that August and replaced with a virtual sparkplug and familiar face to Nettles, Billy Martin. The Yankees soon adopted the fiery attitude of their new manager. In a May 1976 game with the Red Sox, Lou Piniella threw a forearm into Boston catcher Carlton Fisk's face during a play at the plate. During the ensuing brawl Boston pitcher "Spaceman" Bill Lee was seen running his mouth until an irate Graig Nettles ended the conversation with a body slam that put Lee on the shelf for six weeks. It was clear the Yankees had an enforcer when they needed one.

More importantly, this new attitude got results as the Yankees won 97 games and returned to the World Series. Thurman Munson was the unquestioned leader of the Yankees and earned the American League MVP Award, but Nettles had a case for it as well. His 32 home runs, 27 Defensive Runs Above Average, and eight WAR all led the American League. Despite being swept in the Fall Classic at the hands of the Big Red Machine, Nettles was a key cog in the Yankee machine that was finally running smoothly. He was tremendous again in 1977, setting career highs with 37 home runs and 107 RBIs, earning a long overdue Gold Glove, and finishing fifth in the MVP voting. His 5.5 WAR led the team for the second straight year as they returned to the

World Series. This time, they beat the Los Angeles Dodgers in six games thanks to the heroics of Reggie Jackson, a player Nettles would grow to love and hate.

As the Yankees attempted to defend their World Series title, madness within the organization was at a fever pitch. Players, coaching staff, and the front office were all at each other's necks in the press. Martin resigned as manager before Steinbrenner could fire him and the team made it back to the playoffs by the slimmest of margins. Throughout the chaos, Nettles was rock solid. He earned his second consecutive Gold Glove, hit a career high .276, and tied Reggie Jackson for the team lead with 27 home runs. In a World Series rematch with the Dodgers the Yankees found themselves down 2–0 heading into Game 3 at Yankee Stadium and American League Cy Young Award winner Ron Guidry due to pitch. But on baseball's biggest stage, Graig Nettles's star would shine brightest.

Guidry simply didn't have his best stuff, and it was clear early on that he would need help. Nettles led off the second inning with a single and came around to score, giving the Yankees a 2–0 lead, but Guidry was on the ropes in the third. Already having let the Dodgers cut the lead in half, slugger Reggie Smith stepped to the plate with two out and a runner on. He crushed a one-hopper down the third base line that Nettles made a diving stop on and threw him out with ease, ending the threat. Two innings later the score remained unchanged and Smith again came up with two outs, this time with runners on first and second. He hit another hot shot down the third base line that took a wicked hop. Nettles got enough leather on it to keep it in the infield, holding Smith to a single and preventing any runs from scoring. The next batter, perennial All-Star Steve Garvey, hit a nearly identical shot down the line with the bases now loaded. This time, Nettles measured it up with a slick backhand and smoothly threw to second base to end yet another threat. In the sixth inning Guidry was in trouble again as he loaded the bases with two outs, still clinging to a 2–1 lead. It was All-Star Davey Lopes's turn to test Nettles as he roped a low liner that hugged the third base line. A lunging Nettles played the ball perfectly on a short hop as he turned and threw a strike to second base, pulling the plug on the Dodgers' best chance to change the game's momentum.

The Yankees would win Game 3, which proved to be the turning point in a series win to seal back-to-back championships. In the box score, what looked like four groundballs to Nettles made up one of the most impressive performances in World Series history. In victory, a struggling Guidry was thankful, saying "I had to go with something else tonight. I picked on a man who is dependable." In defeat, his two-time victim Reggie Smith added, "It's Dodgers 2, Nettles 1. If we hadn't been losing, I may have applauded myself," while Dodgers third base coach Preston Gomez, who had the best seat in the house, commented, "It was quite an exhibition. I say he's as good as Brooks Robinson."

The 1978 World Series would prove to be Nettles's last hurrah as a true star. As he reached his mid-30s his incredible durability began to take its toll on the quality of his play. Nevertheless, he remained a prominent Yankee figure for the next five seasons, even serving as team captain in 1982 and 1983, before playing for other clubs well into his 40s. During his waning Yankee years his biting, sarcastic sense of humor made him an excellent source of one-liners. When the Yankees traded his old pal and 1977 Cy Young Award winner, Sparky Lyle, he was quoted as saying, "He went from Cy Young to sayonara in one year." When asked about the biggest advantage and disadvantage of playing in New York, to both he answered, "Watching Reggie Jackson play." Perhaps his best line was a reflection on playing for the Billy Martin–led Yankees in the late 1970s and early 1980s. Nettles offered, "Some kids want to run away from home and join the circus. Others want to play baseball. I got to do both."

For all of the nonsense going on with the Yankees during Nettles's tenure, he seemed impervious to it. While he had his fair share of contract squabbles with George Steinbrenner, a rite of passage for any Yankee star of that era, the only true fights he had were with the opposition. Unlike some of his teammates, he steered clear of any drama thanks to a reputation that earned the nickname "Puff" for his ability to disappear from late night parties without a trace. Most importantly, though, Graig Nettles was a hell of a ballplayer, arguably the best on some all-time great Yankee teams, even if he never got credit for it.

RESERVE THIRD BASEMAN—ALEX RODRIGUEZ

Nobody has ever worked harder in my memory than this guy.

—Joe Torre

Few players have ever been blessed with more talent than Alex Rodriguez. Add to it a work ethic that a baseball lifer like Joe Torre called the best he'd ever seen and you have an especially dangerous combination. Rodriguez was the brightest star in baseball when he found his way to New York, a reputation he was well aware of and spent a lot of effort maintaining. As a Yankee he continued his assault on the record books, even if early exits in October were common. It was revealed during

Alex Rodriguez was a two time MVP with the Yankees.
KEITH ALLISON/WIKIMEDIA COMMONS

these years that his pursuit of perfection at all costs included liberal use of performance-enhancing drugs, a revelation that earned him the longest drug-related suspension in major-league history. To his credit, the experience was a humbling one, and he was able to end his career on relatively good terms with the Yankees and their fans.

Born to Dominican parents in New York before ultimately settling in Miami, Rodriguez was a baseball phenom. The first overall pick by Seattle in the 1993 MLB draft, he was the ultimate five-tool shortstop and in 2000 he signed the largest free agent contract in sports history, a 10-year, $252 million deal to play for the Texas Rangers. There he was a perennial home-run king for last-place Ranger teams before he realized that the money alone wasn't enough. In 2003 the Rangers had a deal in place with the Red Sox that involved a pay cut for Rodriguez. The players' union quickly nixed that deal, insisting that he cash in on every cent of his mega-deal.

Enter the evil empire. In January of 2004 the Yankees' incumbent third baseman Aaron Boone tore up his knee while playing basketball. They suddenly had an opening at third base that they soon learned Rodriguez was willing to fill. By February, the Yankees agreed to a deal that sent their star second baseman Alfonso Soriano to Texas in exchange for Rodriguez and roughly $60 million in deferred cash to cover some of his remaining salary.

When news of the trade broke, there was some concern in Yankee Universe about what had become an icy relationship between Rodriguez and Derek Jeter. Once the best of friends, in an interview conducted right after striking it rich in Texas, Rodriguez publicly questioned Jeter's role in the Yankees' recent success. He personally apologized when the regrettable comments were published, yet Jeter's response was lukewarm. During spring training the tension between them was a hot topic, but Jeter quickly squashed it, saying, "It's over with and done with. . . . We don't have problems."

In his first season in pinstripes Rodriguez hit .286 with 36 home runs and over 100 RBIs and runs scored. A great season, but not up to the lofty standard he had set for himself in his career. He did, however, take center stage in the Yankee–Red Sox rivalry again during a July game in which Bronson Arroyo hit him with a pitch. Rodriguez slowly walked to first with some inflammatory words aimed at Arroyo before Boston catcher Jason Varitek stopped him with a mitt to the face. A bench-clearing brawl ensued, stoking the flames of a feud that was already at a fever pitch. Rodriguez was ejected from the game and the Yankees would lose it in walkoff fashion. However, their worst embarrassment at the hands of the Red Sox was yet to come.

In the 2004 American League Championship Series the Yankees took a commanding 3–0 lead in a rematch with the Red Sox. In the top of the eighth inning of Game 6, the Yankees were trailing 4–2. With Jeter on first, Rodriguez had a chance to regain control of the series with one swing. Alas, facing his old nemesis Arroyo he hit a dribbler up the first base line and inexplicably slapped the ball out of Arroyo's glove when a tag was attempted. Amid the chaos, the ball wasn't called dead immediately and Jeter seemingly scored, but an umpire conference ruled Rodriguez out on interference and Jeter back to first. One game later the Red Sox broke the most infamous curse in sports. After Game 3, Rodriguez was one of many Yankees who struggled, going just 2-for-17, but he was poised to come back better than ever.

Right out of the gate in 2005, Rodriguez lived up to his excessive hype and salary. On April 26 the Yankees hosted the Los Angeles Angels, and he made history by going 4-for-5 including three home runs, one of them a grand slam, and 10 RBIs, a Yankee Stadium record. Of his old pal's monster night, Derek Jeter commented, "You don't see too many days like that. That's once in a lifetime." By midsummer he smashed his 400th career home run and finished the season with a robust .321/.421/.610 slash line, good for a 173 OPS+. He also hit 48 home runs, a Yankee record for a righty, and easily won the American League MVP. His performance pushed the Yankees to a first-place finish in a tight race with Boston, yet he showed atypical maturity when asked about it. That September he told reporters, "You throw stats and everything away. The only thing that matters at this point in my career is winning the ultimate prize."

The following season Rodriguez had a great year that got lost in the shine of his MVP campaign. He "only" hit .290 with 35 home runs and 121 RBIs as the Yankees earned their ninth straight division crown. He followed that up in 2007 with a career year. He dominated pitchers from start to finish, sporting an OPS+ of 176 with 54 home runs, 156 RBIs, and 143 runs scored. Each led the major leagues. That August he also joined the exclusive 500-home-run club on his way to another MVP Award. Manager Joe Torre recognized his importance to the Yankee cause. After two Rodriguez homers sealed a victory in Kansas City down the stretch, he said, "The bad side of this is, he does it so often, you're surprised when he doesn't do it. I'm still marveled. It's an honor to watch this stuff. And it's in a pennant race, which makes it special."

The downside of these years for both the Yankees and Rodriguez was that each season ended with a first round exit in the playoffs. While most Yankees struggled during these series, Rodriguez came up conspicuously small given his huge role in getting the Yankees there in the first place. From 2005 to 2007 he hit just .159 in postseason play with rock bottom coming in 2006. Against the Detroit Tigers he was so ineffective that he was moved to eighth in the batting order for the final game as he finished a dismal 1-for-14. Despite the Jekyll and Hyde routine, the Yankees were about to double-down on the Alex Rodriguez experiment.

Rodriguez opted out of the final three years of his contract after the 2007 season. The Yankees publicly vowed not to pursue Rodriguez as a free agent since the Rangers would no longer pay part of his salary. However, less than a month later Rodriguez blamed his agent, the notorious Scott Boras, for the opt-out and met privately with the Yankees to bury the hatchet. It worked. Shortly after Thanksgiving he inked a record 10-year, $275 million deal to remain a Yankee. Unfortunately, they would still miss the playoffs for the first time in 14 years in 2008.

That was the least of his worries when in February 2009 *Sports Illustrated* dropped a bombshell revealing that Rodriguez was one of 104 players who tested positive for performance-enhancing drugs in 2003 during Major League Baseball's supposedly anonymous survey testing. This was especially embarrassing since he had publicly gone out of his way to deny steroid use in the past. Soon after, Rodriguez said in a series of damage control interviews that he used steroids only while in Texas in order to live up to his massive contract. As the Yankees tried to move on from the story, he added injury to insult and missed the first month of the season with a bad hip. When he returned in May, he injected life into a struggling lineup. He reached the 30-home-run and 100-RBI mark in just 124 games as the Yankees amassed 103 wins. He also finally played in the World Series, beating the Phillies in six games. Rodriguez even exorcised his past playoff demons, hitting .365 with six home runs and 18 RBIs. Still, the champagne would have tasted sweeter had his past transgressions not been front and center all year.

For the next three seasons the Yankees remained contenders, even as Rodriguez's production and playing time dipped due to injuries. In 2013 hip surgery kept him out of action for most of the year, but by midseason he was neck-deep in another steroid controversy. He was linked to a shady health clinic supplying athletes with illegal performance enhancers and a circus ensued. Rodriguez, his entourage, the owner of the clinic, MLB officials, and the Yankees' front office engaged in a war of words that involved bribery, lies, and ugly accusations. In the end everybody looked bad, especially Rodriguez. He appeared in 44 games to close out the season, but was suspended for the entirety of 2014.

Rodriguez wisely used that time to take a step back and rehabilitate his career. While he nursed back to full health he apologized in person to Yankee and MLB officials. In 2015 he returned to the playing field to a chorus of boos everywhere he went but handled it with surprising humility. Serving as the Yankees' regular designated hitter, he also had a renaissance season with the bat, reaching 30 home runs for the first time in five years and playing a key role in their return to the playoffs. Miraculously, his newfound attitude and rediscovered power stroke won fans over and by season's end the boos turned to cheers when Rodriguez stepped to the plate.

A year later the 40-year-old Rodriguez found it difficult to stay on the field or be effective when he was on it. He and the Yankees decided that his last game in pinstripes would be an August matchup with the Tampa Bay Rays. Mother Nature honored his Yankee career beautifully when torrential rain interrupted a pregame ceremony dedicated to him. Rodriguez's comments afterwards were equally appropriate for his Yankee career as he said, "It was certainly biblical. You can't make that up. I guess we went out with a bang."

Chapter V

SHORTSTOPS

Starting Shortstop—Derek Jeter

He was more of a leader than anyone knew. We had a relentless nature where nobody gave away an at-bat no matter what the score was, and that's who Derek was.

—David Cone

If someone in the mid-1990s could have built Frankenstein's monster using only Yankee legends, the result would have been Derek Jeter. He had the workmanlike attitude and quiet leadership skills of his immediate predecessors Don Mattingly and Willie Randolph. In clutch situations, he had Reggie Jackson's flair for the dramatic. He was blessed with Joe DiMaggio's pure hitting prowess, grace, and charisma. Off the field, his good looks and reputation as a ladies' man were a page out of Mickey Mantle's book. While not known as a slugger, when the moment called for it he could channel Ruthian power to Yankee Stadium's right field. All of these immense talents were kept in check thanks to a humble nature second only to Lou Gehrig. Derek Jeter was quite simply the ultimate Yankee.

Derek Jeter stroking a trademark opposite field hit.
ONETWO1/WIKIMEDIA COMMONS

Born less than 30 miles from Yankee Stadium in Pequannock, New Jersey, Jeter became a Yankee fan young, even after moving to Kalamazoo, Michigan, at age four. In high school he was a star in cross-country and basketball, but his main focus was on baseball, where his star shone brightest.

Prior to his senior year, he had already earned a full scholarship to play for the University of Michigan. After graduation, he was the consensus top high school player in the country. His coach, Don Zomer, noted, "He's got it all, and I still say he's a better person than a baseball player."

The Yankees had an uncharacteristically high pick in the 1992 draft and selected Jeter sixth overall. Unable to pass up his childhood dream, Jeter skipped college and signed with the Yankees.

As a bright-eyed 18-year-old, Jeter struggled at first in the lower levels of the Yankees' minor-league system. However, in 1993 he found his rhythm by spending the entire season at Single-A Greensboro. The following year he rifled through every other level of the minors, finishing with a combined slash line of .344/.410/.463 and 50 stolen bases.

By season's end he was named the 16th best prospect in the country by *Baseball America*. Better yet, he forged strong relationships with three teammates: Andy Pettitte, Jorge Posada, and Mariano Rivera.

Heading into the 1995 season, the only thing standing between Jeter and becoming the regular shortstop in the Bronx was veteran Tony Fernandez. When Fernandez went down with an injury in late May, Jeter was called up to fill in as the starter. In the 13 games that he started, the Yankees went just 3-10, but at only 20 years old Jeter gained invaluable big-league experience.

Jeter entered 1996 as the starter at shortstop, and he announced his presence with a bang. In his second at-bat of the season on Opening Day in Cleveland, he hit a monster home run to left field off of Dennis Martinez as the Yankees cruised to a 7–1 victory over the defending American League champs. From there, he played like a seasoned veteran on a Yankee team that was poised for something special. Yankee manager Joe Torre noticed: "He's taken on a lot of responsibility. He's playing a key position for a first-place team in New York City. That's a lot." Jeter finished strong with a 17-game hitting streak in September. On the strength of his .314 average, 10 home runs, and 104 runs scored, he was a unanimous choice for the American League Rookie of the Year for the first-place Yankees. As the stage got brighter heading into postseason play, Jeter rose to the occasion.

After hitting over .400 in an easy Division Series win over the Texas Rangers, Jeter and the Yankees took on the Baltimore Orioles in the League Championship Series. In Game 1 they trailed 4–3 in the bottom of the eighth when Jeter stepped to the plate with one out. He hit a flyball to deep right field that appeared to clear the fence and was ruled a home run by the right field umpire, tying the game.

Television replays showed a young fan catching the ball well short of the fence, robbing Baltimore right fielder Tony Tarasco of a chance to make the play. An irate Tarasco pled his case, but the call stood and the Yankees would take the series in five games.

Defending champs the Atlanta Braves pummeled the Yankees in World Series Games 1 and 2, but Jeter and his teammates kept their composure. Jeter helped the Yankees methodically dismantle the Braves in the next four games to end the longest World Series drought in team history. At just 22 years old, Jeter was on top of the baseball world.

In 1997 Jeter's batting average dipped to .291 and the Yankees lost a heartbreaking Division Series in five games to the Cleveland Indians. Most considered the season a sophomore slump for Jeter, although more walks and extra base hits actually made him more productive offensively than the previous season.

The following year, Jeter and the Yankees would remove any doubt about their abilities. They steamrolled through the regular season winning 114 games, 22 more than the second-place Red Sox. They made it 125 after sweeping the San Diego Padres for an easy World Series victory. Throughout it all, Jeter hit 19 home runs with 30 stolen bases and led his league with 127 runs scored. His 7.5 WAR paced his team by a large margin, and he finished third in the American League MVP vote.

Jeter's encore performance in 1999 was even better. As a team the Yankees regressed to 98 wins, but that was still tops in the American League and they swept another World Series, this time over the Braves. Jeter put up numbers that would stand as career highs in runs scored, hits, triples, home runs, RBIs, walks, batting average, and OPS. His 8.0 WAR was best in the majors among position players, yet he finished only sixth in the MVP vote. Joe Torre continued his praise when he told the *New York Times*, "You're watching a Yankee player that's going to rank up there with some of the best."

The Yankees would have a rough go at defending their back-to-back championships in 2000, but Jeter would ultimately get the MVP recognition he deserved. He was named the American League's starting shortstop for that year's All-Star Game in Atlanta and went 3-for-3 with two RBIs as they defeated the National League 6–3. For his efforts, he earned the game's MVP award.

The Yankees won just 87 games during the regular season but won hard-fought battles over Oakland and Seattle to return to the World Series. This time, they would take on their crosstown rival New York Mets in the first Subway Series since their win over the Brooklyn Dodgers in 1956. Overall for the series, Jeter hit .409 with two home runs and was the first player ever to be named the MVP of the All-Star Game and World Series in the same season.

They seemed poised to add a fourth consecutive World Series win to their collection in 2001, and during that year's playoffs, Jeter added two memorable moments to his growing postseason legend. The first came in a Division Series rematch with the Oakland A's. Down 2–0 in a best of five series, the Yankees clung to a 1–0 lead in the bottom of the seventh inning in Game 3.

With Jeremy Giambi on first, Oakland's Terrence Long doubled to right field where Shane Spencer's throw home sailed over the heads of two cutoff men and seemed well off target. From shortstop, Jeter charged to the first base line to intercept the ball and, in one motion, redirect it to catcher Jorge Posada. Giambi was called out by the closest of margins. The Yankees held on to win Game 3 1–0 and take the series in five games. After the game Jeter downplayed his contribution, saying, "I just got there and picked the ball up."

His star would shine again in the World Series when the Yankees needed him most. Down 2–1 in the series against the Arizona Diamondbacks, they headed into extra innings in Game 4 at Yankee Stadium. Due to the tragic events of 9/11 in 2001, the Fall Classic started later than usual and on this day, extra innings meant that the calendar flipped to November for the first time ever in a major-league game.

On a full count with two out in the bottom of the 10th, Jeter drove the next pitch over the short right field fence to win the game and even the series at two games apiece. In an homage to Reggie Jackson's Mr. October moniker, Jeter was dubbed Mr. November. Alas, the Yankees would dramatically lose the series in seven games, ending their streak.

The following season would end no better as a 103-win Yankee team was ousted in the Division Series by a red hot Anaheim Angels team that would go on to win a thrilling World Series. The disappointment for Jeter continued on Opening Day in 2003 when he separated his shoulder sliding into third base and was placed on the disabled list for the first time in his career.

Shortly after Jeter returned to action, George Steinbrenner officially named him captain of the Yankees. That October, Jeter conjured more postseason magic during an intense Game 7 with the Red Sox for the American League pennant. Trailing 5–2 in the bottom of the eighth inning, he stroked a one-out double to right field off of Pedro Martinez to spark a rally that would tie the game. Three innings later Aaron Boone's walkoff home run punched the Yankees' ticket to the World Series.

By 2004, Jeter's 45.1 WAR was the best among major-league shortstops, outside of his new teammate Alex Rodriguez, since his rookie year. His key role in four World Series championships, as well as two other pennants, gave him a reputation as baseball's greatest winner. He was also savvy as they come with the media and extremely humble, especially in victory. Respect and admiration can only go so far though, as the Yankees failed to make it past the first round of the playoffs from 2005 through 2008. The suddenly aging yet still productive Jeter headed into 2009 with a sense of urgency to freshen up the stale atmosphere in the Bronx.

The Yankees spent big in free agency heading into 2009, yet the biggest reason for their return to the World Series was their 35-year-old captain. As expected, he had a stellar year with the bat, hitting .334 with 18 home runs and even adding 30 stolen bases. Yet what made his season stand out was his improved play in the field.

Throughout his career Jeter, a five-time Gold Glove winner, looked smooth playing shortstop and could on occasion make highlight reel plays. The reality is that he was a poor shortstop. In fact, according to Defensive Runs Above Average, for his career Jeter cost his team 243 runs with the glove, the worst mark in major-league history by nearly 50 runs.

In 2009, however, infield coach Mick Kelleher aggressively changed Jeter's pre-play positioning in the field, yielding positive results. He led a 103-win team with 6.6 WAR as they cruised to the World Series. There, he would hit over .400 in his last taste of the Fall Classic, contributing to the 27th championship in franchise history.

While postseason success was lacking for the remainder of his career, Jeter could still draw a crowd to Yankee Stadium. In 2010 he surpassed Lou Gehrig's 2,721 career hits to become the Yankees' all-time hit leader. In 2011 during a game in which he went 5-for-5, he dramatically entered the 3,000-hit club with a home run to left field.

Still a productive player into his late 30s, it seemed he would continue to pile up career milestones until everything came to a screeching halt in Game 1 of the 2012 American League Championship Series, when he broke his left ankle on a routine play. A lengthy recovery and other lingering injuries limited him to just 17 games the following year, and he announced prior to the 2014 season that it would be his last.

He provided one last legendary moment during his final game at Yankee Stadium. With the game tied at 5 in the bottom of the ninth against the Baltimore Orioles, he stepped up to the plate with a runner on second. On the first pitch he went opposite field for a classic Jeterian base hit that won the game and inspired the longest standing ovation of his career.

It's tough to argue that anyone played the role of star athlete in New York City better than Derek Jeter. High expectations never rattled him and success never inflated his ego. When facing the brutal New York media, he was quick to thank his teammates after a victory and would take the blame in defeat. He embraced the high-profile lifestyle, carousing with A-list celebrities and eventually marrying a supermodel, but never took a wrong step along the way.

At 22 years old he carried the burden of saving a once-proud franchise that had lost its way and emerged clean as a whistle 20 years later. His first big-league manager, Buck Showalter, was Baltimore's skipper for Jeter's final walkoff hit and summed it up best saying, "Take a good look because there's not going to be many like this to come our way again."

Reserve Shortstop—Phil Rizzuto

He is the greatest shortstop I have ever seen in my entire baseball career, and I have seen some beauties.

—Casey Stengel

Phil Rizzuto is probably the most unassuming player on this All-Star team. At 5-foot-6 and just 150 pounds, he was more likely to be called a batboy than a big leaguer. Even with his physical shortcomings, he utilized his speed and quickness as an excellent fielder and key member of seven World Series champions over his 13 seasons in pinstripes. During his prime, he was also a good enough hitter to earn an American League MVP Award. After his playing career he became one of the most recognizable play-by-play men in baseball, calling games well into his 70s for his former team. Rizzuto's overall service time with the Yankees spanned seven decades, nearly all of it as a fan favorite. That's a giant shadow to cast for such a short man.

Dubbed "The Scooter," Phil Rizzuto was a world-class bunter. BOWMAN GUM/WIKIMEDIA COMMONS/PUBLIC DOMAIN

A native Brooklynite, Rizzuto was born to Italian immigrants during World War I. Fighting the opinion that he wasn't big enough to play baseball, he let his play do the talking and by his senior year in high school he was playing semipro ball on the side. In New York's melting pot he faced stiff competition during those games, playing the likes of Satchel Paige and other black players whom he would unfortunately not face again in meaningful competition for many years. Reflecting on this time, he would later say, "That was better than any Minor League experience."

Regardless, Rizzuto reported to his first minor-league assignment in Virginia shortly after signing with the Yankees in 1937. Socially, he was a fish out of water in rural Virginia, but on the field played well enough to be promoted to Kansas City by 1939. There, he starred for some all-time great minor-league teams and was named MVP of the American Association in 1940. By 1941 he was named the Yankees' starting shortstop.

Rizzuto quickly found that replacing clubhouse favorite Frankie Crosetti was no picnic. It wasn't until the usually quiet Joe DiMaggio insisted that his teammates give the new kid a chance that he was truly accepted. As it turned out, Rizzuto didn't need the help. In that 1941 season he hit .307 at the bottom of the lineup for the World Series champs and showed why he earned the nickname "Scooter" with his quick hands and feet in the field. He followed that up with a similar season in 1942 when he was named an All-Star for the first time. In both seasons he led the major leagues in Defensive Runs Above Average, backing up his reputation as a superb fielder. He spent the next three years serving in the Navy during World War II. However, the skittish, weak-stomached Rizzuto couldn't handle life at sea and mostly played exhibition baseball for the Navy team.

Both he and the Yankees stumbled their way back into action after the war, but by 1947 he returned to his previous form and hit .308 in a seven-game World Series win over his hometown Brooklyn Dodgers. After another down year in 1948, the Yankees kicked off a five-year World Series win streak in 1949 and their little shortstop was a big reason for their winning ways. Batting leadoff, Rizzuto scored over 100 runs and finished second in the MVP voting behind Boston's Ted Williams. He would avenge that loss in 1950 with an MVP-winning campaign. Combining his usual slick fielding with career highs in runs, hits, doubles, home runs, walks, batting average, and OPS, he was worth 6.7 WAR, which led American League position players. He was called "the 'indispensable man' of the world champion Bombers" by the *New York Times*—high praise on a team that boasted legends Yogi Berra and Joe DiMaggio.

For the next three seasons Rizzuto was his usual productive self to round out the Yankees' World Series streak. A league-average hitter, he continued to play shortstop better than anybody and was named an All-Star each year. He remained the Yankees' starting shortstop for one more season in 1954, but at

36 years old his offensive production fell off a cliff. His playing time slowed to a halt until 1956 when in August the Yankees unceremoniously released him to make room for 40-year-old Enos Slaughter. A devastated Rizzuto left Yankee Stadium in tears. The hard feelings didn't last, though, as he was brought back to call games from the broadcaster's booth a year later and remained there for 40 years.

On the field, Rizzuto's value to the Yankees was obvious to anyone watching. In his definitive account of the Yankees' dynasty years in the 1950s, writer Peter Golenbock noted that "for over ten seasons Rizzuto was the finest shortstop in the major leagues, a defensive genius who won more games with his glove than any of the big hitters won with their bats." His teammate for eight seasons, pitcher Vic Raschi, also supported this notion, saying "My best pitch is anything the batter grounds, lines, or pops in the direction of (Phil) Rizzuto."

Yet Rizzuto also contributed in subtle ways that often meant the difference between winning and losing. A prime example of this occurred in September of 1951 during a heated pennant race with Cleveland. The game was tied at 1 in the bottom of the ninth with Rizzuto facing Cleveland fireballer Bob Lemon and DiMaggio on third base. Never one to ruffle feathers, Rizzuto argued the called first strike with the umpire with the sole purpose of indicating with his hands to DiMaggio that a squeeze play was on. On the next pitch, DiMaggio darted home and Lemon, noticing, fired a pitch at Rizzuto's head. A prolific bunter, he jumped in the batter's box and was still able to get the bunt down the first base line, allowing DiMaggio to score the winning run. Casey Stengel would call it "the greatest play I ever saw."

Whether by being the butt of jokes, or being a truly stand-up guy for his pinstriped peers, Rizzuto was also the consummate teammate. A born omniphobe, it didn't take much to scare the life out of him, which made him easy prey for pranksters in the clubhouse who would litter his locker or equipment with a plastic spider or even a dead mouse. Rizzuto took it all in stride, and if the pranks stopped for any length of time, he'd worry that the team was mad at him. The ironic twist to his phobia was that he was tough as nails on the baseball diamond. His wife, Cora, articulated this observation, saying "It's a funny thing about his fear of mice, I've seen him stand there and get knocked six feet in the air by some big guy in a play at second base, but as for those mice, he's deathly afraid of them."

When it came to Rizzuto being a stand-up teammate, nobody could vouch better than Elston Howard. The first black player in franchise history, Howard broke in with the Yankees in 1955 and struggled playing in the still segregated South during spring training. By that time, Rizzuto was a seasoned veteran in the twilight of his career but did everything he could to comfort his new teammate. Howard noticed, and fondly looks back on Rizzuto, once saying, "I'll never forget [Rizzuto]. I give Phil the most credit of anyone. He would call me up during the day and take me out to various places, go to the movies, meet people around the league. . . . He was the type of man I respected, and I give him a lot of credit."

Even after spending nearly 40 years in the broadcast booth where he crafted lasting memories with rambling stories, endless birthday shout-outs, and healthy doses of his trademark "Holy Cow!", his most lasting impact to the Yankees will always be his selfless dedication. Nobody captured this better than The Scooter himself as he once reflected, "I never felt that I was doing anything extraordinary. I figured that I was doing my job. If I made a good play, I never expected to get written up. My teammates appreciated me, and that's all that mattered."

Chapter VI

OUTFIELDERS

Starting Outfielder—Babe Ruth

*Babe Ruth was the greatest baseball player that ever lived.
I mean, people say he's less than a god, but more than a
man. Like Hercules or something.*

—*Benny Rodriguez in* The Sandlot

As baseball generations churn on, Babe Ruth becomes more
myth than man. These days, a young baseball fan would find
it hard to believe that a portly, beer-swilling, hot dog-gorging,
skirt-chasing night owl could ever become a world-class athlete who took his sport by storm. Yet to say that's what Ruth
did would be an understatement. His unfathomable feats on
the diamond ushered in a new era of high-octane baseball and
made him an American icon. When he was sold to a struggling
Yankees franchise, he single-handedly changed their fortunes
and they've never looked back. Yankee Stadium has since been
called "The House That Ruth Built," and he truly set the foun-
dation on which the unprecedented success of the Yankees lies.

After a tumultuous upbringing in Baltimore that resulted
in him being estranged from his parents at just seven years

Even New York City couldn't contain the larger than life Babe Ruth.
IRWIN, LA BROAD, & PUDLIN/WIKIMEDIA COMMONS/PUBLIC DOMAIN

old, Babe Ruth took solace in baseball. He spent his youth in a Catholic reformatory where he honed his baseball skills and was signed by the Baltimore Orioles, a minor-league club at the time, at 19. The Boston Red Sox purchased Ruth from the Orioles that summer, and within a year he was a star pitcher in the major leagues. By 1918, the Red Sox saw value in his potent bat being in the lineup even on days that he wasn't pitching. In his first full season as an everyday player in 1919, he set a single-season record with 29 home runs. Tired of his off-field exploits and strapped for cash, Red Sox owner Harry Frazee sold Ruth to the Yankees in 1920 for $100,000 cash and a loan of $350,000, sparking a seismic shift in baseball's landscape that would be felt for decades.

The 1920s saw the dawn of the "Live Ball Era" of professional baseball, and nobody embraced the livelier ball better than Babe Ruth. Now playing his home games in New York's Polo Grounds and becoming a full-time outfielder, he belted 54 home runs in 1920, nearly doubling the record he had set the season before. Even more impressive, Ruth's home-run total surpassed that of every other major-league team outside of the Philadelphia Phillies, who hit 64 combined. In 1921 he broke the single-season home-run record for the third year in a row, smashing 59 as he also set the career mark with his 139th that July. In his first two years in New York he also hit .377 with a ridiculous 246 OPS+, drove in over 300 runs total, and scored 177 runs in 1921, a modern era record that still stands. That year he led the Yankees to their first ever World Series appearance but missed most of it with injuries as they lost to the New York Giants.

Ruth was suspended for the first six weeks of the 1922 season for violating baseball's barnstorming rules in the off-season. He returned as great as ever in late May and was even named Yankee captain. However, that reign ended just a week later when he was called out at second seeking an extra base on a single and threw dirt in the umpire's face. When heading back to the dugout, he jumped into the stands and challenged anyone within earshot to a fight. A less than remorseful Ruth said after the game, "I didn't mean to hit the umpire with the dirt, but I did mean to hit that bastard in the stands." Stripped of his captaincy, his temper subsided and he settled back into simply being baseball's best slugger for the rest of the season. The Yankees were swept in another World Series against the Giants as Ruth went just 2-for-17 along the way.

The following season the team opened a massive, state-of-the-art facility of their own, the first triple-decker stadium ever built in North America. The large capacity and hefty price tag of Yankee Stadium was justified by Ruth's drawing power. In 1923 his total of 41 home runs was relatively modest, but he hit .393 and drew 170 walks, which was good for a .545 on-base percentage. All three marks would stand as career highs. Splitting his time between the new stadium's spacious left field and comparatively small right field, the rotund slugger also ranked as the best fielder in the league according to Defensive Runs Above Average. Overall his contributions yielded 14.1 WAR, by far the greatest single-season total in major-league history. He was unanimously named the American League's MVP and led the Yankees to yet another World Series rematch with the Giants. There he hit .368 and belted three home runs during the first World Series win in franchise history.

Ruth had single-handedly revolutionized the game in shocking fashion with his unmatched power and bravado. Ruth biographer Leigh Montville captured this when noting of both teammates and fans that, "They never had seen anything like it. The game they had learned was being changed in front of their faces." He continued his assault in 1924 when he won the only batting title of his career, but the Yankees failed to return to the World Series. A year later the now 30-year-old Ruth experienced a harsh fall from grace. He reported to spring training weighing over 250 pounds and quickly spiked a fever that landed him in the hospital. Amid various rumors that his maladies were due to anything from too many hot dogs to a venereal disease, minor surgery for what was deemed an "internal abscess" got his health back on track.

He began his season that June but the Yankees didn't stand a chance as they were already 10 games under .500. His 25 home runs and .290/.393/.543 slash line would have been a career year for a mere mortal yet was disappointing for Ruth. Had his hard-partying ways finally caught up with him, or was he truly the demigod of baseball?

Between 1926 and 1932 Ruth had arguably the greatest stretch of hitting the major leagues has ever seen. In an average season during this run, he scored 143 runs, drove in 153, slugged 49 home runs, slashed .353/.482/.717 with an OPS+ of 212, and was worth over 10 WAR. Thanks mainly to Ruth and his new bash brother Lou Gehrig, the Yankees added three World Series titles to their collection during this time, sweeping the Pirates, Cardinals, and Cubs in 1927, 1928, and 1932, respectively. During those three series wins Ruth hit .457 with seven home runs and 17 RBIs. In the Game 4 clincher of the 1928 World Series, he became the first player ever to homer three times in a World Series game, adding to his immortality.

During that success, the 1927 season stood far above the others. Still often considered the greatest team in baseball history, the '27 Yankees won 110 games before sweeping the World Series and were dubbed "Murderers' Row" due to their deadly lineup. As dominant as they were, Ruth added a dramatic element to the regular season via a home-run chase for the ages. With a young Lou Gehrig threatening to match The Babe's legendary home-run output, Ruth was inspired to break his own record of 59. They were neck and neck heading into the season's final month, but Ruth pulled away in September, crushing 17 home runs including his record-breaking 60th on the penultimate day of the season.

Ruth was due for a new contract heading into the 1930 season. Acutely aware of the value he brought to the table and keen on continuing his lavish lifestyle, he sought a significant raise on his $70,000 annual salary. With the nation on the cusp of the Great Depression, the Yankees offered only $75,000, which matched US president Herbert Hoover's salary. Ruth settled for $80,000 and in turn fielded numerous questions from the media about earning more than the president. In response, he said, "What the hell has Hoover got to do with it? Besides, I had a better year than he did."

Two years later while playing in his final World Series, Ruth took center stage during the most disputed moment in baseball history. The Yankees would sweep the Cubs in the series, but Game 3 at Wrigley Field was hotly contested. Ruth had opened the scoring with a three-run blast in the top of the first inning, but when he stepped to the plate with one out in the fifth, the score was tied at four and he was engaged in a war of words with the Cubs bench. After two called strikes he made a pointing gesture either toward Chicago's dugout or the center field fence, depending on who is re-telling the story. On the next pitch, Ruth hit a mammoth shot over the center field fence, which has been estimated to have traveled nearly 500 feet. Breaking the tie, an elated Ruth continued to make gestures and verbal jabs toward the Cubs that heckled him as he rounded the bases. The Yankees would go on to hold that lead for a 7–5 victory.

After the game newspaper reports indicated that Ruth indeed pointed to center field before his game-breaking homer, implying that he called his shot, and a legend was born. Initially Ruth told reporters, "I didn't exactly point to any spot, like the flagpole. Anyway, I didn't mean to. . . . All I wanted to do was give that thing a ride . . . outta the park . . . anywhere." As articles continued to portray it as a called shot, he saw the sensational potential in such a story and would say, "It's in the papers, isn't it?" Years later he was fully embracing the embellished version of the story and in his autobiography gave a lengthy account of the home run that confirmed the folktale. No hard evidence has corroborated the "called shot," but it was an impressive feat nonetheless and is still one of the most famous home runs in baseball history.

As a high-profile superstar, carousing and embracing the spotlight in New York City, Ruth was the living embodiment of the Roaring Twenties. With that movement dying down as the 1930s wore on, so did Ruth's baseball career. The Yankees sold him to the Boston Braves in 1935 and after one partial season he retired as a player. He spent his post-playing career attempting to fulfill his long-standing desire to become a big-league manager, but that never came to fruition. At just 51 years old Ruth's carefree lifestyle caught up with him as doctors discovered inoperable cancerous tumors in his skull and neck that would spread to his vital organs. Less than two years later in June of 1948, he helped celebrate the 25th anniversary of Yankee Stadium but needed to use a baseball bat as a cane to stand up. Two months later he would succumb to his ailments and was placed in an open casket at Yankee Stadium for two days while over 70,000 paid tribute.

More than anyone, Ruth helped establish a culture of winning in the Bronx and did it with a style that the New York press ate up. On the other side of the coin, his departure from the rival Red Sox initiated a downward spiral for that organization as they were perennial cellar dwellers in the 1920s and 30s. In fact, thanks to "The Curse of the Bambino," the Red Sox wouldn't win another World Series until 85 years after his sale to New York. He's without doubt the greatest player in franchise history and has a case for the greatest baseball player ever. Former Yankee teammate and longtime manager Leo Durocher once said of him, "There's no question about it, Babe Ruth was the greatest instinctive baseball player who ever lived. He was a great hitter, and he had been a great pitcher."

The advanced metrics back up Ruth's claim as best ever. When combining his contributions as both a hitter and pitcher, his WAR total is tops among all other major-league players. His Batting Runs Above Average is also highest all-time and more than 200 runs better than runner-up Barry Bonds. While Ruth had some clear advantages over Bonds in the time he played, his four years as a full-time pitcher and Bonds's liberal use of steroids levels the playing field. It's hard to argue against Ruth as the superior hitter.

The Babe's positive impact on the Yankees, and baseball in general, extended beyond the field as well. While it didn't get as much press as his party animal reputation, he was a great ambassador. Playing in New York's melting pot, Ruth embraced the children of all backgrounds who worshipped the ground he walked on. He often spent time with kids and shared his wealth whether by playing ball with them, signing autographs, or even visiting hospitals and orphanages. He was also a proponent of racial integration within baseball when that was not a popular opinion. Quoting historian Bill Jenkinson, a recent biographer made this case by noting, "Men of color from Ruth's day were well aware of Babe's efforts on their behalf, and, to a man, told me in numerous interviews of their heartfelt appreciation. In fact, the historical evidence strongly suggests that Babe Ruth did not achieve his lifelong dream of managing a Big League team because of his advocacy of integration."

Ruth was one of the few figures in baseball who truly transcended the sport. Its success can be directly linked to his rise to prominence. As claimed in the first lines of one of his many obituaries in the New York newspapers, "Writing about Babe Ruth is akin to trying to paint a landscape on a postage stamp. The man was so vast, so complex and so totally incredible that he makes mere words so puny and insufficient." Indeed.

STARTING OUTFIELDER—MICKEY MANTLE

Mantle's greatness was built on power and pain. He exuded the first and endured the second.

—Ray Fitzgerald

At just 19 years old, Mickey Mantle was christened the next great Yankee in the vein of Babe Ruth, Lou Gehrig, and Joe DiMaggio. He soon lived up to those lofty expectations. Before his 25th birthday he was a Triple Crown winner and MVP, regularly hitting mammoth home runs that sportswriters spun into the stuff of legend. In his 12 World Series appearances as a Yankee, he helped earn seven series wins and homered a record 18 times.

Even with those accomplishments, the underlying theme of Mantle's career was that he could have reached even greater

Mickey Mantle had impossible expectations to live up to as a rookie in 1951. NEW YORK YANKEES/WIKIMEDIA COMMONS/PUBLIC DOMAIN

heights. Plagued by injuries from his rookie year, he played through chronic pain for the rest of his days. He was also the victim of self-sabotage, living with reckless abandon off the field. The Mick was a painfully relatable character, but a hero nonetheless.

From birth, Mantle was destined to become a big-league ballplayer. His father, Mutt, named him Mickey after Hall of Fame catcher Mickey Cochrane. A semipro ballplayer himself, Mutt lived and breathed the game. After toiling in the mines of Commerce, Oklahoma, he found the time to teach young Mickey America's pastime.

Foreseeing the rise of platoon tactics, Mutt insisted that his son learn how to switch-hit. Mickey developed into such a good hitter that he played semipro ball with grown men at 15.

Signed by the Yankees out of high school, Mantle spent the next two seasons with Yankee minor-league teams in Kansas and Missouri. He hit as well as advertised but struggled at shortstop. He could throw far and field the ball well but could not make accurate throws to first base.

At 19 the Yankees invited Mantle to spring training in 1951, where he impressed manager Casey Stengel enough to keep the youngster. Of his new rookie, Stengel said, "He has more speed than any slugger I've ever seen, and more slug than any other speedster—and nobody has ever had more of both of 'em together."

Since he was unplayable at shortstop, Stengel enlisted the help of former Yankee outfielder Tommy Henrich to convert Mantle into a right fielder. He was named starter and given uniform number 6, following in the sequence of Ruth (3), Gehrig (4), and DiMaggio (5), his teammate who was heading into his last season.

As if the weight of the Yankees' past wasn't enough, Mantle also experienced culture shock coming to New York City from a town of just 2,000 people in Oklahoma. The shy Mantle struggled with the city and the scrutiny that came along with it. He would never grow accustomed.

After some initial success he was slumping badly by mid-July and was sent down to Kansas City to regroup in the minors. His struggles continued there and as a natural introvert, Mantle had a crisis of self-confidence.

Mantle called his father to inform him that he was quitting baseball, which inspired Mutt Mantle to drive straight to Kansas City. Mutt offered only tough love to his son and as he packed his suitcase said, "I thought I raised a man. I see I raised a coward instead." Horrified at the thought of disappointing his father, Mickey vowed to stick with it. His bat caught fire, and he played his way back to the Bronx by mid-August.

Mantle was assigned his now-familiar uniform number 7 upon his return, which lifted a huge figurative weight off his shoulders. His play improved and he started in right field in the 1951 World Series with the New York Giants.

In Game 2 a pop fly from Willie Mays sent DiMaggio and Mantle both charging in. DiMaggio called off the rookie to make the catch. Mantle hit the brakes hard and as he did, his right cleat got stuck on a rubber drain hiding in Yankee Stadium's outfield grass. He dropped, unable to get up, and was rushed to the hospital for knee surgery.

His blazing speed was gone, but more devastating for Mantle was his father's presence in the bed next to him in the hospital. At 39 years old Mutt was diagnosed with Hodgkin's disease and given just months to live. Father and son took comfort watching the Yankees win the World Series from their hospital beds.

Mantle's knee healed in time to open the 1952 season, and he would eventually settle into his now familiar spot in center field. It would be his first of 14 consecutive All-Star seasons, leading the American League with a .924 OPS and finishing third in the MVP vote. In a World Series showdown with the Brooklyn Dodgers, he hit the game-winning home run in a thrilling Game 7 at Ebbets Field.

However, the season would be most notable for how seamlessly Mantle filled the superstar void left by Joe DiMaggio. As sports journalist Peter Golenbock observed, "The Yankees had not forgotten DiMaggio, but they did not really miss him. . . . By July 1952 they were talking about Mantle, and how the

20-year-old kid could hit a baseball—high arching drives that seemed beyond human capability."

Over the next two seasons Mantle was similarly productive. In 1953 the Yankees defeated the Dodgers again in the World Series, but the personal highlight for Mantle during this time happened in just the fourth game of that season.

Facing off against Washington Senators lefty Chuck Stobbs, he batted right-handed and drove a pitch into Griffith Stadium's left field. The outfielders didn't even move. The ball sailed over the fence, cleared the bleachers, and landed in the yard of a house across the street. Players and fans alike stood in awe of the 565-foot masterpiece.

Mantle suffered a setback that August when he reinjured his right knee making a throw from center field. He played through the injury—something that he would do often—but it would linger for the rest of his career.

In 1955 Mantle hit even more show-stopping home runs and kicked his overall production into high gear. His 37 home runs, 11 triples, and 1.042 OPS led the American League. He also led the majors in OPS+ and walks.

Facing the Dodgers for the third time in four years, the Yankees would lose a tough World Series in seven games, in part because a hamstring injury limited Mantle to just three games in the series.

Mantle and the Yankees would come back with a vengeance in 1956. At 24 years old Mantle realized his full potential and had one of the most amazing seasons the game has ever seen. By late May he was knocking the ball out of the park at a swift pace and single-handedly winning games for a Yankee team that was already running away with the pennant. On Memorial

Day at Yankee Stadium, he victimized the Senators again with a heroic blast that garnered national attention.

Down by one with two runners on in the fifth, Mantle stepped to the plate from the left side against righty Pete Ramos. He launched a fastball toward the right field upper deck. The ball struck the façade of the upper deck's roof and ricocheted back onto the playing field. Some estimate that the ball would have traveled 600 feet. As the season wore on, Mantle chased baseball history. His 52 home runs led the majors and were the most by a Yankee since Babe Ruth's 54 in 1928. His .353 batting average and 130 RBIs also led the majors, making him just the fifth player ever to earn the major-league Triple Crown. His OPS, OPS+, total bases, and WAR paced the major leagues as well on his way to his first MVP Award, which he won unanimously. It wasn't even close.

Newsweek's Roger Kahn wrote after the season, "Mantle has come finally to a point where he is generally regarded as the best baseball player in the world and is given a serious chance to become the best ball player of all time."

Mantle continued his otherworldly hitting in yet another World Series matchup with the Dodgers. Of his three home runs that series, by far the biggest was a Game 5 blast that put the Yankees on the board in the fourth inning of Don Larsen's perfect game.

Not known for his fielding ability, Mantle also made a game-saving play to preserve Larsen's gem. With one out in the fifth, Gil Hodges hit a line drive to the deepest part of Yankee Stadium in left-center field. Sprinting all the way, Mantle lunged for the ball in mid-stride and made a backhand snag to spoil the potential game-breaker. The Yankees would win the series in seven games to avenge their 1955 loss.

In some ways, Mantle was even better in 1957. He improved his average to .365 and drew a career-high 146 walks. However his home-run total dropped to 34 due to a mysterious injury sustained that August. Publicly the ailment was diagnosed as shin splints in his left leg. In reality, it was a self-inflicted wound from horsing around on a golf course with his putter. Despite the setback, he played well enough to earn his second consecutive MVP in a close race with Ted Williams.

Mantle earned his third home-run title and fifth World Series ring in 1958 and closed out the 1950s inarguably as the player of the decade. His 68.1 WAR during the span was nearly seven more than runner-up Stan Musial, and he led the majors in WAR each year from 1955 to 1958.

Things were simple on the baseball diamond for Mantle, but his personal life was more complicated. When fans heaped praise on the young slugger he reacted bashfully, which they mistook as apathy and found insulting.

Mantle's inability to handle life in New York and his unfortunate family history were fuel for his self-destructive behavior. When Mutt Mantle died at just 40 years old, Mickey learned that most Mantle men died young. Fearing an early death himself, he vowed to make the most of the few years he figured he had left. He was generous with his money, but took comfort in booze and women.

His drinking escapades with teammates and best friends Billy Martin and Whitey Ford were as legendary as his tape-measure home runs. They lived it up at Toots Shor's restaurant in Manhattan, the place to be for high-rollers. The drinks never stopped. Neither did the women—never mind his wife in Oklahoma.

Heading into the 1960s, Mantle had a new partner in crime on the field: 25-year-old Roger Maris, a left-handed slugger who played right field next to Mantle. Together they formed one of the best one-two punches in the league as Mantle finished with 40 home runs to Maris's 39. When it came to the MVP vote, Maris beat Mantle out by just three points. In the World Series the Yankees trounced the Pittsburgh Pirates yet still lost in seven games thanks to Bill Mazeroski's improbable walkoff home run.

The 1961 Yankees gave the 1927 "Murderers' Row" Yankees a run for their money as the best team of all time. They won 109 games and set a major-league record with 240 home runs. Nearly half of those were accounted for by Mantle and Maris, as they were each in hot pursuit of Babe Ruth's single-season record.

A quiet, humble man from North Dakota, Maris was not an instant hit with the Yankee faithful. When it was clear by midsummer that both players had a shot at the record, Mantle was hailed as the "true" Yankee deserving of the record whereas Maris received death threats in the mail.

Neck and neck all year, by September 10 Maris had 56 home runs to Mantle's 53. Nursing arm and leg injuries—and playing through them as usual—Mantle came down with a cold the following day. He received a penicillin shot in his thigh to try to speed up his recovery. Instead, an abscess at the injection site effectively ended the race for Mantle, although he finished one of his finest seasons with a career-high 54 home runs.

On his own now, Maris broke The Babe's record with his 61st home run on the season's final day. Mantle saw limited action during a World Series where the Yankees would steamroll the Reds.

After falling just short of Maris again in the MVP vote, Mantle would win his third and final MVP in 1962. Although his 30 home runs and .321 average looked pedestrian compared to his previous years, he was clearly the best player on a 96-win team that would win their second straight World Series.

He missed the majority of 1963 thanks to a broken foot but returned for one last superstar year in 1964. His OPS and OPS+ led the majors as he brought the Yankees back to the World Series one last time. There, he put up a heroic effort with three homers and eight RBIs in a tough seven-game loss to the Cardinals. At just 32 years old, his best days as a Yankee were behind him.

The wear and tear on Mantle's legs caused his play in center field to deteriorate rapidly. After first shifting to left field, he was relegated to first base for his final two years in 1967 and 1968. His batting average dropped, but he was still a productive hitter in his waning years. He averaged 20 home runs per season with a slash line of .254/.386/.450 and a 149 OPS+ over his last four years in pinstripes.

Still, these were sad times for a once proud player and franchise. On Mothers' Day 1967, the Yankees were 11-13 as they took on the Baltimore Orioles. In the seventh inning Mantle drove a Stu Miller pitch deep to right field for the 500th home run of his career. He limped around the bases, clearly favoring the bad knee as a mostly empty Yankee Stadium cheered their aging slugger. He didn't even take a curtain call.

Two years later he would get the send-off he deserved. The Yankees held Mickey Mantle Day at the stadium for their freshly retired star in June of 1969 before a capacity crowd. When Mantle was introduced, fans erupted into a standing ovation that lasted nearly 10 minutes.

For the rest of his life, Mantle was shown the love typically reserved for Gehrig, Ruth, and DiMaggio each time he appeared at Yankee Stadium. Warts and all, his unprecedented power displays and dedication to the Yankees helped fulfill a prophecy forced upon him when he was a teenager. The Mick's status on the Yankees' Mount Rushmore is forever sealed.

STARTING OUTFIELDER—JOE DIMAGGIO

There was an aura about him. He walked like no one else walked. He did things so easily. He was immaculate in everything he did. Kings of State wanted to meet him and be with him. He carried himself so well. He could fit in any place in the world.

—*Phil Rizzuto*

Baseball scouts often refer to the "five tools" when evaluating talent. Speed, power, hitting for average, a sound glove, and a strong arm make up the components of a perfect player. Few players have ever exhibited those skills better on a baseball diamond than Joe DiMaggio. After taking the reins of the Yankees from Lou Gehrig in the late 1930s, he brought the team to new heights, earning nine World Series rings in his 13 years. During that journey he became an American icon thanks to his grace on the field and the almost mystical nature of his reserved personality. For baseball fans, he embodied everything that a player should be and was appropriately dubbed "baseball's greatest living player" for the last 30 years of his life.

The eighth of nine children, DiMaggio came from a large Sicilian family who settled in the San Francisco Bay Area in the 1910s. Rather than follow in the footsteps of his father, a

For many, Joe DiMaggio was baseball perfection.
BOWMAN GUM/WIKIMEDIA COMMONS/PUBLIC DOMAIN

skilled fisherman, Joe sought a career in baseball along with his older brother Vince and younger brother Dom, who all found success in the major leagues. By age 17 Joe was playing professionally for the San Francisco Seals, a high-profile minor-league team. In 1933 he remarkably hit safely in 61 consecutive games, a record that would become more significant later in his career. After a major knee injury in 1934, he responded well in 1935 and the Yankees agreed to send a stable of prospects and cash to the Seals for DiMaggio's services.

At 21 years old, DiMaggio came to the Bronx a polished baseball player. Manager Joe McCarthy was notoriously hard on rookies, but made an exception for his new phenom. He trusted DiMaggio as a starter early on and never felt a need to "coach" the kid. In fact, McCarthy trusted his bat so much that when asked whether DiMaggio could bunt or not, he simply replied, "I will never know." In 1936 DiMaggio rewarded his manager with over 200 hits, a .323 average, 29 home runs, and 125 RBIs all while navigating Yankee Stadium's spacious center field with ease. He was named an All-Star, as he would be in each of his 13 major-league seasons, and kept his form in the Fall Classic. During the first of four consecutive World Series wins for the Yankees, he hit .346 as the number three hitter in the lineup.

DiMaggio rose to major-league supremacy in 1937. His 8.2 WAR led all position players in the American League and his 151 runs scored, .673 slugging percentage, 418 total bases, and 46 home runs each led the majors. The home runs were especially impressive for a right-handed hitter in Yankee Stadium, whose fence in left-center was more than 450 feet from home plate. His 46 longballs stood as the record for a right-handed-hitting Yankee for nearly 70 years.

After another productive season in 1938, DiMaggio hit a career high .381 in 1939, which led the American League and resulted in his first MVP Award. He was also dubbed the "Yankee Clipper" that year by Yankees' radio announcer Arch McDonald, who compared DiMaggio's speed and range to that of the popular *Clipper* series of airliners. The Yankees had a down year in 1940, finishing third in the American League, but DiMaggio earned his second consecutive batting title with a .352 average and reached the 30-home-run plateau for the fourth straight year.

The personal success meant nothing to DiMaggio, whose perfectionist style consumed him. He was deadly serious, emotionless, and eerily silent. When confronted by a reporter about this he once replied, "I am a ball player, not an actor." While he seemed aloof to his teammates, he was actually fighting a daily struggle within himself on their behalf. If the Yankees lost, regardless of the circumstances, in his mind he had let down his entire team. That struggle was put to the test in 1941 and DiMaggio responded the way only legends can.

By the middle of May the Yankees were a .500 club and sitting in fourth place in the American League. Worse yet, DiMaggio was slumping as the team was struggling to score runs. After going 1-for-4 in an embarrassing 13–1 defeat at the hands of the White Sox on May 15, he homered in a 6–5 victory the next day. That sparked a hot streak for DiMaggio and the Yankees as they found themselves in the win column more often than not. During a doubleheader sweep of the St. Louis Browns on June 8, DiMaggio had two hits apiece including three home runs. The Yankees had climbed to six games above .500 and into second place while writers started to notice that DiMaggio had hit safely in 24 consecutive games.

Two weeks later he singled and doubled in a 5–4 win over the Detroit Tigers that extended his streak to 34 games, surpassing Rogers Hornsby's National League record. On June 29 DiMaggio had the chance to both tie and break George Sisler's modern era record 41-game streak during a doubleheader in sweltering heat against the Washington Senators. He struggled but went 1-for-5 in both games, breaking the record in the seventh inning of the second game before a roaring crowd at Griffith Stadium. After the game he let his usually iron-clad guard down when he said, "Sure, I'm tickled. It's the most excitement I guess I've known since I came into the majors." Sisler himself told him, "Congratulations. I'm glad a real hitter broke it. Keep going." Three days later he would extend the streak to 45 games with a screeching line drive home run during a win over the Red Sox at Yankee Stadium. That hit set the all-time record, surpassing Willie Keeler's record of 44 games set in 1897.

DiMaggio extended the streak to an absurd 56 games by mid-July. On July 17 in Cleveland he scorched two hot shots down the third base line that would be hits on most days. However, slick-fielding third baseman Ken Keltner ended the streak on spectacular plays. During one of the most remarkable achievements in baseball history, he had hit .408 with 15 home runs and 55 RBIs while the Yankees won 41 of 56 games. DiMaggio catapulted the team from fourth to first place, which they now held by seven games. As a postscript, he started a 16-game hit streak the next day during which the Yankees would go 13-3 and extend their lead to 12½ games. They would go on to easily win the World Series over the Brooklyn Dodgers, but DiMaggio's streak was the thrill of 1941. Years later, renowned scientist and author Stephen Jay Gould called the streak "the most extraordinary thing that ever happened in American sports."

For his efforts DiMaggio earned the American League MVP over Ted Williams despite Williams's .406 batting average. Teddy Ballgame felt no ill will as he said during the streak, "I really wish I could hit like that guy Joe DiMaggio. I'm being honest. Joe's big and strong and he can club the ball without any effort. These hot days I wear myself out laying into it."

With the respect of his peers at an all-time high, DiMaggio was worth more than six WAR in 1942. However, he suffered the only World Series loss of his career and would have to live with it for the next three years. At 28 years old he interrupted the prime of his professional baseball career to join the Air Force, where he would entertain American troops by playing exhibition baseball across the globe. By 1945 it was discovered that he suffered from stomach ulcers, no doubt a consequence of the immense pressure that he put on himself. That September he was given a medical discharge and returned home a hero.

Fans flocked to Yankee Stadium to see DiMaggio again and the Yankees' total attendance surpassed two million in 1946, nearly doubling the previous record set in 1930. Still, DiMaggio found it difficult to shake off the rust. His .290 average was a career low and the Yankees stumbled to a third-place finish. After the season DiMaggio would have surgery to remove a painful bone spur on his left heel.

When DiMaggio returned to the lineup in late April of 1947, he again slumped, but by June he found his stride. His hot streaks coincided with Yankee win streaks as they took home the American League pennant by 12 games. DiMaggio hit a modest .315 with 20 home runs and 97 RBIs, but based on his role in his team's success he earned the MVP by a single point over his rival in Boston. Ted Williams won the Triple Crown and his WAR more than doubled DiMaggio's, but his Red Sox finished third, 14 games back of the Yankees. In a thrilling seven-game World Series, the Yankees would beat the Brooklyn Dodgers, but DiMaggio displayed the only show of emotion on a baseball diamond during his playing career.

With a chance to tie Game 6, DiMaggio hit a deep flyball to Yankee Stadium's left-center field that was snagged by Al Gionfriddo at the fence, just a few feet from the 415 foot sign. As he rounded first base, DiMaggio saw that he was out and kicked the dirt in front of second base, furious that he had let his team down.

In 1948 DiMaggio returned to superstar form, smashing 39 home runs and driving in 155 runs, both of which led the league. Alas, the 94-win Yankees finished third behind the Cleveland Indians and Boston Red Sox. Over the winter he had more bone spur surgery, this time on his right heel. The surgery was apparently unsuccessful as the pain that persisted was unbearable. Seething at the thought of letting his teammates down, he became a recluse. He quarantined himself in his New York hotel room, pondering if he would ever play again until one June day when he miraculously felt no pain in the surgically repaired heel. He eyed a return for a series with the Red Sox in Boston on June 28. The Yankees had held onto first place without their leader, but the usually reserved DiMaggio jubilantly returned to the Yankee clubhouse ready to put the team on his back one more time.

DiMaggio homered in all three contests, collecting five hits in 11 at-bats with five runs scored, nine driven in, and four home runs total. The performance inspired cheers even from the rival crowd in Boston as the Yankees swept the Red Sox. With a productive DiMaggio, they cruised through the regular season until September 18 when pneumonia sidelined the Yankees' star again. On October 1 they began a two-game series at Yankee Stadium against the Red Sox, now trailing them by a game in the standings. It also happened to be Joe DiMaggio

Day as the man of the hour returned to the lineup. Before the game DiMaggio gave a speech that included the now famous line, "I want to thank the good Lord for making me a Yankee."

The Red Sox took a 4–0 lead heading into the bottom of the fourth inning when DiMaggio jump-started the offense with a leadoff ground rule double and scored two batters later. They chipped their way to a 5–4 victory and in a winner-take-all game for the pennant the next day won 5–3. They flattened the Dodgers in a five-game World Series, but wouldn't have gotten there without DiMaggio. In half a season he hit .346 with 14 home runs, 67 RBIs, a 178 OPS+, and inspired a championship run with a team-leading 4.4 WAR.

DiMaggio was healthy enough to play full-time and had a fine season in 1950, but was no longer the MVP of the Yankees, giving way to the likes of Yogi Berra and Phil Rizzuto. In 1951 injuries took their final toll on DiMaggio as he hit just .263 with 12 home runs. However, he did win one last World Series and passed the torch of Yankee superstardom to rookie Mickey Mantle. In December he retired and became a living legend.

DiMaggio remained in the spotlight thanks to a brief and tumultuous marriage to Marilyn Monroe in 1954. However, the baseball community didn't need a reason to keep his name relevant. To this day, DiMaggio is celebrated as having the sharpest batting eye in baseball history. Combined with his insatiable desire to come through for his team, he was nearly impossible to strike out. In fact, during his epic 1941 season, he struck out just 13 times while drawing 76 walks. For his career he walked more than twice as often as he struck out and never whiffed more than 39 times. These are unheard of accomplishments in baseball today.

More impressively, DiMaggio maintained superlative respect from his fiercest rivals. During his playing days, baseball's holy trinity included Ted Williams, Stan Musial, and himself. Two-thirds of that group would later concede supremacy to the Yankee Clipper. Williams once said of him, "I have to say that he was the greatest baseball player of our time. He could do it all." Meanwhile, Musial offered, "There was never a day when I was as good as Joe DiMaggio at his best. Joe was the best, the very best I ever saw."

For nearly 50 years after retiring, DiMaggio was adored for being as close to a perfect baseball player as anyone had ever seen and his legacy was literally set in stone after he passed away in 1999. The Yankees made DiMaggio just the fourth Yankee player to have a monument dedicated in his honor at Yankee Stadium. He didn't break the mold of what a baseball player could be; Joe DiMaggio is the mold.

RESERVE OUTFIELDER—CHARLIE KELLER

He wasn't scouted. He was trapped.

—Lefty Gomez

To put it lightly, Charlie Keller looked nothing like a baseball player. His robust, muscular physique could not be contained by his 5-foot-10 frame and the thick black hair that covered his head only got slightly less thick as it covered the rest of his body. He was aptly nicknamed "King Kong," but even with less gorilla-like features it would have been appropriate. For a brief period in the 1940s, Keller was a beast on the baseball diamond, serving as one-third of arguably the greatest outfield trio in baseball history along with Tommy Henrich and Joe

Charlie Keller impressed anybody who saw him play.
STATE LIBRARY AND ARCHIVES OF FLORIDA/WIKIMEDIA COMMONS/PUBLIC DOMAIN

DiMaggio. Like DiMaggio, he was a complete player with no weakness in his game and expected perfection from himself. Unfortunately, a back injury all but ended his career at just 30 years old. Short as his career was, few players were ever better than Keller at his best.

Growing up on a farm in Maryland, Keller began developing his immense strength at a young age by milking cows and pitching hay. In high school he excelled in every sport he tried his hand at, but especially stood out in baseball as both a pitcher and catcher. He earned a scholarship to attend the University of Maryland where he played baseball, basketball, and even football, a sport he had never tried before. By the time he was a junior, he had become one of the best prospects in baseball and was playing semipro ball during his summer breaks.

The Yankees signed Keller prior to graduating and in 1937 he reported to the Newark Bears, their minor-league affiliate.

There he hit .353 with 13 home runs and impressed in right field, a position he was playing for the first time in his life. He was named the minor-league player of the year and was in high demand around the majors. However, the Yankees weren't fielding offers and with no room in the Bronx sent him back to Newark in 1938. He improved to a .365 average with 22 home runs, essentially forcing the Yankees to promote him in 1939.

A thigh injury delayed the start of the 1939 season for Keller, and when he was ready to play he was eased into the lineup. Yankee manager Joe McCarthy recognized the star potential in Keller and took him under his wing. He deployed him in left and right field as part of his corner outfield rotation. Keller made his first start in a Yankee uniform on May 2 during a game that was most famous for breaking Lou Gehrig's consecutive games streak. During a 22–2 rout of the Detroit Tigers, Keller still made his presence felt with a triple, home run, and six RBIs. As the season wore on playing time increased for Keller. In 111 games played he hit .334 with 11 home runs, 83 RBIs, and 4.6 WAR for a 106-win Yankee team. The rookie sensation saved his best for last as he hit .438 with three home runs in a World Series sweep of the Cincinnati Reds. In Game 3 he made baseball history when he became the first rookie to hit two home runs during a World Series game.

At the urging of McCarthy, Keller began during the 1940 season to embrace the full power potential of his bat as a left-hander in Yankee Stadium, even if it meant sacrificing a few batting average points. McCarthy also made him a more permanent fixture in the lineup, and he didn't disappoint. His batting average dipped to .286, but that was offset by his 21 home runs, 15 triples, and 106 walks, the latter leading the

American League. He was named an All-Star for the first time and at just 23 years old was the most productive player on the team outside of Joe DiMaggio and Joe Gordon. Despite his bulky stature, he had also put his athleticism on full display as evidenced by his ability to leg out triples and his excellent range in the outfield. By the start of the 1941 season, McCarthy noticed as he gave him the everyday job in left field, which in Yankee Stadium required someone with the skills of a center fielder.

For the season, Keller hit .298 and set career highs with 33 home runs and 122 RBIs. His 6.6 WAR was also third best among all position players in the majors, behind Ted Williams with his .406 average and DiMaggio with his 56-game hitting streak. DiMaggio's magical season overshadowed the fact that the Yankees won over 100 games on the strength of one of the best starting outfields ever. Keller, DiMaggio, and right fielder Tommy Henrich each hit 30 or more home runs, scored over 100 runs, and played an excellent outfield. All three received MVP consideration with Keller finishing fifth in the vote. The Yankees cruised to another World Series win over the Brooklyn Dodgers where Keller hit .389 and drove in five runs.

Keller's 1942 and 1943 seasons were virtual carbon copies of his stellar 1941 campaign. While his batting average wasn't eye-popping, he continued to consistently hit with power, handle Yankee Stadium's left field with ease, and draw walks at league-high rates. The Yankees reached the World Series both years, losing to and then beating the St. Louis Cardinals. Over the course of five seasons, Keller had been a major contributor to four American League pennant winners and three world championships. From 1940 to 1943, the average season for Keller included 28 home runs, 11 triples, 102 runs both driven in and scored, 107 walks compared to just 63 strikeouts, and a .287/.410/.531 slash line. On the advanced side of things, he was good for a 158 OPS+, more than six WAR per year, and a total of 25 Defensive Runs Above Average over that period.

While he did make a conscious effort to utilize Yankee Stadium's unique dimensions to his favor, he was more than a one-trick pony pulling home runs to the short right field fence. In fact, former Yankee pitcher Herb Pennock once scouted Keller and noted that of all the left-handed batters he had ever seen, only Babe Ruth could hit the ball as hard to left field. Healthy, extremely productive, and squarely in the prime of his career, Keller was likely to continue wreaking havoc on the American League. Instead, like most ballplayers of his generation, he got the call to serve his country as part of the war effort.

For the entire 1944 season and most of 1945, Keller was a purser on Merchant Marine ships spanning the Pacific Ocean. When he returned to the Yankees in mid-August of 1945, he had spent 20 months without even picking up a baseball. That didn't seem to affect him, as he picked up right where he had left off in 1943. In just 44 games, Keller hit over .300 with 10 home runs, 34 RBIs, and a 181 OPS+, albeit for a middling Yankee team. The following year he played a full season that was representative of his pre-war years. He hit 30 home runs, a career-high 29 doubles, and 10 triples with 101 RBIs and 113 walks. His 6.1 WAR led the third-place Yankees, but that would be the last full season of his career. In June of 1947 he was a major part of a Yankee team that was finally back on a championship path; however during a game in Detroit he felt a sharp pain in his back during a rundown. A slipped disk ended his season early.

Keller recovered enough to return to the Yankees in 1948 but was limited to part-time duty. When able to take the field, he wasn't nearly as effective as he had been before back surgery, and during a late September game the Yankees held Charlie Keller Day at the stadium. During what was intended to be the final send-off for the once-great slugger, he was showered with a plethora of parting gifts. Stand-up guy that he was, the only gift Keller accepted was the plaque dedicated to him. He insisted the other gifts be returned and the money be used for scholarships at his alma mater. After another lackluster season in 1949, the Yankees released him. After an unsuccessful stint with the Detroit Tigers, the Yankees took one more chance on their former star in 1952. Alas, his comeback lasted only two games before his body called it quits. Out of respect for his previous accomplishments and dedication, the Yankees still awarded him a full World Series bonus share after the season.

The greatness of Keller's career has rarely gotten its due after the fact thanks largely to its relatively brief peak and six years of part-time play due to injury and his military service. However, that doesn't make his career any less great. In his *New Historical Baseball Abstract*, Bill James named Keller the 17th best left fielder in baseball history. James said of Keller that, "had he not been injured, would have been one of the greatest power hitters in the history of baseball; he would rank, if not with Williams and Ruth and Aaron, certainly with Ott and Schmidt and Reggie and Willie McCovey and Al Simmons." In a direct comparison of Keller with his far more popular teammate, Joe DiMaggio, James gave a surprisingly favorable review, noting, "In 1942 and in 1946, in my opinion, Keller was actually a better player than DiMaggio." That's quite a compliment when considering that

DiMaggio was widely regarded as the best player in the game during those years.

A farmer by nature, Keller used his career earnings to buy what would become a horse farm near his hometown in Maryland. It would also serve as his connection back to his baseball career as he named it Yankeeland Farms. For 35 years until his death the farm would yield a bevy of champion racehorses, leaving a legacy worthy of its founder.

RESERVE OUTFIELDER—BERNIE WILLIAMS

Bernie was a son of a bitch; the pressure of the game never bothered him.

—*Joe Torre*

The Yankees' run of championships in the late 1990s are often lauded as the product of their homegrown Core Four who were rookies at the beginning of the run. However, there was a fifth element just as important to the cause and whose roots with the Yankees went even deeper. Bernie Williams saw his first action as a Yankee during one of the darkest periods for the franchise in the early 1990s. As Bernie improved his game, so did the Yankees. By the end of the decade they ruled the baseball world, and in true New York fashion, he did it his way.

Born in San Juan, Puerto Rico, Williams fell in love with music and baseball as a child. A musician in high school with aspirations of becoming a doctor, he displayed his raw athletic ability in track and field and earned four gold medals in the under-17 group of the 1984 Central American and Caribbean Junior Championships in Athletics. On his 17th birthday he signed with the Yankees and sacrificed his med-

Bernie Williams anchored the Yankee dynasty of the late 1990s.
CLARE_AND_BEN/WIKIMEDIA COMMONS

ical career to focus on baseball. From 1986 through 1988 he enjoyed more ups than downs in the minor leagues, proving it was a wise choice.

Williams received his first invite to spring training in 1989 amid some fanfare. Michael Martinez of the *New York Times* wrote of him, "He is their phenom this spring, their kid with unlimited talent and untapped potential." That season he learned how to hit left-handed, and thanks to his superb work ethic became a viable switch-hitter, adding to his ever-increasing potential. In 1991 *Baseball America* named Williams the number 11 prospect in the country and Joel Sherman, beat writer for the *New York Post*, noticed that he had his general manager drooling: "[Gene Michael] loved that such a young player worked at-bats from both sides of the plate with a keen-eyed savvy." When Yankees center fielder Roberto Kelly was injured that July, Michael called on Williams to replace him. He struggled adjusting to the majors, but remained there for the rest of the season.

The Yankees signed All-Star outfielder Danny Tartabull the following season, and Williams wasn't recalled until August when injuries cleared roster space for him. He showed significant improvement at the plate and in the field, but it was no picnic for Williams thanks to Mel Hall, a fellow Yankee outfielder. In a profile of Hall for the SB Nation website, Greg Hanlon wrote, "With Williams, Hall took rookie hazing to abusive extremes. . . . He called Williams 'Bambi,' mocking his large doe eyes, which were magnified by his bulky glasses. Alternately, he called him 'Mr. Zero,' Hall's assessment of Williams' value." At one point Williams was nearly reduced to tears before Don Mattingly stepped in and encouraged him to believe in himself. Williams took the message to heart and continued to improve on the field, while karma came back to bite Hall, who eventually landed in jail for sexual assault.

Early on during his first full season with the Yankees, Williams experienced two things that would become a career trend. He slumped early, and George Steinbrenner publicly threatened to trade him. However, Gene Michael wasn't ready to swap his favorite prospect just yet. By season's end he had worked himself into a league average hitter with some power as the Yankees finished in second place for the first time since 1986. In 1994 he improved even more, posting a 120 OPS+ and a .289/.384/.453 slash line whose components all represented career highs. On June 6 during a game in Texas, he became just the fifth Yankee to homer from both sides of the plate in the same game. The Yankees also improved, sporting the American League's best record when the season abruptly ended due to the players' strike.

When play resumed in 1995, the Yankees settled for the first ever wild card playoff spot in the American League. Williams led the charge, again establishing career highs in nearly every meaningful offensive category thanks to his ever-improving plate discipline and power. He also had a career year with the glove as his 14 Defensive Runs Above Average were top 10 in the majors. In total, he posted a 6.4 WAR, which would serve as his career high and paced the team by more than two full wins. Although they lost a painful ALCS in five games to the Seattle Mariners, Williams shined in the playoffs. He hit .429 with five RBIs and became the first ever major leaguer to homer from both sides of the plate in a playoff game during Game 3.

Building on that success, Williams became a serious home-run threat in 1996. His 29 home runs led the team, and as a result he was used in the cleanup spot throughout the season. He helped the Yankees return to the playoffs and set off on a magical playoff run that yielded the first World Series victory for the franchise in 18 years. In the Division Series the Yankees faced off against a formidable Texas Rangers team, but Williams was the star of the show, homering from both sides of the plate again during the Game 4 clincher. In Game 1 of the American League Championship Series against the Baltimore Orioles, he drilled a dramatic, no-doubt-about-it shot to left field for a walkoff victory in the 11th inning. After the Yankees won in five games, Williams was named the series MVP and had hit .471 with five home runs in the playoffs. An anonymous scout noted, "Forget that border on superstar thing. This guy has crossed the border." Bernie would have none of it. After receiving the award he said, "The real MVP is this team."

His 1997 season was just as impressive, although he endured two DL stints because of hamstring injuries. He was named an All-Star for the first of five straight years, but struggled in a Division Series loss to the Cleveland Indians. A season later Williams and the Yankees would have no such struggles. During a record-setting year they won 114 games during the regular season and went on to sweep the World Series. Williams played a starring role by winning the batting title with a .339 average and posting a 160 OPS+, which was a team high and a personal best.

At 29 years old Williams was a free agent following the season and was armed with notorious super-agent Scott Boras. After enduring annual trade rumors, Boras and Williams played hardball with the Yankees. While neither side budged in a contract standoff, the Red Sox had a whopping $91.5 million offer for Williams on the table. Luckily, the Yankees acquiesced, agreeing to bring Williams back on a record contract worth $87.5 million over seven years.

The Yankees had no regrets as they completed a World Series three-peat with wins in 1999 and 2000 while Bernie continued his ambidextrous assault on American League pitching. In 1999 he hit a career-high .342, third best in the league, and made more Yankee history. Behind Ruth, Gehrig,

Mantle, George Selkirk, and Charlie Keller, he became just the sixth player in franchise history to compile over 100 walks, runs scored, and RBIs in the same season. The following year he set career highs with 30 home runs, 37 doubles, and 121 RBIs. In six playoff series over those two years, all wins, he hit four home runs with 13 RBIs. Williams was also an effective leader, albeit obliviously, as Joe Torre would later note, "Bernie, I had to tell him he was a leader. He didn't know it. But he played every day and you relied on him."

In 2001 Williams had a representative season, but the Yankees fell inches short of winning their fourth World Series in a row as the Arizona Diamondbacks outlasted them in seven games. He was great again in 2002, hitting .333, collecting a career-high 204 hits, and both scoring and driving in over 100 runs. However, the 103-win Yankees shockingly lost the Division Series to the Anaheim Angels. At 34 years old, Williams was done as an elite player.

From 2003 through 2006, Williams's once great bat regressed to a league-average level and could no longer hide his subpar fielding. Despite the four Gold Gloves he won in his prime, according to Defensive Runs Above Average he cost his team more than 10 runs per year in the field after he turned 30. He was still a fan favorite though, and in 2004 he collected his 2,000th hit and 250th home run. In each case he became just the seventh Yankee to reach those career milestones.

Williams desired to stay with the Yankees in 2007, but the feeling was not mutual. A well-respected jazz guitarist, he found solace in focusing on his music. After retirement, he recorded a Latin Grammy–nominated album in 2009, but his post-career accolades wouldn't end there. In 2015 the Yankees honored his baseball career by retiring his number 51. An underappreciated player in his time—David Cone once said, "The thing I appreciated more and more from the other side was how good Bernie and O'Neill and Jeter were after facing them. How good Bernie was really caught me."—Bernie appropriately acknowledged three other underappreciated Yankees in Gene Michael, Roy White, and Willie Randolph during his ceremony. Each played a key role in cultivating his career.

When looking back on his struggles as a young man, Bernie once said, "I always had to prove I could play. They all saw me and always thought I was too mild, that I wasn't tough enough, that I didn't care, that my mind was not into baseball. But none of that was true." The truth is, Williams is an all-time great Yankee. He ranks within the top 10 in franchise history for games played, runs scored, hits, home runs, runs batted in, walks, extra base hits, and WAR. His playoff performance includes ranking second all-time in hits, runs, home runs, and walks while being the all-time leader in playoff RBIs, albeit with more opportunities than players whose careers pre-date him. Regardless, those rankings stand as a testament to how tough and composed a hitter Williams was in the middle of a Yankee lineup that ruled baseball in the late 1990s. Much to Mel Hall's chagrin, he was more Bambino than Bambi.

RESERVE OUTFIELDER—ROY WHITE

If you really don't watch him, and you really don't figure out what he does, he can easily be overlooked. But his biggest asset to the club, is that here's a guy who's going to do his job and not make mental mistakes.

—Reggie Jackson

Sometimes incredibly talented ballplayers aren't blessed with one skill that defines them. Roy White wasn't a true slugger, but he could hold his own as a cleanup hitter. He didn't have blazing speed, but he was a great baserunner. His arm was ordinary, but his range and sure hands made him one of the best left fielders of his generation. Add it all up and he was as productive as most superstars in baseball, even if he wasn't recognized as one. For most of his career, White toiled for middling Yankee teams that went nowhere. By all accounts he was a class act during those years and got his just deserts, albeit in anonymity, winning back-to-back World Series championships with the Bronx Zoo Yankees.

A native of Compton, California, White grew up playing baseball in empty lots with makeshift balls that would twist and turn more than any pitch he would see in the major leagues. In high school he was a switch-hitting second baseman and spurned scholarship offers from UCLA and Long Beach State to sign with the Yankees. He stumbled out of the gate in the minor leagues but steadily improved as he moved up the Yankee ladder. By 1965 he was named the Southern League MVP at Double-A Columbus.

White earned a September callup to the Bronx to finish the season. He played well, but set impossible expectations heading into 1966. After winning just 77 games in 1965, the Yankees and their fans looked to their young prospect as a savior. Coming out of spring training, the *New York Times* suggested that White "seemed destined for a fine Yankee career, [and that] he may turn out to be cut from the same mold as Mickey Mantle or Yogi Berra." Ironically, his desire to live up to that was his undoing. White found the appeal of Yankee Stadium's shallow right field enticing and tried to pull the ball too often. He hit just .225 with seven home runs and 20 RBIs. Worse yet, the Yankees finished last in the American League.

In 1967 White rediscovered what made him successful when sent back to Triple-A. The following May he earned the Yankees' everyday left field job, setting a high standard that he met consistently for the rest of his Yankee career. On the surface, his 17 home runs, 62 RBIs, and .267/.350/.414 slash line were not impressive. However, in the suppressed run-scoring environment of the late 1960s, that yielded a 137 OPS+ and by August he was batting cleanup behind Mickey Mantle. With Mantle gone in 1969, White's importance increased. His home-run total dipped to just seven, but he was no less productive thanks to improvements in other areas with 30 doubles, 81 walks, and a .290 batting average. At 25 years old, he was selected to his first of back-to-back All-Star teams and entered his prime.

White's 1970 season was his best. His 22 home runs, 94 RBIs, 109 runs scored, 180 hits, .296 batting average, and .860 OPS would all stand as career highs. He also stole 24 bases and played a solid left field that yielded a 6.8 WAR, again a career high. Despite being one of the best players in the league, Yankee fans were underwhelmed with White due to his lack of flashy numbers or team success. Even the endorsement of a legend wasn't enough to sway the fans in White's favor. In an article written for *SPORT* magazine during the offseason, Mickey Mantle wrote, "People ask me: what happened to all the Yankee stars? I tell them that Roy White is as good a player as any of the old players we used to have."

Undeterred, White's 1971 season was a near carbon copy of his 1970 effort. His 6.7 WAR was second in the American League among position players, behind only Graig Nettles.

He helped win games any way he could and set an American League record with 17 sacrifice flies, a mark that still stands. The following year he owned the strike zone and led the American League with 99 walks while striking out just 59 times. This was especially impressive when considering that he was no power threat with only 10 home runs all year.

George Steinbrenner purchased the team in 1973 and for the next two years White's production and playing time decreased while the roster around him was rebuilt via a flurry of trades. As the team started to take shape and improve, White emerged as a guiding light in the clubhouse for the revolving door of new players. To outsiders, he kept the Yankees respectable. In *The Yankee Encyclopedia*, Mark Gallagher noted that, "Roy's soft-spoken, sophisticated manner added class to the Yankee club. Intelligent and dignified, he was most cooperative with the press and Yankee fans."

Billy Martin was hired as manager during the 1975 season, and one of his shrewdest moves was making White the starting left fielder. Martin recognized the value of his all-around game and penciled him in near the top of the lineup often. White rewarded him by slashing .290/.372/.430, good for a 128 OPS+, and smacking a career-high 32 doubles. He was similarly spectacular the following year, and even added a career-high 31 stolen bases. Better yet, the team around him coalesced into a cohesive unit. White was sandwiched between Mickey Rivers and Thurman Munson at the top of the order and the trio served as perfect table-setters in front of sluggers Chris Chambliss and Graig Nettles. White scored an American League–leading 104 runs and the Yankees reached the playoffs after an 11-year drought.

At 32 years old White was finally able to play meaningful October games. The Yankees took on the Kansas City Royals for the American League pennant in a best of five series. White reached base safely each game and in a Game 5 thriller he plated the first Yankee run with an RBI single and later scored in the bottom of the first. He also drew two walks and scored again to tie the game at 3 before a walkoff home run from Chris Chambliss punched the Yankees' ticket back to the World Series. They would get swept by the Reds, but the Yankees were back.

The Yankees carried that momentum into the 1977 season and won 100 games, which earned another playoff berth. White had a solid year but by October he took a back seat to the hot-hitting Lou Piniella. He mostly watched from the bench as his team earned the first World Series win for the franchise since 1962, but he knew that he had been instrumental in their climb back to respectability. During one of the most dramatic pennant races in baseball history in 1978, he remained a reserve as the Yankees stormed from 14 games back in July to tie the Red Sox for first place in their division.

White's hot bat forced his way back into the lineup down the stretch, and he played a key role in the do-or-die tiebreaker game in Boston. His single to center field in the seventh inning made him the tying run when Bucky Dent hit his infamous home run. White started again in the playoffs and hit .325 with two home runs and five RBIs across the League Championship and World Series as the Yankees cruised to back-to-back championships. White's value as a quiet leader was needed more than ever as a civil war brewed between Yankee players, management, and ownership. In his autobiography, pitcher Sparky Lyle said, "Roy White is probably the nicest Goddamn guy on the club. He's quiet. He's well-respected by everybody, and he's very classy."

In spring training of 1979, the Yankees would not extend the 35-year-old's contract. Knowing his importance to the club, Yankee veterans stood up for White. Reggie Jackson said, "Sometimes management can't accept his kind of player because they're looking for loud players, guys who do things in a big way." Even the loudest player of the bunch pleaded with the Yankees to keep their humble leader around. Alas, he and the Yankees faltered during the 1979 season, and he was not brought back.

After playing in Japan for three years, White was welcomed back to the Yankee family and served on the coaching staff at points from 1983 through 1986 and again from 2004 to 2005. However, he has never been adequately celebrated as one of the all-time great players for the franchise. Willie Randolph and Rickey Henderson are the only Yankees to exceed 35 runs above average in the three main components of WAR: batting, baserunning, and fielding. Lowering that bar to 25 runs above average in all three categories, White is the only other Yankee who qualifies. Combined with the fact that he effectively navigated the Yankees from rags back to riches, the lack of recognition he gets from a team that loves a good ceremony is criminal.

As of 2001, Bill James ranked White as the 25th greatest left fielder of all time and noted, "Roy White has been a tremendously underrated player, for three reasons: 1) His skills were subtle, and not easily summarized into two or three statistics. 2) Like Ralph Kiner, he was blamed for the failures of his teams. 3) He was measured, for much of his career, against a standard of Joe DiMaggio and Mickey Mantle." He continued by comparing White favorably to a contemporary Hall of

Famer. "Roy White, in context, was actually a more productive hitter than Jim Rice . . . I think if you put both players in the same park in the same years, a lot of fans would be able to see that White was a better all-around player." Few players mastered the art of baseball like Roy White. Unfortunately, very few people seemed to notice.

RESERVE OUTFIELDER—EARLE COMBS

If you had nine Combses on your ball club, you could go to bed every night and sleep like a baby.

—*Miller Huggins*

When Babe Ruth and Lou Gehrig ruled baseball in the 1920s and spearheaded the first successful Yankee teams, they couldn't do it all by themselves. By the middle of the decade, help came in the form of an athletic center fielder at the top of the order who served as a perfect complement to the two sluggers. Literally playing in the shadow of Ruth in Yankee Stadium's outfield, Earle Combs's personality was diametrically opposed to his, and he may have been the only Yankee whose wholesomeness exceeded even Lou Gehrig's. Because of that, he won the hearts of fans, teammates, and managers alike. It didn't hurt that he was consistently productive for some all-time great Yankee teams.

Earle Combs was born in Kentucky on a family farm where his father made his own baseball equipment. Later he attended Eastern Kentucky University where he excelled at basketball, track and field, and, of course, baseball. Upon graduating he became a schoolteacher but soon recognized that baseball would be a more lucrative option. The minor-league Louisville

Colonels offered him a contract that he couldn't refuse, and at 23 years old he embarked on a professional baseball career.

Early on Combs hit well but made frequent errors in center field. After a particularly egregious error that cost his team a win, he began to doubt his ability but Joe McCarthy, his manager in Louisville, encouraged him by saying, "Look, if I didn't think you belong in centerfield on this club, I wouldn't put you there. And I'm going to keep you there." With his manager's confidence, Combs turned his game around and impressed during his time with the Colonels. He and McCarthy would cross paths again years later in New York.

The Yankees purchased Combs from the Colonels in 1924 and he impressed, hitting over .400 in a brief audition before a fractured ankle ended his season on June 15. He recovered from the injury in time for the 1925 season and became the leadoff hitter manager Miller Huggins craved. Although Combs was blessed with great speed, Huggins had no need for it with power threats Ruth, Gehrig, and Bob Meusel behind him in the lineup. He only needed him to focus on being patient, getting on base, and letting the big bats drive him in. Combs did that and then some, collecting 203 hits with 117 runs scored and a .342/.411/.462 slash line. It was all for naught, though, as the Yankees stumbled to a seventh-place finish.

The following season would be Combs's worst as a starter, but even at that he was a solid contributor. His bat was still above average with a 104 OPS+, and he scored over 100 runs for a pennant-winning team. They would lose the World Series in seven games to the Cardinals, but were primed to dominate baseball the following season. The 1927 Yankees are often considered the greatest team ever assembled, and Combs served as the ultimate table-setter. He collected a league-high 231 hits, scored 137 runs, hit a career-high .356, and set an American League Live Ball Era record that still stands with 23 triples. His career-high 6.8 WAR was third best on the team behind the titanic seasons of Ruth and Gehrig as the Yankees won 110 games and swept the World Series over the Pittsburgh Pirates.

During the 1927 season Combs received admiration on two occasions from unlikely sources. He tripled three times against Philadelphia in a close victory at home that September. Ty Cobb, his counterpart in center field for the Athletics, marveled at Combs's ability to use his speed, especially as it translated to patrolling the outfield between two big, lumbering men in Babe Ruth and Bob Meusel. At one point during the game, Cobb yelled to Combs, "You're crazy! Those two big guys stand out there and point out the ball so that you can go after it. In another season you'll have your legs worn off clear up to the knees." Just five days earlier between games of a doubleheader, a group of fans who often sat in the right field bleachers at Yankee Stadium had taken up a collection to purchase a gift for their favorite center fielder. That day they presented him with a gold watch. Naturally, Combs accepted it with humility and grace.

For the next five seasons Combs produced with remarkable consistency as the Yankees were perennially among the best teams in the major leagues. His average season during this period saw him hit .327 with 126 runs scored and 74 walks compared to just 28 strikeouts. As a left-handed hitter in Yankee Stadium he surprisingly hit few home runs, never exceeding nine in a season. Rather than trying to take advantage of the short porch in right field, Combs opted to spray the ball to left and center field. That supplemented his lack of home runs with a healthy dose of doubles and triples. He stroked more than 30 doubles each of those five years and averaged 16 triples, surpassing 20 in a season twice. The only hole in Combs's game was his comically weak throwing arm. However, thanks to his speed and dedication to improving his glove he was a respectable center fielder in his prime. With such a high-quality player in a premium position like center field, the Yankees bookended this five-year period with two more World Series wins.

By 1931, a familiar face in Joe McCarthy had taken the reins of the Yankees, and at 34 years old, Combs was still a serviceable player. McCarthy continued to deploy him as the everyday center fielder, but he lost a step that season and his numbers dropped across the board. His decline accelerated in 1934 when during a July game at Sportsman's Park in St. Louis he ran into the outfield wall tracking down a flyball. The crash caused injuries to his shoulder and knee, but the worst of it was a skull fracture. Combs's condition was thought to be life-threatening, and he spent two months in the hospital recovering. In a display of uncommon toughness, Combs was back in the lineup for Opening Day the following season. Now 36 years old, he valiantly tried to regain his previous form to no avail. That August he broke his collarbone, which ended both his season and career.

During his time with the Yankees, Combs proved a worthy sidekick to the superheroes he played with, but he was the antithesis of Babe Ruth off the field. While Ruth and other stars in New York during the 1920s and 1930s lived a hedonistic lifestyle, Combs, often referred to as the "Kentucky Colonel" for his gentlemanly appearance, put altar boys to shame. A quiet, humble, and deeply religious man, he simply did what was asked of him on the field and never so much as cursed off of it. When he was elected to the Hall of Fame in 1970, he put his trademark modesty on display saying, "I thought the Hall of Fame was for superstars, not just average players like me."

Combs was a manager's best friend for much of his career, as Miller Huggins and Joe McCarthy could attest, and that continued after his playing days. He served as a coach for numerous franchises across baseball, but his best work was with the Yankees. In his debut as a coach in 1936, his first task was to instruct a promising young prospect on how to effectively navigate Yankee Stadium's spacious center field. Joe DiMaggio's education may have been Combs's greatest achievement.

RESERVE OUTFIELDER—TOMMY HENRICH

Tommy is the smartest player in the big leagues.

—Joe DiMaggio

Baseball is supposed to be a fun game, but Tommy Henrich never got that memo. He played with a stern discipline that demanded winning at all costs and expected as much from his teammates. A player who wasn't pulling his own weight would often hear about it from Henrich before even his own manager. He put his money where his mouth was, though, meeting and exceeding his own absurd standard. A dual threat, when he couldn't physically beat an opponent, he would outsmart them. Yet his true trademark was an uncanny knack for coming through in clutch situations for the Yankees, so much so that he earned the nickname "Old Reliable."

Henrich was born and raised in Northeast Ohio, but didn't play baseball as a child because there were no teams in his hometown. He had to settle for playing softball when he could and after high school played semipro ball while working at a steel mill. In late 1933 he signed his first professional contract with the Cleveland Indians and soon became a top prospect. When the Indians failed to invite him to spring training in 1937, he sent a letter of complaint directly to Kenesaw Mountain Landis, the commissioner of baseball. Landis agreed and granted Henrich free agency. Coveted by most major-league teams, Henrich grew up a Yankee fan admiring Babe Ruth and chose to join a crowded Yankees outfield.

Henrich was given his first taste of major-league action in New York, and as a left handed bat off the bench was a key reserve. In 67 games he slashed .320/.419/.553 and showed great plate discipline with 35 walks compared to just 17 strikeouts. A knee injury limited him down the stretch, and he was held off the World Series roster for the eventual champions.

A season later Henrich earned the regular job in right field and was trusted to bat third in the lineup more often than not. Although his batting average dipped to .270, he was a steady run producer with 22 home runs, 109 runs scored, 91 driven in, and a career-high 92 walks. He was able to play in October this time and sealed the first World Series three-peat in franchise history by homering in the final game of a sweep over the Chicago Cubs. He homered in every World Series he played in thereafter.

The knee injury Henrich suffered in his rookie year lingered throughout his career, but affected him most in 1939 and 1940. He played in less than 100 games each season, but was a weapon in the middle of the order when able. Thanks to an undying work ethic, he also became an excellent fielder. In fact, when Joe DiMaggio was injured during this period Henrich filled in admirably in center field. Finally healthy he fulfilled his potential in 1941. He hit a career-high 31 home runs and formed one of the greatest outfields of all time with Charlie Keller in left and DiMaggio in center. All three were deadly with the bat and killed most balls that sailed into the outfield. Together they led the Yankees to over 100 wins and another World Series berth where Henrich's awareness proved priceless.

With a 2–1 series lead over the Brooklyn Dodgers, the Yankees were down 4–3 with two out in the ninth at Ebbets Field. Hugh Casey then struck out Henrich for what should have been the final out, evening the series. However, Brooklyn catcher Mickey Owen couldn't handle the third strike, and the ball rolled all the way to the fence. Henrich alertly darted to first base and reached safely. That brought up DiMaggio who singled and Keller who doubled them both home to give the Yankees a lead they wouldn't surrender. Henrich homered in the series clincher a game later. In his brief career to this point he was already one of the most dependable players on the team. As a result Yankee radio announcer Mel Allen coined his "Old Reliable" nickname for him after a trusty train line that ran from Ohio to Alabama. Henrich was just happy to be a part of a winning team: "I get a thrill every time I put on a Yankee uniform. It sounds corny, but it's the gospel truth."

In 1942 Henrich was named to his first All-Star team but joined the US Coast Guard that August in support of America's involvement in World War II. During his military service years, he was stationed at a training base in Michigan and played exhibition baseball. Like many players of his generation, he lost three of his prime years to the war and returned to the Yankees in 1946. He played in a career-high 150 games and was a steady run producer, but showed some signs of rust with a .251 batting average.

Henrich bounced back and made the All-Star team each season from 1947 through 1950. In 1947 he raised his average to .287, led the American League with 13 triples, and saved his best for a thrilling seven-game World Series against the Dodgers. He contributed a team-high 10 hits and drove in five runs, including the series-winning RBI in Game 7. A season later he had a career year with the bat and again led the league with 14 triples, scored a major-league-high 138 runs, hit .308 with 25 home runs and 100 RBIs, and posted a career-high 151 OPS+.

In 1949 the Yankees were on the verge of an unprecedented run of success. In his account of those teams, author Peter Golenbock highlighted Henrich's importance when he noted, "In right was Tommy Henrich, Old Reliable, an excellent fielder who, while not as charismatic as Joe DiMaggio, was to DiMaggio what Gehrig was to Ruth, a dangerous batter overshadowed by a star. In the late innings in clutch situations Henrich, too, could kill you." He continued his stellar play in 1949 but back and toe injuries limited him to just 115 games. He was healthy enough at season's end to play in a heated pennant race and the World Series.

Taking on the Brooklyn Dodgers again, Game 1 featured a classic pitchers' duel between Don Newcombe and Allie Reynolds. The game was scoreless heading into the bottom of the ninth when "Old Reliable" stepped to the plate. He deposited the first pitch he saw from Newcombe deep into the right field stands for the first walkoff home run in World Series history. That set the tone for the Yankees as they would take the series in five games.

In 1950 Henrich's chronic knee problems reached a tipping point and he was only able to play in 73 games, most of them as a pinch-hitter. He retired that December and in a *New York*

Times article covering the news, Arthur Daley wrote, "Henrich has never been the captain of the Yankees. But the other players just gravitated to him as their natural leader. . . . It is to be doubted if any player studied the game with as much intensity as Old Reliable." In retirement he varied his time as a coach, broadcaster, and businessman but maintained a strong relationship with the Yankees. Just as Earle Combs had trained Joe DiMaggio to play the outfield, Henrich, reliable as ever, took a young Mickey Mantle under his wing and molded him into a competent center fielder.

For all the words said about how clutch Tommy Henrich was during his career, the numbers actually back it up. Win Probability Added (WPA) is a stat that captures the overall change in probability of winning that a player has accounted for with his bat. Since clutch situations have a larger impact on winning or losing than average ones, a high WPA for a player indicates that they have produced a positive result in tight situations more often than not. For Henrich, his 30.4 WPA in a Yankee uniform ranks eighth in franchise history behind a who's who of superstars: Mickey Mantle, Lou Gehrig, Babe Ruth, Joe DiMaggio, Yogi Berra, Charlie Keller, and Derek Jeter. Tommy Henrich's clutch abilities were truly legendary.

RESERVE OUTFIELDER—REGGIE JACKSON

The thing about Reggie is that you know he's going to produce. And if he doesn't, he's going to talk enough to make people think he's going to produce.

—*Catfish Hunter*

In the mid-1970s the Yankees emerged from baseball obscurity with a group of players whose considerable talent was not eye-grabbing. To borrow a term from George Steinbrenner, they didn't have guys who "put meat in the seats." That all changed when Steinbrenner paid top dollar to lure a man whose overwhelming home-run power was outsized only by his ego and ability to sell himself. When Reggie Jackson came to New York, Steinbrenner risked destabilizing a clubhouse that was on the verge of accomplishing great things. In the end, the risk was worth the reward. Amidst a perpetual civil war between Yankee players, management, and ownership, Jackson put his money where his mouth was, so much so that he is now the quintessence of success in October baseball.

Reggie Jackson grew up in the northern suburbs of Philadelphia. There he attended Cheltenham High School where he starred in football, basketball, baseball, and track and field. He then attended Arizona State University on a football scholarship, but by his sophomore year had also talked his way onto the baseball team. After the season he was drafted second overall by the Athletics, then in Kansas City, and decided to leave school after a long contract negotiation with the team. Drama at the negotiating table would become a career staple.

In 1968 the 22-year-old Jackson broke in as an everyday major leaguer for the Athletics, now in Oakland. Early on he caught the eye of the A's new hitting instructor, Joe DiMaggio, who said, "Reggie is still green as grass. We've just got to bring his talents to the surface. They're all there, no question." By 1969 he was a rock star. With a muscular upper body that dwarfed his average frame, he regularly hit tape-measure blasts reminiscent of Mickey Mantle in his heyday. He finished the season with

47 home runs, which would stand as a career high. During his time in Oakland, he was a major contributor to three consecutive World Series championships won from 1972 to 1974. He was at his best when all eyes were on him, taking home both regular-season and World Series MVP honors in 1973.

After annual contract squabbles and a trade to the Baltimore Orioles in 1976, he prophetically said, "If I played in New York they'd name a candy bar for me." After the season he became a free agent, and so began George Steinbrenner's courtship of Reggie Jackson. One was a loud, deep-pocketed owner eager to overpay for premium talent and the other was an outspoken, egocentric player eager to get paid for his star power. It was a match made in heaven. They agreed on a record five-year deal that would pay nearly three million dollars.

Thanks to his new salary, which overshadowed those of incumbent sluggers Chris Chambliss, Graig Nettles, and especially Thurman Munson, Jackson was received coldly by his new teammates. At his introductory press conference he quipped, "I didn't come to New York to become a star. I brought my star with me." He couldn't understand why his showboating ways, which had played so well on the West Coast, ruffled feathers with teammates and fans in New York who were fiercely loyal to Munson. Jackson reacted the only way he knew how. During spring training he was famously quoted in a *SPORT* magazine interview as saying that he was the "straw that stirs the drink" for the Yankees. When the story was published that June, it fueled the fire. Even Willie Randolph at one point gave Jackson the silent treatment when he asked what time batting practice started.

That was nothing compared to his relationship with his new manager. Billy Martin was firmly against the acquisition of

Jackson and wasn't shy about expressing his displeasure when he seemingly failed to hustle. During a key June 18 matchup in Boston, Jim Rice popped up to right field and Jackson failed to catch or even retrieve the ball in a timely manner. Rice took second base thanks to Jackson's hesitation. A livid Martin pulled a perplexed Jackson from the game in mid-inning. When Jackson returned to the bench, the volatile Martin frothed at the mouth and laced into him as he said, "You want to show me up by loafing on me. Fine. Then I'm going to show your ass up. Anyone who doesn't hustle doesn't play for me." Jackson retaliated with some choice words and, ready for a fight, removed his glasses. The diminutive Martin beat him to the punch and lunged at him. Yankee coaches separated them to restore order as Jackson retreated to the clubhouse and said to Martin, "You don't like me—you've never liked me." He wasn't wrong. The Bronx Zoo was in full swing.

When it came to his bat, Jackson's teammates and manager had nothing to complain about. He hit .286 with 32 home runs and a team-high 110 RBIs and 150 OPS+. That helped the Yankees win 100 games and another division title. In a tight American League Championship Series rematch with Kansas City, Jackson had just one hit in 14 at bats through four games and was benched for the decisive Game 5. Called on to pinch-hit down two runs in the eighth inning, Jackson delivered an RBI single to spark a comeback win and a trip to the World Series. During another close series Thurman Munson once redirected an interviewer to Jackson by sarcastically saying, "Go ask Mr. October," alluding to his past exploits in the World Series.

True to his reputation, Jackson homered in both Games 4 and 5 as the Yankees headed into Game 6 with a chance to win their first Fall Classic since 1962. Down 3–2 in the fourth inning, Jackson stepped to the plate against Burt Hooton with Munson on first base. He drilled the first pitch he saw into the right field seats to give the Yankees a 4–3 lead. One inning later he stepped in against Elias Sosa with Willie Randolph on first and a 5–3 lead. Again, he crushed the first offering for a liner that cleared the right field fence by just a few feet. Jackson then led off the eighth inning against Charlie Hough with a chance at history. The flamboyant slugger would bring the goods. Hough floated a knuckleball to open the inning and Jackson put a charge into a towering flyball that landed in the old center field bleachers at Yankee Stadium, nearly 500 feet away. Three pitches, three swings, three home runs, three different pitchers, and three aggressive trots around the bases later, Reggie Jackson went from mortal to legend. He joined Babe Ruth as the only other player to hit three home runs in a World Series game and sealed the series victory for the Yankees. The Mr. October nickname would stick.

In 1978 Jackson had another quality season in the middle of the Yankees' lineup. His 27 home runs tied for the team lead with Graig Nettles and his 97 RBIs led the team outright as they won 100 games for the second consecutive season. That April he also got his own candy bar, just as he said he would if he played in New York. On April 13th all fans at Yankee Stadium received a free Reggie! Bar, peanuts and caramel covered in chocolate with Jackson's name and face on the wrapper. Naturally, Jackson homered in the first inning as a delighted crowd roared his name and showered the field with their now famous treats.

Despite the success, a return to the playoffs wouldn't be easy. The Yankees crawled from 14 games back of the Red Sox to tie them for first place in the American League East, which required a 163rd game to determine a winner. In a game with a far more famous home run, Jackson hit a solo shot in the top of the eighth, scoring what would stand as the winning run in a 5–4 victory. His October heroics continued in matchups with the Royals and Dodgers in the League Championship and World Series, respectively. He hit a pair of home runs in each series with a .417 batting average and 14 RBIs as the Yankees successfully defended their World Series title. For all the bragging and boasting, Jackson was worth every penny of his mega-deal.

Though Jackson had another fine season at the plate, the sudden and tragic death of Thurman Munson derailed the Yankees in 1979. In a tender reflection Jackson would later note of Munson in an autobiography: "Our wars were behind us then and if we weren't best friends, I at least thought of us as battle scarred comrades, who'd finally achieved a warm measure of respect and formed a basis of understanding." In 1980 Reggie had his finest season in pinstripes. His 41 dingers led the American League, his 111 RBIs led the team, and he hit .300 for the first and only time. Unfortunately, that success wouldn't carry over to October as the Yankees were swept by the Royals in the American League Championship.

The strike-shortened season of 1981 was mostly forgettable for Jackson. He hit just .237 with only 15 home runs, but the Yankees snuck into the playoffs. They took on the Milwaukee Brewers in a divisional playoff where Jackson channeled his Mr. October alter ego. He hit home runs in Games 2 and 5, both Yankee wins, as they advanced to the American League Championship Series against his old team in Oakland. The Yankees swept the Athletics to return to the World Series, but

Jackson sustained an injury in Game 2. Limited to just three games played against the Dodgers, the Yankees lost in six.

The Yankees did not re-sign Jackson after his contract was up, but he continued to play for another six years. As explosive and fleeting as his time in New York was, few could argue with its success. Every superstar free agent the Yankees have signed since has stood in the shadow of Mr. October and fallen short of eclipsing it.

Chapter VII

PITCHERS

Starting Pitcher—Whitey Ford

If you had one game to win and your life depended on it, you'd want him to pitch it.

—*Casey Stengel*

Any list of great Yankees is typically scarce on pitching. However, when a pitcher is finally chosen, it's inevitably Whitey Ford. Whether it was Opening Day, the dog days of summer, or the World Series, Ford's demeanor never changed. Nobody was more confident in his ability to get the job done than he was of himself. While winning was second nature, no matter the outcome of a game he was equally affable afterwards with both the media and his teammates, ready to toast the town. Not only is he an all-time great Yankee, he's one of the most successful players in baseball history.

Born in Midtown Manhattan and raised in Queens, Edward Ford was a New Yorker through and through. He grew up rooting for the Yankees and like many young fans of his day worshipped Joe DiMaggio. In high school he was a first baseman, but by his junior year he began pitching as well. As a

Nobody was cooler under pressure than Whitey Ford.

senior he participated in a tryout camp hosted by the Yankees, who deemed him too small to play first base yet saw potential in him as a pitcher. That summer he dazzled the competition pitching in a local semipro league, which inspired the Yankees to sign him.

In 1947 Ford reported to spring training under the tutelage of Yankee legend, and fellow left-handed pitcher, Lefty Gomez. Forgetful manager Bucky Harris often referred to Ford as "Whitey" because he couldn't remember his name and only knew him by his blond locks. The name would stick. Armed with a strong curveball, Ford needed help with the rest of his repertoire and spent a stint playing winter ball in Mexico where he learned how to throw an effective changeup, but also contracted a mean case of dysentery. After a lengthy hospital stay back in the United States, he led his league in ERA and strikeouts for the Yankees affiliate in Binghamton.

The following spring Ford displayed a cockiness that stood in stark contrast to his 5-foot-10, 170-pound physical presence. Eddie Lopat, a veteran lefty junkballer, was tasked with mentoring Ford. He soon found that the young lefty was resistant to change and wasn't shy about it. Lopat eventually said, "What the hell am I breaking my ass for? Take him back. He's too much for me." Ford didn't start the 1950 season with the Yankees, but by June they were in desperate need of pitching and called up the 21-year-old.

When Ford first arrived with the Yankees, manager Casey Stengel used him as a utility pitcher, either starting or coming out of the bullpen depending on team need and Ford's recent form. As the season wore on, Stengel's trust in the rookie grew and on September 16 he turned to Ford for the rubber game of a crucial series in Detroit. He matched Dizzy Trout pitch for pitch as the game was tied 1–1 heading into the ninth inning, Ford's only run support being a home run from his idol Joe DiMaggio. The Yankees rallied for seven runs, and Ford sealed a complete game victory that gave the Yankees a lead in the American League they wouldn't surrender.

In half a season's work Ford went 9-1 with a 2.81 ERA that was 53 percent better than average per his 153 ERA+. He was the runner-up for the Rookie of the Year award and was trusted to start Game 4 of the World Series against the Phillies with a chance to complete the sweep. Ford, confident as ever, shut the Phillies out through 8⅔ innings before surrendering two unearned runs and was pulled while his teammates sealed the 5–2 victory.

With the Korean War in full swing, Ford was drafted into the US Army in November of 1950. He spent the next two years as a radar operator and played exhibition baseball to stay in shape. He returned to the team prior to the 1953 season and rejoined a pitching staff that had earned two more World Series wins in his absence on the strength of Allie Reynolds, the aforementioned Lopat, and Vic Raschi. No one of that group was a true ace, but together they formed one of the best trios of pitchers in baseball. Ford would become the top dog of a fearsome foursome.

Ford paced the Yankees with 18 wins, 207 innings pitched, and 110 strikeouts. He helped the Yankees reach and win their remarkable fifth straight World Series as they bested the Brooklyn Dodgers in six games. The following year he struggled early but was named to his first All-Star Game and was unstoppable in the second half. He was a big reason that the Yankees won 103 games, yet they fell well short of the pennant thanks to the 111-win Cleveland Indians.

By 1955 Ford was one of baseball's best pitchers. He led the American League in complete games and wins with 18 of each and had a particularly dominant stretch that September. In a home game against the Washington Senators on September 2, he took a no-hitter into the seventh inning before surrendering a one-out single. That would stand as the only blemish as Ford held on for a complete game victory. The following week he repeated that feat against the Kansas City Athletics, whose only hit would be a seventh inning double. It was just the fifth time in baseball history that a pitcher spun consecutive complete game one hitters. Facing the Dodgers in the World Series, Ford won a close Game 1 and got the ball again for Game 6 where he pitched a complete game gem, striking out eight and allowing just one run in a 5–1 victory. Afterwards, curmudgeonly Hall of Famer Ty Cobb said to Ford, "I'd hate to have been hitting against you myself." Alas, the Yankees lost the series in seven.

Ford was the veteran leader of a rotation that no longer included Reynolds, Lopat, or Raschi in 1956. Before the season started *Sports Illustrated* raved about Yankee pitching and praised Ford as "a left-hander with all the pitches." In his description of the 1956 Yankees, Peter Golenbock also noted, "Ford was the best left-hander in the American League." He responded with his best season yet, winning 19 games with a major-league-leading 2.47 ERA as the Yankees cruised to another pennant. His 5.2 WAR was also by far a career high to that point. He finished third in the Cy Young Award vote but uncharacteristically struggled in the World Series, losing Game 1 in a rematch with the Dodgers. Ford would win a Game 3 nail-biter as the Yankees got their revenge, winning a seven-game series.

Lingering shoulder soreness limited Ford to just 24 games in 1957, but he made two high-quality starts in a World Series loss to the Milwaukee Braves. In 1958, Ford's 2.01 ERA, 177 ERA+, and seven shutouts all led the major leagues. His stellar performance was thanks in large part to improved accuracy on his curveball as he recorded a career-high 145 strikeouts with a career-best walk rate. In a rematch with the Braves in the World Series, Ford was not personally responsible for any victories in his three starts, but pitched well enough for the Yankees to win another seven-game series.

Ford was typically brilliant in 1959, but after going the distance in a 14-inning marathon with the Senators that April, he experienced chronic arm trouble that caused him to miss starts over the next two seasons. Despite winning that 14-inning classic 1–0 thanks to Ford, the Yankees struggled the rest of the season. In 1960 Ford fell short of his standard, but thanks to a stacked lineup that now featured Roger Maris alongside Mickey Mantle, the Yankees returned to the World Series. There, they took on the Pittsburgh Pirates and Ford found his confidence. He pitched complete game shutouts in Games 3 and 6, but the team was blindsided in Game 7 as they lost 10–9 after Bill Mazeroski's improbable walkoff home run. Things might have turned out differently had Casey Stengel given Ford the ball three times instead of two, and Ford would later say that was the only time he was ever mad at his old manager.

The disappointing 1960 World Series marked the end of a Yankee era that flourished through the 1950s. Mickey Mantle may have been the face of the team, but Ford was the heart and soul. He was among the best starting pitchers of his generation and had the deserved reputation of being even deadlier when stakes were highest. Recognizing these traits in his diminutive lefty, Casey Stengel used it to his team's advantage. Stengel would often schedule Ford's starts to coincide with games against top teams in the American League rather than waste them against bottom-dwellers. As a result, Ford could go a week or more between starts. As good as Ford's results were, it's remarkable to think that they could have been even better had he pitched every fourth day, and against good and bad teams alike, as his peers did.

A major factor in Ford's ability to shine under pressure was his comfort in being a star in New York. Unlike most Yankees, he was accustomed to the harsh coverage high-profile players were subject to in the New York media because he read those same articles at a young age and knew how to handle it. To his best friends on the team, shy country bumpkin Mickey Mantle and hot-headed Californian Billy Martin, this made him a priceless asset. As young, successful, well-paid athletes they soaked up the nightlife New York City had to offer, sometimes to their detriment. In fact, Ford once said, "Hell, if I didn't drink or smoke, I'd win twenty games every year. It's easy when you don't drink or smoke or horse around." In that lifestyle, dicey situations were commonplace and his pals could rely on the streetwise Ford to get them out of a jam.

Luckily for Stengel, Ford's composure also translated to the baseball diamond so he turned a blind eye to most of their antics. As Peter Golenbock noted, "Though [Ford] was a witty man off the field, on it he was serious and almost arrogant, exuding a confidence in himself that suggested infallibility." Stengel gave Ford the nickname "Slick" for that reason, while others referred to him as "The Chairman of the Board" before Frank Sinatra earned the nickname too. Still, it was Stengel's reluctance to rely on Ford in 1960 that probably cost the Yankees the World Series.

Ford's career significantly changed when Ralph Houk took over as Yankee manager in 1961. Unlike Stengel, Houk started Ford on regular rest, regardless of who they were playing. After never starting more than 33 games in a season through 1960, Ford led the majors with 39 starts in 1961 and started a minimum of 36 games over the next four years. In a season far more famous for Mickey Mantle and Roger Maris chasing Babe Ruth's home-run record, Ford was quietly dominant thanks to the increased usage. He won a major-league-leading 25 games and earned the only Cy Young Award of his career as the Yankees went 109-53. During the World Series he earned victories over the Cincinnati Reds in Games 1 and 4 without surrendering a run. At 32 years old Ford found a second wind and was named the World Series MVP for an all-time great team.

Ford continued to pitch like an ace in 1962 and 1963, although his performance in the Fall Classic dipped a bit as the Yankees beat the San Francisco Giants, then lost to the Los Angeles Dodgers. He followed that up with arguably the best season of his career in 1964. Ford would say around this time, "My greatest asset as a pitcher is knowing the hitters." He outsmarted hitters on his way to a minuscule 2.13 ERA, which yielded a 170 ERA+. He also led the Yankees in WAR for the only time of his career. However, in the World Series he made only one disappointing start due to numbness in his throwing hand caused by a clogged artery. He never pitched in the World Series again.

After surgery, Ford returned to the Yankees in 1965, but he wasn't the ace that he had been. His lingering circulation issue required more surgery, and he pitched in a limited capacity for the next two seasons while also serving as an invaluable mentor to young pitchers Mel Stottlemyre and Al Downing. He officially retired in May of 1967 as the best pitcher in franchise history.

Whitey Ford can best be described as a winner. His 236 regular-season victories are a Yankee record and his .690 winning percentage is the best of any pitcher with at least 200 starts in the modern era. He was even better in October, and from 1955 through 1958 he became the only pitcher ever to start Game 1 in four consecutive World Series, then did it again from 1961 through 1964. At one point during those series he pitched 33⅔ consecutive scoreless innings, breaking a record set by Babe Ruth. Ford's desire to win burned so deep that late in his career he resorted to discreetly scuffing the ball with a strategically sharp wedding ring or even his catcher's shin guard. Some would call that cheating, but a slick kid from New York City would just call it being resourceful.

STARTING PITCHER—RON GUIDRY

You know how you can spot those left-handers who are going to have super control? They're exceptionally graceful. Remember Guidry on the mound, how graceful he was? He was like a dancer.

—*Bill James*

Nothing about Ron Guidry's appearance would convince someone that he could be a dominant pitcher. Standing under 6 feet tall with a wiry, bow-legged frame, he would look more at home as a midfielder on a soccer pitch than perched atop a pitcher's mound. He fought that perception for years, despite his otherworldly ability to throw a baseball. When Guidry did finally get a chance to prove his value, he became one of the most dominant forces in the game. During a period of great success amid chaos for the Yankees in the late 1970s, he anchored a pitching staff that was in constant turnover. Against all odds, he finished his career without doubt one of the greatest pitchers in franchise history.

Born and raised in southern Louisiana, Ron Guidry came by his leathery skin and Cajun accent honestly. When he wasn't perfecting a recipe for frog legs with his father or watching baseball on TV with his Yankee-obsessed mother, he was an elite track star in high school. As it turned out, he could also generate an inordinate amount of torque from his slight frame and could throw a baseball over 90 miles per hour. Thusly, he pitched for the University of Southwestern Louisiana and was the third round pick of the Yankees in the 1971 draft. Guidry was thought of as nothing more than a potential left-handed reliever by the Yankees' front office. However, he impressed during his slow plod up the organizational ladder as both a starter and reliever.

At 24 years old, Guidry finally earned his first callup to the big leagues in 1975. The only notable occurrence during this stint was an exchange with fellow Yankee relievers Sparky Lyle and Dick Tidrow. Lyle informed the rookie that in the Yankee clubhouse, everyone needed a nickname. When asked where he was from, he described his upbringing in the bayou, where snakes and alligators were prevalent. Tidrow dubbed him "Gator," and a lasting moniker for Guidry was born. He was called up for another brief stint the following season that nearly saw his Yankee career end prematurely.

In a game that May, Guidry blew a two-run lead in the ninth inning to give the Red Sox a win. Naturally, George

Steinbrenner wanted him traded immediately, but general manager Gabe Paul vehemently defended his young pitcher who thankfully stayed in pinstripes. Despite the poor results, all was not lost for Guidry. During a bullpen session with Lyle, known for having one of the most effective sliders in baseball, Guidry learned how to throw the pitch as a complement to his blazing fastball.

Guidry made the Yankee Opening Day roster in 1977. Before the season was even a month old, he was thrust into the starting rotation of the defending American League champs. With no other healthy arms at his disposal, Billy Martin gave Guidry the ball for a home game against the Seattle Mariners on April 29. In his first career start, he used his slider to perfection, tossing 8⅓ scoreless innings with eight strikeouts in a 3–0 victory. That start helped ease Yankee concerns about Guidry as a starter, and he was soon a mainstay in the rotation.

His benefactor Sparky Lyle may have earned the American League Cy Young for his 26 saves, but Guidry was the Yankees' best pitcher. This was a notion asserted by his manager after earning a complete game win over Boston in mid-September. Billy Martin said after the game, "He has been our most consistent pitcher since he started." Both traditional and advanced metrics substantiate the claim. His 176 strikeouts, 16 victories, and 4.8 WAR led the pitching staff and his 2.82 ERA was second only to Lyle. A metric called Fielding Independent Pitching (FIP) paints an even brighter picture. Designed to approximate ERA, FIP uses only walks, strikeouts, and home runs allowed in its calculation to remove any fielding quality bias for pitchers. Guidry's 2.73 FIP mark led all qualified starters in the major leagues. In the postseason he earned complete game victories in the League Championship Series against

Kansas City and World Series over the Dodgers. He was vital in ending the longest World Series drought in franchise history.

Guidry's 1978 season was simply one of the best in baseball history. Having mastered his fastball-slider combination, he mowed down everything in his path. Regardless of what Reggie Jackson had said about straws and drinks, Guidry became the most valuable Yankee. He led the major leagues by surrendering just six hits per nine innings. His 25 wins, 9 shutouts, microscopic 1.74 ERA, and astounding 208 ERA+ were also the best in baseball. During a June 17 game against the California Angels, he etched himself in Yankee lore.

Guidry had extra life on his fastball and bite on his slider as he struck out 18 of 35 batters faced in a complete game shutout. That set a franchise record for a single game and included a staggering 16 Angels that went down swinging. The Yankee Stadium crowd stood and clapped in anticipation each time Guidry had two strikes on a batter, which has become a lasting tradition. Guidry even earned praise from Angels pitcher Nolan Ryan, unquestionably the greatest strikeout pitcher in baseball history, who was watching from the opposing dugout and said, "That kid was overpowering." No longer considered too small to be a durable starter the "Louisiana Lightning Man," as Phil Rizzuto nicknamed Guidry, became a household name.

The Yankees needed Guidry more than ever during a crucial weekend series that September in Boston. They trailed the Red Sox by just a game after being as many as 14 games behind them that summer. Guidry started the third game of what later would be called the "Boston Massacre" and tossed a two-hit shutout. A week later he faced them again in Yankee Stadium and delivered another two-hit shutout. After back-to-back gems from Guidry, the Yankees had a 2½-game lead.

When the season came down to the wire and required a 163rd game to decide the division winner, Guidry was the obvious choice to start. After carrying his teammates all year, he needed a little help. He surrendered two runs over 6⅓ innings before giving way to Goose Gossage as the Yankees hung on for a 5–4 victory and a berth in an American League Championship rematch with the Royals.

In the Game 4 clincher over the Royals, Guidry pitched eight innings for a 2–1 victory. He then threw a complete game victory over the Dodgers in Game 3 of the World Series. The Yankees would repeat as World Series champs and couldn't have done it without Guidry. After the season he was unanimously named the American League Cy Young Award winner and was runner-up in the MVP vote behind Boston's Jim Rice. Perhaps most impressively, he had earned the public praise of a curmudgeonly owner who had wanted to run him out of town just a couple of years prior. At an awards banquet that winter George Steinbrenner offered this about his prized pitcher: "I almost made a big mistake in 1976 by trading this young man. I'm so glad I was talked out of it, because, as it turns out, we would never have accomplished what we did in the last couple of years if it wasn't for him."

The good vibes ceased when Yankee captain Thurman Munson crashed his plane and died suddenly in August of 1979. The Yankees understandably faltered thereafter, though Guidry did everything he could to help the team. When the Yankees needed bullpen help, he volunteered to fill in on days between starts. Across the 1979 and 1980 seasons he made 11 relief appearances and earned three saves while winning 35 games total. In the latter season they returned to the playoffs by winning 103 games. Unfortunately, Guidry put up a dud in

Game 1 of the American League Championship Series to kick off a sweep at the hands of the Royals.

During a whirlwind, strike-shortened year in 1981, the 30-year-old Guidry combined with 22-year-old Dave Righetti and nearly over-the-hill Tommy John to form one of the best, and most unlikely, trios of starters in the majors. Each posted an ERA well below 3.00, and they combined to account for nearly half of the Yankees' wins in the abbreviated schedule. The Yankees snuck into the playoffs and found themselves taking on the Dodgers in the World Series again. Guidry pitched spectacularly in a Game 1 victory and got the ball for Game 5 with the series tied at two. He pitched valiantly, surrendering two runs over seven innings, but lost a 2–1 heartbreaker and the series a game later. Guidry would never pitch in the playoffs again.

He continued as a dependable starter for the next two seasons. During both years he led the team in wins, was named an All-Star, and earned the first two of five consecutive Gold Gloves. Guidry was often cited as the best athlete on the Yankees. As a result, any dribbler or bunt that stayed in his vicinity was a sure out. All the athleticism in the world couldn't save his ailing arm a season later though. The undue stress of firing 90-mile-per-hour fastballs from a jockey's frame finally caught up with Guidry. For the first time since becoming a starting pitcher, he had a losing record in 1984 with an unsightly 4.51 ERA. He also missed a month of action due to his sore arm.

An offseason full of rest did Guidry well and he had a career renaissance in 1985. His 259 innings pitched was his highest since setting the world on fire in 1978 and his 22 wins led the American League. Boasting a 3.27 ERA, he was also runner-up in the Cy Young Award vote. Even better, he contributed to a 10-win team improvement as the Yankees won 97 games, albeit two games shy of the division crown. At spring training the following year Guidry was named co-captain of the Yankees along with Willie Randolph, a position that had not been filled since Munson's death. It was a long overdue honor for the two players most responsible for keeping the Yankees respectable since their last championship run. Guidry had a fine season in 1986 as the Yankees finished second again, but his 36-year-old arm didn't have much mileage left.

In 1987 Guidry missed significant time due to shoulder woes, but was effective when able to take the hill. Offseason shoulder surgery kept him out until July of 1988. When he did return, he was limited to only 10 starts. After more offseason surgery, Guidry intended on returning in 1989. However, the Yankees sent him to Triple-A Columbus for a de facto tryout. He underwhelmed in seven starts and when the Yankees didn't call him up, he announced his retirement after 14 seasons in pinstripes.

Despite getting a late start to his major-league career, Guidry's pitching numbers are among the all-time Yankee greats. His 170 career wins rank fifth in franchise history, his 26.3 Wins Above Average rank third among pitchers, while his 2,392 innings pitched rank just seventh best. Like Hall of Famer Sandy Koufax, his dominance during his relatively short career more than made up for his relatively modest career totals. In fact, in *The Politics of Glory*, Bill James made the case that Guidry was on Koufax's elite level when he wrote, "You may be surprised to learn that Ron Guidry's career record is comparable to Sandy Koufax's. Koufax's ERA is a little better, but half of that difference is created by league ERAs."

Although Guidry will never receive the acclaim that Koufax has, he did earn the respect and admiration of those he went to war with in pinstripes. Fran Healy, reserve catcher on the Bronx Zoo Yankee teams, once noted, "Oh man, was he first class. He threw extremely hard, with good control—which was unusual. And a very nice guy." On the other hand, former Yankee pitcher Brian Fisher offered, "He was a gamer. Not very big, but full of fire. The kind of guy I wouldn't want to meet in a dark alley—even as small as he was, he was fiery." When Louisiana Lightning was about to strike, nobody could see it coming.

Starting Pitcher—Lefty Gomez

Gomez had as much to do with my success as any man who ever played for me.

—*Joe McCarthy*

If Lefty Gomez never touched a baseball, he might still have been a popular figure and American icon. His sharp wit and irresistible personality would have landed him a successful career in entertainment. As it turned out, though, he could throw the hell out of a baseball. Thanks to that skill, he got a gig in New York right near Broadway, but it was pitching for the Yankees rather than performing in theaters. As a Yankee he had a lasting impact on legends like Joe DiMaggio. But to define his greatness, look no further than his work on the mound. The flame-throwing Gomez was the greatest strikeout pitcher of his era and was the Yankees' ace for most of his career. He was also a fierce competitor, especially in the World Series where he was 6-0 lifetime.

Lefty Gomez was as talented on stage as he was on the mound.
GOUDEY GUM/WIKIMEDIA COMMONS/PUBLIC DOMAIN

Vernon Gomez grew up near the San Francisco Bay Area on his family's farm. The son of a Spanish-Portuguese cowboy, he grew up riding horses, but his true passions were aviation, playing the saxophone, and most of all baseball. He saw the best means to pursuing that passion as joining the famed San

Francisco Seals of the Pacific Coast League and tried out for them at age 14. After high school he played semipro ball until finally getting a contract offer from the Seals. Although they deemed his 6-foot-2, 125-pound body too thin, he talked his way onto the Seals' roster in 1929 and after a torrid 11-game winning streak was purchased by the Yankees.

The Yankees shared the Seals' concerns about Gomez's weight and ordered him to bulk up before reporting for spring training. When he arrived, he weighed just under 150 pounds and pitched well, although a comebacker to his face required significant dental work. When the regular season started he was effective as both a reliever and spot-starter, but his mouth needed more surgery that June. Upon Gomez's return his ERA swelled to over 5.00 and he was sent to the minors to finish out the season. In 1931 the Yankees eased him in again as a reliever, but he soon became one of their most trusted starters. Gomez, colloquially known as "Lefty" by this time, won 21 games and his 2.63 ERA was runner-up to Lefty Grove for best in the majors. The Yankees finished second behind Grove's Athletics, but they had a new ace of the pitching staff.

In 1932 Gomez surrendered what would be a career-high 23 home runs, which contributed to a below average 4.21 ERA. That didn't matter to MVP voters as he finished fifth in the vote thanks to his 24 victories for a dominant 107-win Yankee team. Gomez fared even better in his first World Series as he twirled a complete game victory over the Chicago Cubs in Game 2, striking out eight and allowing just one earned run. The Yankees swept the Cubs and that offseason Gomez set the stage for a career off the diamond as well. Shortly after arriving in New York, the sweet-talking Gomez married a Broadway actress. With a firsthand connection to show business, he joined a vaudeville act in the winter of 1932. As part of the show he delivered a humorous monologue about being a base-ball player and performed slapstick comedy skits.

Any concerns the Yankees had about Gomez's slender frame were behind them by 1933. He boasted an impressive 3.18 ERA with an American League leading 163 strikeouts, and his strikeout rate was tops in the majors. He attributed his strikeout ability to his jovial nature off the field with com-petitors, which lulled them into a false sense of security. "I talk them out of hits," he once said. Gomez also had the distinction of starting the first All-Star Game in major-league history. His first truly dominant campaign would come a year later. Behind his scorching fastball, he was 14-2 at the All-Star break and again started the Midsummer Classic. Around this time he also became the first pitcher ever to grace the cover of *Time* magazine. By season's end he had earned the American League pitching Triple Crown with 26 wins, a 2.33 ERA, and 158 strikeouts, just the fifth pitcher ever to do so. His six shutouts and extraordinary 8.3 WAR led all major-league pitchers. In 1935 Gomez suffered the only losing record of his career with 12 wins and 15 losses. However, his 128 ERA+ indicates that he had some tough luck.

The Yankees boasted a bona fide superstar pitcher in Gomez and the immortal Lou Gehrig in his prime, but had frustratingly finished in second place each year from 1933 through 1935. The frustration would finally end in 1936. Although he dealt with arm soreness all year, Gomez pitched solidly for a Yankee team that won 102 games and returned to the World Series. His most important contribution to the team, though, was taking a young, shy kid from San Francisco under his wing. Gomez made sure that Joe DiMaggio didn't succumb to the pressure of living and playing in New York City, and even roomed with him on the road. For the rest of DiMaggio's career, Gomez proved to be the only player who could joke around with him without getting under his skin. With Lefty's help DiMaggio flourished and the Yankees beat the New York Giants in a World Series that featured two Gomez victories. During his lopsided 18–4 victory in Game 2, Lefty stopped the game dead in its tracks from the mound during the seventh inning to stare up at the sky above the Polo Grounds. His childhood love of aviation got the best of him as he admired the rare occurrence of a plane flying over a baseball game, much to the bewilderment of everybody watching. It was just another case of Gomez being "El Goofo," as he would come to be known.

With his arm soreness gone, Gomez returned to dominant form in 1937. For the second time he earned the American League pitching Triple Crown with 21 wins, a 2.33 ERA, and a career-high 194 strikeouts. His 9.3 WAR also led a Yankee team that returned to Gomez's favorite stage, the World Series. Manager Joe McCarthy conceded as much when he said, "Lefty loved to pitch against the tough clubs. When he thought he should pitch, he would give me that look . . . put the bead on me. Even if my back was turned, I could feel his eyes boring into me." He got the ball for the first and last games of the series, earning complete game victories in each and surrendering just three runs between them. Gomez was on top of the baseball world.

During the offseason Gomez dealt with a messy divorce that extended into the 1938 season. It clearly affected even the gregarious Gomez as he struggled through the first half. However, by midseason he had convinced his wife to reconcile and took the league by storm thereafter. He finished with 18 wins, including a league-leading four shutouts as the Yankees earned their third straight trip to the World Series. In a sweep of the Cubs, he earned the final World Series victory of his career.

In May 1939 a back injury turned into more arm trouble after Gomez changed his pitching motion to compensate. While not at 100 percent, he was still an important part of a starting rotation that helped the Yankees to their fourth straight World Series. He also provided some needed comic relief when Lou Gehrig ended his consecutive games streak in Detroit. Gehrig got a standing ovation after handing in a lineup without his name to the umpire, and the entire team was overcome with emotion along with him. Gomez then said to Gehrig, "Hell Lou, it took fifteen years to get you out of there. Sometimes I'm out in fifteen minutes." Everyone, including Gehrig, had a laugh. However, Gomez's ailing arm was no laughing matter. At 30 years old with over 2,000 innings logged on it, he was done as an elite pitcher.

Gomez played three more years with the Yankees, but was there more in spirit. Jokes still flowed through Lefty with ease. Among the best was a classic about his diminutive shortstop: "Phil Rizzuto was so short that he had to stand on a stool to take a shower, otherwise the water would be cold before it got to him." However, he was relegated to the back of the rotation and was left off the 1941 World Series roster entirely. The Yankees beat the Brooklyn Dodgers, but the snub hurt Gomez who had pitched so admirably in his five prior World Series. After 80 subpar innings in 1942, the Yankees released him that winter.

In retirement Gomez remained a part of the Yankee family as he coached and managed in the minor-league system in the late 1940s. But he found that the best use of his gift of gab was traveling the world to spread the good word of baseball. He entertained troops as part of a USO tour in Africa and Italy, served as a pitching instructor in Venezuela and Cuba, administered baseball clinics throughout Latin America, and even returned to Japan where he had been popular during a visit as a player in 1934. In his spare time when back in the States, he had no trouble finding work as a speaker at banquets, where he could dip into his reservoir of baseball stories. He was even a guest of Johnny Carson on *The Tonight Show*. In some ways, his retirement was even more successful than his stellar playing career.

When Gomez was inducted into the Baseball Hall of Fame in 1972, he put his self-deprecating sense of humor on full display. Upon being asked why he was so successful he responded, "Clean living and a fast outfield." Yet, his lasting impact on baseball goes far beyond any one-liners. Pee Wee Reese, former Brooklyn Dodger and key figure in Jackie Robinson breaking baseball's color line in 1947, once recalled, "Lefty never saw color. He only saw ability. That's why, in 1945, when black players were still banned in major league baseball, he went to Caracas. It was his way of telling the brass back home that 'Hey, there's talent here and it has nothing to do with skin color.'" That's no joke.

STARTING PITCHER—ANDY PETTITTE

Andy is a big game pitcher. That's the bottom line.

—*Derek Jeter*

Yankee Stadium's unique dimensions give a distinct advantage to left-handed batters, but historically, left-handed pitchers have also benefitted greatly as well. Most great pitchers in Yankee history have been lefties, and when Andy Pettitte burst on the scene in the mid-90s, he became their next southpaw star. Unlike those before him, Pettitte looked the part of a big-league pitcher. Tall and thick as a Texas steer, he was a formidable presence on the mound, but his greatest assets were his nerves of steel. He had the uncanny ability to focus only on what it took to win, and winning is what he did best. His 219 victories as a Yankee are third best in franchise history, and his 18 playoff wins in pinstripes is the all-time major-league record.

Andy Pettitte grew up just outside of Houston, Texas, by way of Baton Rouge, Louisiana. They say everything's bigger in Texas, and Pettitte was no exception. In high school he played center and nose tackle for his football team and also approached 90 miles per hour with his fastball. Upon graduating he was drafted by the Yankees in the 22nd round of the 1990 MLB draft, but chose not to sign right away. Instead he enrolled at San Jacinto Junior College, where he began an intense workout regimen that dropped weight from his 6-foot-5 frame, but added velocity to his fastball. With Pettitte's stock on the rise and his draft rights still with the Yankees, they pushed to sign him prior to the 1991 draft and succeeded at the bargain price of $80,000.

Over the next four years, Pettitte utilized his fastball and changeup to great results as he rose to the top of a Yankee farm system brimming with talent. *Baseball America* named Pettitte the 49th best prospect in baseball leading into the strike-shortened 1995 season. That year he and the other Core Four members Mariano Rivera, Derek Jeter, and Jorge Posada would each make their major-league debut.

Pettitte fought for the fifth spot in the starting rotation during spring training, but lost out to fellow left-hander Sterling Hitchcock. The intensely competitive Pettitte vowed to prove that was the wrong decision. Minor-league pitching instructor Tony Cloninger recognized this drive and had his general manager's ear as Gene Michael once said, "[Cloninger] told me Pettitte is a mentally tough guy that has big inspirations [*sic*] to be better than Hitchcock. He wanted to pass him in the organization." When injuries opened a spot in the rotation, Pettitte did just that and filled in admirably for the balance of the year. He truly shined under pressure, going 5-1 with a 3.38 ERA in September as the Yankees won a heated wild card race.

A soul-crushing loss in the Division Series to the Seattle Mariners resulted in significant changes to the Yankee roster, but Pettitte wasn't going anywhere in 1996. He got the ball for the Yankees' home opener in the middle of an April snowstorm. Unfazed, he gutted out a victory over the Royals and quickly became new manager Joe Torre's only reliable arm in the rotation. Pettitte's newly developed cutter made him especially effective against right-handed hitters, and he was a late-season savior for the second straight year. By August the Yankees were losing their grip on the American League East, but he earned four victories in five starts, each of them following a Yankee loss. Torre bluntly said, "We don't make the postseason without Pettitte, period." He led the league with 21 wins and was runner-up for the Cy Young Award.

In the 1996 playoffs Pettitte struggled early, but he quelled any doubters in the World Series. After getting shelled by the Braves in Game 1 at Yankee Stadium, he started Game 5 in Atlanta against world-beater John Smoltz. A Cecil Fielder double in the fourth inning scored the only Yankee run, but an unfazed Pettitte ensured that it would stand up. Yankee catcher Joe Girardi saw that focus firsthand: "Andy had an incredible ability as a young man to focus on just the next pitch, not the one before, not the one still to come. He could block out bad stuff."

Already an intimidating figure on the mound, Pettitte displayed the composure and resourcefulness of a seasoned veteran. In the bottom of the fifth, he used his all-time great pickoff move to nab a leadoff baserunner. An inning later Smoltz and Marquis Grissom, both good baserunners, led off with a pair of singles. Mark Lemke then bunted to force the lumbering Pettitte into action. Showing world-class moxie he barehanded the ball and shocked everybody at Fulton County Stadium by throwing a strike to third base, not first, for the tougher out. Nearly a decade later Smoltz would say, "I still don't believe he made that play." On the next pitch Chipper Jones grounded back to Pettitte, who smoothly started a double play, officially killing the rally. His gutsy plays sealed the win, and a game later the Yankees ended an 18-year World Series drought.

Pettitte followed up his breakout year with the finest regular season of his career. In 1997 he won 18 games, boasted the best home-run rate in the major leagues, and posted a 2.88 ERA, which in the high-scoring late 1990s yielded an impressive 156 ERA+. His 8.4 WAR also ranked second among all American League pitchers. Alas, he and the Yankees struggled with the Cleveland Indians' potent lineup in the postseason as they faltered in the Division Series.

Pettitte was never a lights-out pitcher after that as his low-90s fastball was ordinary and his cutter was better suited for inducing groundballs than for missing bats. Instead, he was a dependable workhorse who remained unflappable in any situation. That type of pitcher is vital to winning championships.

His average regular season from 1998 through 2000 saw him go 16-10 with over 200 innings pitched, 131 strikeouts, a 4.42 ERA, and 105 ERA+. With that modest stat line, naturally George Steinbrenner wanted Pettitte traded and needed to be talked out of several potential deals. The fact that he was indispensable to three straight World Series wins was lost on The Boss, but not on sportswriters covering him. Prior to Game 4 of the 1998 World Series, Jerry Crasnick of *Bloomberg News* wrote, "Pettitte, 26, is one of the most accomplished young starters and elite left-handers in the game."

The Yankees won 10 of the 11 playoff games that Pettitte started in that three-year stretch. This included a momentum-shifting victory over the Red Sox at Fenway Park in Game 3 of the 1999 American League Championship Series. A year later he got the ball for Games 1 and 5 in the Subway Series against the crosstown Mets and kept each game close as the Yankees sealed a three-peat. Derek Jeter, the MVP of that World Series, deflected praise to Pettitte afterwards: "Think of how tough Andy was in this series, in every big game he's ever pitched for us."

By 2001 Pettitte had spent two years forging a close friendship with teammate, fellow Texan, and San Jacinto alumnus, superstar Roger Clemens. Clemens was a maniacal gym rat, which meant the ultra-competitive Pettitte had to step up his workout routine to keep up. With a more chiseled physique and a renewed command of his pitches, he started seeing better regular-season results. His strikeout rate increased while his walk rate and ERA decreased as the Yankees sought a fourth straight World Series win.

One of baseball's best pitchers in 2001, Pettitte's performance in the playoffs was uncharacteristically volatile. In the

Division Series against Oakland and League Championship against Seattle he was superb, and even earned series MVP honors for his two victories over the Mariners. However, he was roughed up by the Arizona Diamondbacks in the World Series, especially during a pivotal Game 6 when he surrendered six runs in just two innings. It was later revealed that he was unknowingly tipping his pitches, but the damage was done and the Yankees' World Series streak was over, devastating the big lefty.

After another early exit from the playoffs in 2002, Pettitte matched his career high with 21 wins in 2003 for a 101-win Yankee team that returned to the World Series. Ever the gamer, Pettitte recaptured his previous form in the Fall Classic and dominated the Florida Marlins in a Game 2 victory. He got the ball again for Game 6 with the series on the line and pitched his heart out, allowing just one earned run across seven innings. Unfortunately, Yankee bats failed to score as they lost the game and the series.

A free agent after the 2003 season, Pettitte wanted to remain a Yankee, but Steinbrenner did little to convince him that the feeling was mutual. Other contending teams were in hot pursuit of the durable 31-year-old lefty, especially the hated Boston Red Sox and Pettitte's hometown Houston Astros. He ultimately spurned the Yankees' lowball offer for the comfort of pitching near home on a three-year contract. His buddy Roger Clemens followed him to the Astros, leaving the Yankees scrambling to reassemble a starting rotation. Over the next three years the Yankees failed to return to the World Series while Pettitte, Clemens, and the Astros earned a spot in the 2005 Fall Classic. By the winter of 2006, both Pettitte and the Yankees were keen on a reunion.

Pettitte's years in Houston made him miss the constant pressure that fueled him as a competitor in New York. Earlier in his career he once said, "Whatever I do, I love to win. I don't care if it's tennis or ping pong, I'll kill myself to win it." Unfortunately, upon his return to the Yankees he found that aside from his fellow Core Four members, most players in the Yankee clubhouse no longer shared that mentality. Regardless, Pettitte gave the Yankees exactly what they expected: 200 solid innings at the top of the rotation and a high-quality start in the playoffs. However, the Yankees would be ousted in the first round again.

That winter, Pettitte had bigger problems to deal with. When the Mitchell Report on steroid use in baseball was released, it revealed that Pettitte had used human growth hormone (HGH) in 2002. The straight-shooting Texan handled the situation about as well as one could. After the report was released, he publicly admitted to using HGH in 2002 and again in 2004 as an Astro in order to accelerate the recovery of an ongoing elbow injury. He was honest, unambiguous, and mostly remorseful about his actions, which helped quickly bury the hatchet. Clemens, also exposed in the report, took the opposite approach and continues to fight all accusations with little success in the court of public opinion.

Pettitte's image remained mostly intact in 2008, but the Yankees failed to reach the playoffs for the first time in 13 years. In 2009 the Yankees' pitching staff was the beneficiary of a massive spending spree that landed the two best pitchers on the market in A. J. Burnett and CC Sabathia. Pettitte served as the veteran leader of a revamped staff that helped the Yankees back to the playoffs.

By that time it was clear that Pettitte, Burnett, and Sabathia were the only reliable starters on the Yankee roster, so manager Joe Girardi shortened the playoff rotation to just those three. At 37 years old, Pettitte earned series-clinching wins in each of the first two rounds of the playoffs and on just three days' rest started a potential World Series–clinching game against the Phillies at Yankee Stadium. Naturally, Pettitte got the job done and became the first pitcher to earn three playoff series–clinching wins in the same season. He also set the record for playoff series–clinching wins in a career with six.

Pettitte pitched three more seasons for the Yankees, broken up by a brief retirement in 2011. He was serviceable on the mound each of those years and turned in trademark performances in the playoffs, albeit in losing causes for the Yankees. In late September of 2013, Pettitte made it publicly known that he would be retiring at season's end along with Mariano Rivera.

A week later Pettitte made the last start of his career in front of his hometown fans in Houston. A gamer until the end, he went the distance in a 2-1 victory despite the Yankees being well out of playoff contention. Yet that performance didn't give Pettitte's career the justice it deserved. His lasting image will always be that of a menacing pair of eyes staring down an opponent from behind his glove, ready to do whatever it takes to win a big game.

STARTING PITCHER—RED RUFFING

Sure, he's the best pitcher around.

—*Joe McCarthy*

Babe Ruth's sale to the New York Yankees is pointed to as the seminal moment of the power shift in the American League from the Red Sox to the Yankees, and for good reason. However, the Yankees' dominance could not have been perpetuated for so many years without other blundering moves by Boston. The most important of those was a 1930 trade that landed Red Ruffing in pinstripes. A strong, silent right-hander, Ruffing was a mainstay in the Yankees' pitching rotation for 15 seasons, which yielded six World Series championships. Not only was he an extremely effective pitcher during those years, but he worked like a mule. Thanks to his durability and longevity, by the end of his career he had set numerous Yankee pitching records that still stand.

Hailing from a small coal mining town in northern Illinois, Charles Ruffing experienced a life of hard labor at an early age. At 13, with a head of hair that inspired the nickname "Red," he began working the mines with his father, who also happened to manage the company baseball team where Ruffing stood out as a right-handed pitcher and outfielder. Two years later at work, he was hooking two mine cars together when his left foot was crushed in between them. His doctor salvaged the foot, but he lost four toes to the accident and his days as an outfielder were over. After he recovered he focused primarily on pitching, and by the time he was 18 he had signed with a local minor-league team in Danville, Illinois. In just one season he impressed enough to earn a major-league contract with the Boston Red Sox.

By 1925 Ruffing was a full-time member of the Red Sox, who were still reeling from the infamous sale of Babe Ruth five years prior. Armed with a quality fastball, Ruffing mostly underwhelmed for awful Red Sox teams over five years. He compiled an unsightly 39-96 record with a below-average 4.61 ERA while his team finished last in the American League each year. During the *best* season the Red Sox had in this span, they won 58 games, which was 48 games behind the first-place

Philadelphia Athletics. By 1930 the franchise was in financial ruin and agreed to trade Ruffing to the Yankees for $50,000 in cash, a spare outfielder, and another $50,000 in loans.

The Yankees' gamble in acquiring a pitcher with such a miserable résumé paid off. Ruffing's first start with the Yankees was not a showstopper as he gave up six runs, but he did throw a complete game and earned the victory thanks to seven runs of support from a formidable lineup. From there his confidence grew and by season's end he was the best pitcher on the Yankees' roster. After years of losing he had gone 15-5 with a 4.14 ERA, which in the booming offensive environment of 1930 was actually above average. And speaking of offense, Ruffing helped himself considerably with the bat. While his foot injury stunted his running ability, he was still a capable hitter and slashed .374/.415/.596 with a 157 OPS+, four home runs, and 21 RBIs for the Yankees in 1930. He would often be used as a pinch-hitter on days he didn't pitch and hit over .300 five more times with 31 home runs as a Yankee.

After regressing on the mound in 1931, Ruffing bounced back in 1932. With his fastball running on all cylinders, his sparkling 3.09 ERA and 132 ERA+ were by far career bests as his 190 strikeouts led the American League. He also won a career-high 18 games and was chosen by manager Joe McCarthy to start the first game of the World Series for the 107-win Yankees. At Yankee Stadium he earned a complete game victory with 10 strikeouts in his first World Series action, setting the pace for a sweep of the Chicago Cubs.

There were three main contributing factors to Ruffing's career turnaround in New York. The most obvious was the increased run support he got from the potent Yankee lineup; in Boston there was no room for error. He also had much better fielders behind him with the Yankees as well as Bill Dickey, one of the best catchers in baseball, behind the plate. Lastly, when Ruffing arrived in New York former Yankee pitcher and manager at the time, Bob Shawkey, observed that his mechanics put undue stress on his arm, which caused fatigue late in games. This was likely the result of Ruffing compensating for his disfigured left foot. Shawkey retooled his delivery to positive results.

From 1933 through 1935 Ruffing averaged 238 innings pitched with a 3.67 ERA, 110 ERA+, and 15 wins per season. The Yankees finished in second place each of those years, but Ruffing along with a young Lefty Gomez were among the best dynamic pitching duos in the major leagues. Gomez was a lefty with dazzling stuff when he was healthy and the life of the party off the field. Ruffing, literally on the other hand, was a strong, dependable, and durable righty who was happy being the workhorse and mostly kept to himself when not pitching. In fact, Joe McCarthy once said of him, "If Ruffing has nothing to say he doesn't bother to say it." Of the pair, outfielder Tommy Henrich let it be known that only one was looked upon as the go-to Yankee pitcher when he said, "You know, there wasn't that much difference between [Gomez] and Ruffing, but Ruffing was always looked upon as the ace."

After adding a slider to his pitch arsenal, Ruffing kicked his career into another gear at the age of 31 in 1936. Of his new pitch, longtime American League umpire Joe Paparella would later say, "The first game I ever worked behind the plate in the major leagues was against the guy who invented the slider and had the best slider ever seen—Red Ruffing." On the strength of that pitch, Ruffing won at least 20 games for the next four years and went the distance in at least 20 every season. His ERA improved to 3.29, which yielded a 137 ERA+, and his nearly 20 pitching WAR ranked fourth among all major-league pitchers in that span. Not coincidentally, the Yankees won the World Series all four years, and Ruffing led the charge. He started Game 1 in three of the four series and overall went 4-1 with a 2.34 ERA in World Series play during this time.

By 1939 Ruffing was widely considered one of the best pitchers in baseball. After an Opening Day complete game shutout over his former team, New York sports columnist Joe Williams wrote, "There may be better pitchers in baseball than Mr. Ruffing, but we can't name two offhand. He has more poise than a head waiter, and he can do more with a baseball then [*sic*] FDR can do with a radio voice." Richard J. Tofel, sportswriter for the *Wall Street Journal*, took it a step further in his book on the 1939 Yankees. He made the following point regarding Ruffing clinching his fourth straight 20-win season: "The string firmly established him (perhaps along with Bob Feller) as the leading pitcher in the game, succeeding Carl Hubbell . . . and in the American League following Lefty Grove." He had come a long way since those dark days in Boston.

At 35 years old in 1940, chronic arm trouble began to limit Ruffing. He was still a fine pitcher when able, though, and won 15 games for a third-place Yankee team. He helped the Yankees return to the World Series in both 1941 and 1942. As usual, he got the starting nod for Game 1 of both series. In 1941 he pitched a complete game gem at Yankee Stadium to defeat the Brooklyn Dodgers by a slim 3–2 margin. The Yankees would take the series in five games. A year later he had a no-hitter going through 7⅔ innings against the Cardinals in St. Louis, but an eighth inning hit and ninth inning rally chased Ruffing from the game. The Yankees held on to win, giving Ruffing the seventh World Series win of his career, a record that would stand until Whitey Ford broke it in 1960. Alas, the Cardinals won the next four games for the series win.

Despite being 37 years old and having a severely handicapped left foot, Ruffing was cleared for noncombat duty and drafted into the Army prior to the 1943 season. His service was limited to physical fitness training in California and playing baseball to entertain troops in Hawaii. He was discharged immediately following V-E Day, and in July of 1945 he returned to the mound for the Yankees at 40 years old. As the Yankees struggled to get back on their feet after the war ended, Ruffing went 12-4 with a 2.43 ERA in 19 starts across 1945 and 1946. However a comebacker off the bat of the Athletics' Hank Majeski shattered his kneecap in June of 1946 and ended his Yankee career. After retiring he remained in baseball as a manager, scout, and coach for various organizations, but never returned to the Yankees.

Red Ruffing wasn't blessed with the great raw pitching skills that some of his peers had, but he made up for it with an iron arm that consistently churned out quality innings. His 231 career victories as a Yankee were a franchise record until broken by Whitey Ford, and still stand as the record for a Yankee right-hander by a margin of over 60 wins. With a record 261 complete games in a Yankee uniform, he bested runner-up Lefty Gomez by an impressive 88 games.

What truly stands as a testament to Ruffing's character, though, is that he accomplished it all after suffering a horrific accident as a young man. Even the most resolute among us would be discouraged from becoming a professional athlete after losing four toes to a mining cart, but Red persisted and thrived in the face of adversity. One can only imagine what he could have accomplished had he been able to play the field as well. In more ways than one he might have followed in Babe Ruth's footsteps.

STARTING PITCHER—WAITE HOYT

The secret of success as a pitcher lies in getting a job with the New York Yankees.

—Waite Hoyt

The fact that Waite Hoyt had the luxury of pitching for some of the greatest lineups ever assembled was not lost on the outspoken hurler. But his value as a quality pitcher that contributed to the success of those teams shouldn't be forgotten. One of many players shipped from the Red Sox to the Yankees for peanuts at the dawn of the 1920s, Hoyt's career took off in New York. Throughout the decade he was the team's most dependable arm and integral in winning the first World Series championships in franchise history. A skilled performer, he also had a successful secondary career in show business, which led to him being a prominent figure in baseball as an announcer for decades after his playing days.

Hoyt was born on the cusp of the 20th century in the Flatbush section of Brooklyn. In his formative years he learned to play baseball in that concrete jungle, and by the time he was in high school his fastball had caught the attention of major-league scouts. With the help of his father, a semipro player in his younger years, he secured a tryout with the New York Giants at the Polo Grounds and impressed manager John McGraw. At 15 years old he became the youngest man ever to sign a big-league contract and made national news. Sporting

Waite Hoyt was an unsung hero of the 1927 Yankees.
BAIN NEWS SERVICE/WIKIMEDIA COMMONS/PUBLIC DOMAIN

a baby face that would stay with him into his older years, he was given the nickname "Schoolboy," but soon proved he was anything but.

During his minor-league career, Hoyt displayed the reputation of a typical New Yorker. He was quick-witted, hardheaded, and eminently confident in his abilities. After a brief callup to the Giants in 1918, he rejected his assignment back to the minors and forced McGraw's hand. Hoyt would not accept any trade to another minor-league team, so he was sold to the Boston Red Sox. Their agreement included a provision, demanded by Hoyt, that he be given a big-league start within four days of a signed deal.

In his first major-league start, he took on the Detroit Tigers in July of 1919. Showing resolve that would become a trademark, he went the distance in a 12-inning marathon and earned the victory, 2–1, during a game where, "Cobb called me every name in the book," as he would later recall. For the next season and a half Hoyt toiled for the Red Sox with mixed results. The team, still strapped for cash since the Babe Ruth deal, went back to the well and made a cost-saving deal with the Yankees that centered on Hoyt going to New York for second baseman Del Pratt. The trade seemed even at the time.

By 1921, the Yankees were coming off of a 95-win season and ready to contend for the World Series. They needed no help offensively, as Ruth anchored a powerful lineup, but they lacked quality pitching depth. Hoyt was just what the doctor ordered. In what would stand as a career-high 283⅓ innings, he went 19-13 with a 3.09 ERA and 136 ERA+ as the Yankees took home the American League pennant and a spot in the 1921 World Series.

Taking on the New York Giants in what was then a best-of-nine series, Hoyt got the ball three times, each on just three days' rest. The pressure and fatigue didn't faze the young hurler. He went the distance in each start and surrendered no earned runs for the entirety of the series. After his two-hit gem in Game 2, the *New York Times* praised the diversity of his repertoire, as they reported, "He exhibited to the startled Giants a complete line of fast shoots of varying height, but almost unvarying accuracy, as well as floaters of aggravating slowness, drops, and speedy and languid curves." Nevertheless, his final start in the decisive Game 8 ended in heartbreak for the Yankees as the Giants scored the only run of the game on an error by Yankee shortstop Roger Peckinpaugh. Still, the *Sporting News* noted that he was "most sensational of all the hurlers" during the series.

The Yankees would return to the World Series to take on the Giants again in 1922 and 1923. In both seasons Hoyt was part of a small stable of pitchers that manager Miller Huggins exclusively relied on. He won 36 games across those two seasons and his 3.02 ERA in 1923 was best on the team and second best in the American League. While he wasn't able to match his previous success in the World Series during these years, the Yankees did finally beat the Giants in 1923 for the first World Series championship in franchise history.

Hoyt and the Yankees struggled to maintain a championship-caliber level of play. In 1925 the Yankees fell below .500 and Hoyt followed suit, finishing just 11-14 with an ERA over 4.00 for the first time since his Boston days. A year later he suffered an elbow injury, but the Yankees returned to the World Series to face the St. Louis Cardinals. There, Hoyt regained his previous stellar form. In St. Louis for Game 4, he pitched a complete game, surrendering five runs, but only two were earned as Yankee bats slugged their way to a 10–5 victory. Four days later he dominated through six innings at Yankee Stadium for Game 7, but again was undone by errors in the field. The Cardinals scored three runs thanks to two errors in the fourth inning and won the game 3–2, taking the series.

A young, handsome man living in New York City during the Roaring Twenties, Hoyt had the reputation of being a night owl. Like Ruth, he enjoyed both ladies and drinks in abundance, and as the son of a vaudevillian he used his baritone voice to perform during the offseason, a side job which no doubt helped fuel his nocturnal habits. Those distractions combined with his obstinance contributed to his decline on the field.

At 27 years old during spring training for the 1927 season, Hoyt had a moment of clarity triggered by some fatherly advice from his manager. He decided to tone down his hot-headedness and off-field antics to rejuvenate his career. Publicly, Huggins expressed confidence in Hoyt's new attitude when he said, "He has stuff and he knows how to use it. That fellow should win 20 or more games for me every season. He should be as good a pitcher as there is in the league." He returned to the Yankees a better teammate. During the 1927 season, the Yankees' "Murderers' Row" lineup battered American League pitching to the tune of nearly 1,000 runs scored. But they could not have won 110 games without a formidable pitching staff.

Hoyt served as the Yankees' bona fide ace as they led the league in fewest runs allowed. His 22 wins paced the American League and his 2.63 ERA was second best. Throughout the season, the *New York Herald Tribune* gushed about Hoyt's performance and once reported, "Hoyt's pitching has been a treat, a treat for those who can appreciate something other than hitters murdering the ball. Such control, such transition from one speed to another, such art in the pleasure of his slow curve." In the World Series he started Game 1 against the Pittsburgh Pirates but struggled, giving up four runs in just over seven innings. Luckily, his lineup helped him to a 5–4 victory. The Yankees would sweep the Pirates and seal their destiny as the greatest team of all time.

Hoyt continued his career turnaround in 1928 and won a career-high 23 games with a bonus. He, like most pitchers of this era, was available out of the bullpen on days he didn't start. In 1928 Hoyt was unstoppable when called upon to close out games, and in his 11 relief appearances he sported a 1.61 ERA with a major-league-leading eight saves. Thanks in part to Hoyt's heroics, the Yankees won their third straight American League pennant. He started Games 1 and 4 against the Cardinals in the World Series, pitched a complete game in each, and allowed just three earned runs as the Yankees made it back-to-back World Series sweeps. After the series, sportswriter James R. Harrison wrote, "[Hoyt] justified the claim that he is in the front rank of right-handed pitchers." Unfortunately, at just 28 years old, these would be the last great moments of his Yankee career.

Hoyt slipped back into his old habits off the field in 1929 and his on-field results suffered. His ERA ballooned to 4.24, and after a particularly bad start in mid-September Miller Huggins shut him down for the remainder of the season. Just days later Huggins passed away suddenly. Without his most ardent supporter, Hoyt was dealt to Detroit for spare parts in 1930 and pitched for eight more years as a journeyman.

When his playing days were over, Hoyt put his quality pipes to good use and served as the radio voice of the

Cincinnati Reds for 24 years. As an announcer he would often tell embellished stories of his playing days with the Yankees, especially those involving Babe Ruth. His years spent in the broadcast booth helped him gain entrance into the Hall of Fame via the Veterans Committee in 1969.

While his Yankee career may have ended on a sour note, from 1921 through 1929 no Yankee pitcher compiled more WAR than Hoyt's 35.6. That mark was also eighth best in the majors over that span. He saved his best performances for the World Series when the pressure was greatest. As sportswriter Tom Meany once wrote, Hoyt "appeared almost casual on the mound, never creating the impression that he was bearing down with any great amount of sweat or strain, games when the chips were down brought out the best in him." His six Fall Classic victories would stand as the all-time record when he retired. However, his crowning achievement was his overlooked role on the 1927 Yankees. Murderers' Row would not have been as successful without a "Schoolboy" from Brooklyn doing the dirty work on the pitcher's mound.

STARTING PITCHER—MEL STOTTLEMYRE

He doesn't embarrass you. He doesn't overwhelm you. He's an annoying kind of pitcher. He just gets you out.

—Roy White

Due to unfortunate circumstances, tragic is the word that best describes Mel Stottlemyre's playing career with the Yankees. As a righty he had a disadvantage pitching in Yankee Stadium, and on top of that had an anemic offense supporting him. During his prime he was relied on too heavily and logged more innings than any arm should be expected to handle. As a result his career was cut short, just a few years shy of the Yankees returning to championship glory. However, in the end the team officially recognized Stottlemyre for what he was, one of the greatest pitchers in Yankee history, albeit 40 years too late.

After a nomadic early childhood, Mel Stottlemyre's family settled in Washington's Yakima Valley, about 150 miles southeast of Seattle. Growing up he would often play baseball with his siblings and they would recreate highlights of their favorite team, the New York Yankees. Mel didn't play organized baseball until high school, but by his senior year he was 13-0 and earned a scholarship to play for the local Yakima Valley Junior College. After a successful sophomore campaign, he worked out for pro scouts who claimed he didn't throw hard enough to warrant an offer. As fate would have it, while later working on a farm he was paid a surprise visit from a Yankee scout who was interested in signing Stottlemyre to a minor-league contract. He jumped at the chance, and at 19 years old he embarked on his professional baseball career.

Stottlemyre quickly became one of the best prospects in the Yankee organization. From his lanky frame he administered a steady diet of fastballs and sliders, but what separated him from the pack was his sinker. By 1963 he had dominated in the lower levels of the Yankee system and was promoted to the Yankees' Triple-A affiliate in Richmond. Despite early struggles he went 13-3 with a 1.42 ERA in 1964. At the same time, the Yankees were in a dogfight for the American League pennant and desperately needed pitching help as Whitey Ford had suffered a hip injury. Stottlemyre was called up and made his major-league debut on August 12th against the White Sox, who sat just ahead of the Yankees in the standings. The rookie earned a complete game victory, 7–3, and frustrated batters with his sinker, recording 19 of his 27 outs via groundballs.

Stottlemyre was by far the Yankees' best pitcher down the stretch. For the season he posted a team-leading 2.06 ERA and 177 ERA+ and went 9-3 as the Yankees edged the White Sox by just one game to win the pennant. His stellar debut had earned the respect of his teammates as outfielder Tom Tresh reflected, "Here's a twenty-one-year-old kid nobody knew coming out of nowhere with this great arm and super control who has all this confidence—not a big head, mind you, but a quiet self-assurance—of a Whitey Ford." He had become so vital to the team that in the World Series against the Cardinals, manager Yogi Berra handed him the ball three times in seven games, each time against Hall of Famer and notorious clutch pitcher Bob Gibson.

In Game 2 at Busch Stadium Stottlemyre went the distance while Yankee bats torched Gibson for an 8–3 victory. With the series tied heading into Game 5, he matched Gibson blow for blow. He surrendered two runs that the Yankees later matched with a two-run blast by Tresh off Gibson in the bottom of the ninth. However, the bullpen blew it for the Yankees in the 10th. On just two days' rest, he was back in St. Louis for Game 7 and cruised until an error by shortstop Phil Linz turned a sure double play into a team-wide implosion. Stottlemyre covered first on the play and dove to reach Linz's errant throw, injuring his shoulder in the process, but he stayed in the game. Two batters later catcher Tim McCarver stole home and by the end of the inning the Yankees trailed 3–0.

Stottlemyre left the game after four innings as the Yankees lost, 7–5, giving the Cardinals the series. After the game, Leonard Koppett lamented, "The fielders sabotaged [him]. . . . With a little support, Stottlemyre could have been the hero." Cardinals third baseman and National League MVP Ken Boyer heaped praise on the young righty: "The kid's got the best sinker and curve I've seen. There isn't a pitcher in the National League with this kind of stuff."

On a 1965 Yankee team that included Hall of Famer Whitey Ford and former All-Star and 20-game winner Jim Bouton, Stottlemyre was the ace at just 23 years old. He handled an enormous workload, pitching a league-high 291 innings including 18 complete games, also tops in the league. Across those innings he pitched magnificently with 20 wins, a 2.63 ERA, and 129 ERA+, which yielded a team-high 6.9 WAR that ranked second among all American League pitchers. He came crashing down to earth the following year. His ERA ballooned to 3.80 in 1966 and his combined record that year and in 1967 was well below .500 at 27-35.

Part of the reason for Stottlemyre's poor record was the overall deterioration of the Yankees. Since his rookie year, the team had a losing record and outside of a waning Mickey Mantle had little offensive firepower to speak of. Injuries also limited him as he required foot surgery and developed soreness in his right shoulder. Unfortunately, these maladies would follow him for the rest of his career.

Stottlemyre was never a pitcher who relied on overwhelming stuff to get by. As such, he took a cerebral approach, outsmarting hitters rather than blowing them away. In 1968 he made two adjustments that got him back to what made him successful in the first place. He extended the placement of his plant foot on the follow-through of his delivery, which prevented his arm from finishing across his body and following through wildly. Secondly, he all but removed his curveball from his repertoire. This assuaged the soreness in his shoulder, improved his command, and meant that he would double down on his best pitch, the sinker.

Stottlemyre's 1968 walk rate was a career best as were the 21 wins he recorded. Yankee manager Ralph Houk made the case that he was once again among baseball's elite pitchers when he said, "There is no question that Mel rates with the top five pitchers in baseball." Over the next three seasons, Stottlemyre was the ace of the pitching staff and de facto leader of an inexperienced Yankee team after Mickey Mantle and Whitey Ford retired. He was a class act, never throwing his teammates under the bus, and the most respected player on the team. As a fiercely competitive workhorse, he led best by example. In 1969 he led the American League with 24 complete games and his 303 innings pitched were the most by a Yankee in over 40 years. A season later he was selected to his fifth and final All-Star team as the Yankees won 93 games but settled for second place.

In 1971 Stottlemyre compiled the last winning record of his career at 16-12 with a career-high seven shutouts. For the next two seasons the Yankees continued to hover around .500 as Stottlemyre dealt with ever-increasing shoulder pain and received cortisone shots regularly. He still pitched well and maintained his huge workload as he racked up 533 innings over 74 starts. In 1974 it seemed possible that he would pitch in the playoffs for the first time since his rookie year. However, after 15 starts he was diagnosed with a torn rotator cuff. Without his help, the Yankees finished just two games out of first place and Stottlemyre never pitched again.

During a rare dark period for the Yankees, Stottlemyre was one of the few bright spots. He pitched his heart out, mostly in futility, and found ways to be successful as a right-handed pitcher in Yankee Stadium. His sinker kept the ball on the ground, which defused power hitters and made him an infielder's best friend. Perennial All-Star second baseman Bobby Richardson said of him, "I liked playing behind him, he was always ahead of the hitters. . . . When a pitcher is throwing a lot of strikes, you're up on your feet, ready all the time." In the 10 seasons from 1964 through 1973, Stottlemyre's 40.1 pitching WAR was eighth best in the major leagues. With more run support, he would have earned more victories, saved his arm from having to go deep into games, and extended his career into the Yankees' championship years of the late 1970s. However, luck was not on his side and his greatness remained under the radar.

Ten years after his playing career Stottlemyre returned to baseball as the pitching coach for the New York Mets. He finally earned a World Series ring in 1986 and by 1996 the Yankees came to their senses by bringing him on to handle the pitching staff. They would win four World Series over the next five years and quality pitching was paramount. From 1996 through 2004, Stottlemyre's staff finished no worse than sixth in the American League in ERA. After the 2005 season, a battle with blood cancer and a strained relationship with George Steinbrenner unceremoniously forced him away from the Yankees again.

After leaving the Yankees for the second time, Stottlemyre was invited back for Old-Timers' Day in 2015. As part of the pregame ceremonies, the Yankees surprised Stottlemyre with a plaque dedication. Ailing from his cancer bout, the usually reserved Stottlemyre was emotional in his acceptance speech as he said, "It's been a thrill over the years for me to wear this uniform. I can honestly say that every time I put this uniform on—even when we weren't—I felt unbeatable." He also noted that when his time on earth ends, he'll be ready to rejoin the Yankees in spirit: "I will start another baseball club, coaching up there, whenever they need me." Early in 2019 that time came, which means now that club won't lose because of poor pitching.

STARTING PITCHER—DAVID CONE

No one on those championship Yankee teams occupied a more important dual role—on the field and in the clubhouse combined—than Cone.

—Tom Verducci

The 1994 players' strike temporarily halted Yankee progress, but by 1995 they had emerged from baseball's basement, poised to end their postseason drought by fielding a homegrown team. Yet championships aren't built on homegrown talent alone. When they acquired David Cone that summer, the Yankees went from a solid team to a force to be reckoned with. A bona fide ace, he was also a media-savvy leader whose winning attitude permeated the team. His arrival sparked a championship run the Yankees had been chasing for decades.

David Cone grew up in a hard-working, blue collar family from Kansas City, Missouri. Sports were a big part of Cone family life, and David took to pitching as a youngster while playing Wiffle ball with his siblings. In high school he was a standout athlete, leading his team to the district finals in both football and basketball during his senior year. His school had no baseball team, so he joined the local amateur league instead. At 15 years old he faced off against college-age players and impressed enough as a right-handed pitcher to gain

David Cone about to unleash "The Laredo" slider.
CLARE_AND_BEN/WIKIMEDIA COMMONS

the attention of Kansas City Royals scouts. They selected Cone in the third round of the 1981 MLB Amateur Draft.

Generously listed at 6-foot-1, fresh-faced, and sporting slumped shoulders, Cone was never an intimidating presence on the mound. He got by with great natural movement on his pitches and a willingness to change speeds and arm angles often. As former Yankee beat writer Joel Sherman once noted, "Cone imagined himself a great jazz musician, capable of conjuring what worked as he went along, able by sense of feel to know what was in his repertoire that day and adjust." His best pitches were a split-finger fastball and a sweeping sidearm slider that he affectionately dubbed the "Laredo."

Cone broke into the major leagues with the Royals, then spent a highly successful stretch in New York with the Mets before winning the World Series as a rental with the Toronto Blue Jays in 1992. In free agency after that season he lobbied for a contract with the Yankees, but they were distracted in their fruitless pursuit of Greg Maddux. Instead, he signed with the Royals again, earned a Cy Young Award in 1994, and was traded back to the Blue Jays in 1995.

At this point in Cone's career he had the reputation of being a gun for hire. By July the Yankees were within striking distance of the new wild card spot in the playoffs. General manager Gene Michael felt that a quality pitcher would get them over the hump and knew just the man for the job. He sent three prospects to Toronto for Cone, who fulfilled his wish of returning to New York. As a young bachelor, he abided by the work hard, party harder lifestyle of the 1980s Mets and was a great source of quotes in the press, always shooting from the hip. A ready-made ace experienced in handling the Big Apple, he went 9-2 in 13 starts down the stretch. In turn the Yankees earned their first playoff berth in 14 years.

Cone got the call for Game 1 of the American League Division Series against the Seattle Mariners at Yankee Stadium. He earned a victory after eight strong innings and was called upon again with the series on the line in Game 5. Without his best stuff he gutted through seven innings, as the Yankees built a 4–2 lead, before faltering in the eighth. His pitch count crept over 120 as he surrendered a solo home run to Ken Griffey Jr. With two outs he loaded the bases and allowed the tying run to cross frustratingly via a walk. The Yankees would lose the game and the series in the 11th inning. Downhearted as he was, Cone set a good example for his teammates as he took all questions head-on from reporters after the game.

Cone continued his "Have Gun—Will Travel" routine in 1996 as he seriously considered a contract offer from the Baltimore Orioles. That inspired George Steinbrenner to personally negotiate a three-year deal for Cone to stay in pinstripes. With high expectations to fulfill, he opened the season strong. Despite his success, Cone had felt numbness in his throwing hand since his Opening Day victory. Just days after a complete game masterpiece over the White Sox at Yankee Stadium on May 2, an angiogram revealed that what was misdiagnosed as blood clots was actually a potentially life-threatening aneurysm in his right shoulder. He missed four months of action after a graft procedure from his thigh while the team struggled to stay afloat.

Cone was scheduled to return for the opening game of a series in Oakland on September 2 and as Bernie Williams would reflect, "Once the game began, there was never any messing around with David." Through seven lights-out innings he surrendered no hits. However, he had reached his quota of 85 pitches and was yanked without a chance to complete his no-hit bid. With their ace back in the hole, the Yankees hung on for a first-place finish as Cone pitched to a 2.88 ERA, 175 ERA+, and a 7-2 record in his abbreviated season. With his help the Yankees earned their first pennant since 1981.

In Games 1 and 2 of the World Series at Yankee Stadium, they were mauled by the Atlanta Braves. That meant the Yankees' survival depended on Cone's surgically repaired shoulder in Atlanta for Game 3. Wild throughout, he walked the bases loaded in the sixth, clinging to a 2–0 lead, when Atlanta's slugger Fred McGriff stepped to the plate with one out. Manager Joe Torre visited the mound and said, "I need the truth. How do you feel?" Naturally, Cone said he could get McGriff, to which Torre said, "Don't bullshit me." Unflinchingly, Cone stared back and said, "I can get him. I can get out of this inning." Torre relented and Cone obliged by getting McGriff out on a pop fly. He left the game with a lead in what would be a 5–2 win. The team didn't look back, winning three straight to bring a World Series title back to the Bronx.

Cone pitched spectacularly in 1997, forming one of the best pitching duos in baseball with Andy Pettitte. He enjoyed the best strikeout rate of his career and his 2.82 ERA and 159 ERA+ each ranked third in the American League. The season would end on a sour note, though, as he spent the final month on the disabled list with shoulder issues. He returned for the playoffs, but the Yankees couldn't handle the Cleveland Indians' formidable lineup in a tight series. His shoulder problem was later diagnosed as a bone spur that required surgery in the offseason.

Finally healthy, Cone played a full season for the first time as a Yankee in 1998, but the surgery sapped the velocity on his fastball. Already a resourceful pitcher, Cone doubled down on changing arm angles with his offspeed and breaking pitches. It worked as he won a major-league-leading 20 games, his first 20-win season since 1988 with the Mets. The 10 years between 20-win seasons is a major-league record, but more importantly he earned them for a 114-win Yankee team. In the playoffs Cone started the series winner against Texas in the first round and in the next round did enough against the Indians to get the Yankees back to the World Series. He made one more start in a sweep over the San Diego Padres as the 1998 Yankees sealed their legacy as one of the greatest teams of all time.

In the first half of the 1999 season Cone pitched like a man possessed to get the Yankees back to the World Series. He made his final All-Star appearance that July, but his first start after the break provided the defining moment of his career. During Yogi Berra Day at Yankee Stadium, the ceremonial first pitch was thrown by Don Larsen, who pitched the first perfect game in Yankee history during the 1956 World Series. In the presence of Yankee royalty, Cone allowed no Montreal Expos to reach base through 8⅔ innings while striking out 10. On the game's final play, Orlando Cabrera popped up toward third base where an incredulous Cone looked on with both hands on his head. In a flash the crowd erupted as Cone fell to his knees and bear-hugged catcher Joe Girardi. The rest of his teammates triumphantly carried him off the field. Cone had pitched the third perfect game in Yankee history.

For the balance of the season, he endured an extended hangover from that magical day, winning just two of his final 13 starts. He found his form come playoff time and won a 3–2 nail-biter over the Red Sox in Game 2 of the American League Championship Series. Taking on the Braves in the World Series he tossed seven shutout innings as part of a sweep that sealed back-to-back rings for the Yankees. At 37 years old he had a forgettable season in 2000 but worked out of the bullpen in a World Series win over the Mets, clinching a three-peat. He would never pitch again for the Yankees, but since 2008 has served as a color analyst on the YES Network. One of the best commentators in baseball, he has embraced advanced analytics as a part of the game while serving up entertaining anecdotes with his trademark sense of humor.

Cone was acquired to be the final piece of a championship puzzle and was just that. In his six seasons with the Yankees, they made the playoffs each year and dominated with four World Series wins. That's an unheard of yield for a trade deadline deal. He was tailor made for the big city as Joel Sherman alluded to when he wrote, "Cone's value transcended his elite pitching . . . [he] was a New Yorker in every way. . . . He thrived in this atmosphere, wrapping his arms around the idea of being the spokesman for a team in the biggest media market in the world." Cone was as comfortable on the mound with his team's life on the line as he was lazing on a sunny afternoon, shooting the breeze with anyone willing to listen, cold beer in hand and jokes in abundance. The Yankees have been trying to land the next David Cone ever since he left, but it's a futile effort. He was one of a kind.

STARTING PITCHER—MIKE MUSSINA

You try to give kids a Mike Mussina wind-up so they never get hurt, they throw the ball over the plate, everybody likes them and they like what they're doing.

—*Jim Palmer*

The greatest starting pitchers in Yankee history generally fall into one of two categories. Ron Guidry and Lefty Gomez had unhittable stuff, but lacked durability. On the other hand, Whitey Ford and Andy Pettitte, through sheer will, outlasted and outsmarted hitters more so than dominated them. When the Yankees signed Mike Mussina as a free agent in 2000, they finally had a pitcher who struck a perfect balance between those two profiles. The diversity and quality of his repertoire

Mike Mussina putting his perfect mechanics on display.
MANDALATV/WIKIMEDIA COMMONS

was second to none, while his physicality and brains kept him effective over a long career. Though not as celebrated as other Yankees mound greats, he might be the most talented pitcher the team has ever employed.

The oldest son of a lawyer and a nurse, Mike Mussina grew up in a small town just outside of Williamsport, Pennsylvania, the home of the Little League World Series. In high school he was a three-sport star and even earned a spot on the USA Junior Olympic baseball team prior to his senior year. Painfully shy, he was among the smartest in his class, but legend has it that he purposely fell just short of being valedictorian to avoid giving a speech at graduation. Despite being closely scouted by major-league teams, Mussina spent three years at Stanford University where he pitched in the College World Series twice, winning it as a freshman. He was selected 20th overall in the 1990 draft by the Baltimore Orioles and signed a hefty contract to turn pro.

During Mussina's minor-league career he found time to complete his economics degree at Stanford, where his senior thesis covered the economy of baseball players attending college versus signing a professional contract out of high school. How appropriate. After just 28 minor-league starts he became a mainstay in Baltimore's big-league rotation.

In the period from 1992 through 2000 Mussina made five All-Star appearances, earned four Gold Gloves, finished in the top five in the Cy Young Award vote five times, and twice more finished sixth. A remarkably durable pitcher, his 45.5 WAR total over this time was sixth best among major-league pitchers, but he did it mostly for mediocre Oriole teams. In 1996 and 1997 Baltimore made the playoffs and Mussina was nearly unhittable despite the team's inability to reach the World Series. A free agent in 2000, he left for greener pastures.

On a deal that would pay him $88.5 million over six years, Mussina joined the defending World Series champions for three years running. The Yankees drooled over their new prize.

Athletically built at 6-foot-2, Mussina could simply overpower hitters. Other times, he would outsmart them. In a 1994 profile on Mussina for *Sports Illustrated*, Tom Verducci aptly described his mastery: "Mussina can dot the i in his autograph with any one of six pitches. He has three fastballs (a cutter, a sinker and a riser), two curveballs (a slow curve and the knuckle curve) and an astonishingly deceptive changeup that is his best pitch." In that same profile, he noted that Mussina developed his cutter on the fly to get out of a jam, to which his catcher Chris Hoiles said, "Well, I guess if you're going to use that pitch, we ought to have a sign for it."

Mussina was as superb as ever in 2001. This culminated with one of the best games of his career that September in Boston. He racked up 13 strikeouts and had a perfect game going through 8⅔ innings. With two strikes on Carl Everett, Mussina left a fastball up in the zone, which Everett blooped to left field for a single. He retired the next batter and settled for a 1–0 shutout victory, but fumed to the point that he didn't talk to reporters after the game. It was the fourth time in his career that he carried a no-hitter into the eighth inning or later, only to have it slip away. For the season, he posted a 7.1 WAR, which was the best mark among American League pitchers that year, as was his 143 ERA+. Despite being more deserving, he lost out on the Cy Young Award to teammate Roger Clemens, who rode superior run support to a 20-3 record compared to a 17-11 showing for Mussina.

Come playoff time Mussina proved his worth. Down 2–0 in a best of five Division Series against the Athletics, the Yankees traveled to Oakland with their historic streak of playoff series wins in jeopardy. Mussina changed the tone of the series, shutting Oakland out through seven innings while

Mariano Rivera finished off a dramatic 1–0 victory. The Yankees would beat Oakland in five games and Mussina earned a victory over Seattle as part of the team's fourth straight American League pennant. In the World Series he bounced back from a rough start in Game 1 to go eight innings in Game 5 as the Yankees would win in 12 innings. Unfortunately, the Yankees would lose one of the best World Series ever played in seven games.

Over the next two seasons, Mussina remained the Yankees' best starting pitcher for teams that would win over 100 games. After a forgettable early exit in the 2002 playoffs, he had a chance to redeem himself in Game 7 of a classic American League Championship Series against the Red Sox in 2003. Down 4–0 in the fourth inning of the sudden death game, Joe Torre called on Mussina to make the first relief appearance of his career. On three pitches he disposed of Jason Varitek via strikeout, then induced an inning-ending double play groundball from Johnny Damon. In total he pitched three innings of scoreless relief as the Yankees chipped away at Boston's lead. When he returned to the dugout after the sixth inning, Torre said to him, "All I can tell you is you pitched the game of your life here. If anybody ever questions how you handle pressure, you answered that right here. Don't you ever forget that."

Even Aaron Boone, who hit the game's now famous walkoff home run in the 11th inning, recognized Mussina's importance to the win: "[Mussina]'s kind of the consummate pro—all business, always prepared. . . . We all know I never get the chance to hit that home run if not for him." The Yankees would face the Florida Marlins in the World Series, and in Game 3 Mussina went seven strong innings, striking out nine and allowing just one run. The Yankees held on for a win to take a 2–1 series lead but faltered thereafter. Had there been a Game 7, Mussina would have taken the mound, but he would never pitch in the World Series again.

At 35 years old Mussina began to experience tightness in his elbow as he failed to reach the 200-inning plateau in 2004 for the first time in 10 years. He missed it again in 2005. When he did pitch he performed well short of his career standard and was only slightly better in October. Finally healthy again in 2006, he rebounded with a 129 ERA+ and five WAR for a 97-win Yankee team. Thanks to more team-wide struggles, he lost his only playoff start that year.

The Yankees brought back the 38-year-old Mussina on a two-year deal, at least in part because he was valuable in showing new teammates how to handle playing in the Big Apple. As Joe Torre noted, "Moose had been through the New York wringer when he first got here. He had figured out how to deal with it all. Not everyone does that." However, the Yankees would soon regret it. In the midst of what was by far the worst season of his career, he had a two-start stretch in late August where he failed to reach the fourth inning in either game and surrendered 13 runs combined. He was banished to the bullpen before injuries forced him back to the rotation.

Always thinking, Mussina changed his approach upon his return as a starter. He made a concerted effort to challenge hitters inside and as a result won three of his last four starts. That success continued into 2008 during a season that would be notorious for the Yankees ending their 13-year playoff streak. He reached 200 innings for the first time in five years, and his 3.37 ERA and 131 ERA+ were his best marks since his Cy Young–worthy 2001 season. He also finished strong, allowing just one run over his final three starts, the last of which was his 20th win of the season. With that, he became the oldest pitcher ever to post the first 20-win season of his career. As a cherry on top, he also earned his seventh Gold Glove Award.

Mussina decided not to pitch into his 40s and retired a criminally underappreciated pitcher. During his eight years in New York, his 35.2 WAR total was eighth best among all major-league pitchers, and that included three full seasons that were subpar for him. Still, he was never considered an elite pitcher because he fell short of many traditional standards. He had only one 20-win season, fell short of 300 wins for his career, and never won a Cy Young Award. His career 3.68 ERA, including a 3.88 mark with the Yankees, seems pedestrian. He also lacked a World Series ring, but to judge Mussina on these facts alone is unfair.

Mussina's win totals were suppressed due to consistently inferior run support throughout his career, even with the Yankees. In the Cy Young Award vote he finished in the top six nine times in his career, including getting robbed blind in 2001 as a Yankee. His pedestrian ERA was actually more than 20 percent better than average despite facing above average hitting in the American League East with mostly porous fielding behind him. As for his missing World Series ring, he was brilliant more often than not in October and might have had a career-defining performance in Game 7 of the 2003 World Series. Alas, his team couldn't get him the ball.

Despite the detractors he may have, Mussina himself is not the type to let such things bother him. Tyler Kepner, former Yankee beat reporter for the *New York Times*, wrote after Mussina's retirement that, "Mussina's head guides his heart, not the other way around. He was always able to put his success in perspective. . . ." Luckily, baseball writers finally found that perspective in 2019 and voted Mike Mussina into the Hall of Fame. An honor he no doubt deserves.

RELIEF PITCHER—MARIANO RIVERA

He needs to pitch in a higher league, if there is one. Ban him from baseball. He should be illegal.

—*Tom Kelly*

During the Yankees' championship run from the late 1990s into the early 2000s, there was a lot of talk about the "mystique" and "aura" when a clutch hit or lucky bounce was needed. In actuality, that mystique and aura came in the form of a skinny Panamanian right-hander named Mariano Rivera. Other teams had a quality lineup and strong starting pitching just like the Yankees during those years, but nobody else had an ace in the bullpen who could consistently shut down the opposition in late-inning, high-pressure situations quite like Rivera. The stone-faced reliever's repertoire consisted of a single pitch that was as unassuming as he was, but carried with it the force of Thor's hammer, driving the nail in his opponent's coffin more times than anyone in baseball history.

The Mariano Rivera story has a humble beginning. He grew up in a poor fishing village in Panama and by 16 had quit school to work with his father as a fisherman. When not fishing his true passion was soccer, but he also played baseball as a kid with makeshift gloves fashioned out of old milk cartons. Soccer injuries forced him to focus on baseball, and he eventually latched on with a local amateur team as a shortstop. During a playoff game his team's starting pitcher got rocked

Mariano Rivera achieved legendary status with a single pitch.
KEITH ALLISON/WIKIMEDIA COMMONS

early and Rivera was called upon as an emergency replacement. He pitched so well that he was tipped off to a Yankee scout who was holding a tryout camp in Panama shortly thereafter. At 20 years old, 6-foot-2 and just 155 pounds with a fastball that topped out in the high-80s, there was seemingly nothing special about this shortstop turned pitcher. However, the Yankee scouts loved the fluidity of his pitching motion and saw a world of potential. They signed him for just $2,000.

Rivera spent the next five years working his way through the Yankees organization. His scrawny frame, lack of an elite fastball, advanced age for a prospect, and elbow surgery in 1992 meant that he was never regarded as a top prospect. Despite the lack of publicity, no one could argue with Mariano's results. Pitching mostly as a starter, he compiled a 2.32 ERA over more than 400 innings during his minor-league career. He also possessed something that couldn't be quantified. As Mike DeJean, a minor-league teammate of Rivera and future major-league pitcher, would later reflect, "I never saw him get mad. I never saw him sweat. When he pitched, it was like he was acting as if he were the only guy on the field."

In 1995 Rivera finally got his first taste of major-league action at 25 years old but proved to be overmatched by major-league hitters. After four spot starts for the Yankees and a bloated 10.20 ERA, he was sent back to Triple-A Columbus and rumored to be included in a potential trade that would bring David Wells to the Yankees. However, during a rain-shortened no-hitter he had suddenly added about five miles per hour to his fastball. Once Yankee general manager Gene Michael substantiated the claim from that game, he called off the trade and brought Rivera back to the Bronx.

Now armed with a fastball in the mid-90s, he shut out the White Sox over eight innings in his first start back. By September, he found his groove as a setup reliever, making scoreless appearances in four of his last six outings. That continued in the playoffs as the Yankees ended a 14-year drought by getting in via the new wild card spot, but he probably could have been utilized better in a soul-crushing first series loss to the Seattle Mariners.

The Yankees were a much different team heading into 1996. Former stars Tony Fernandez, Jack McDowell, and Mike Stanley were not brought back. Yankee legend and captain Don Mattingly retired, and manager Buck Showalter was ousted in favor of Joe Torre. Amidst that change, Torre wisely kept Rivera as a big part of the team's plan to return to the playoffs. Paying no attention to the trade rumors that continued to swirl around him, Rivera had proven to be the most dependable arm out of the bullpen. Since he still had the arm strength and stamina of a starting pitcher, Torre eventually saw no need to rely on anyone else as the ever-important bridge between his starters and closer John Wetteland.

Rivera was doing it all with just one pitch, the mid-90s fastball that appeared out of nowhere. The key to it was the deception of him uncorking it from such a skinny frame and with such ease. By season's end he had pitched over 100 innings in relief to the tune of a 2.09 ERA and a staggering 240 ERA+, compiled five WAR, and finished third in the American League Cy Young Award vote. Along with minor-league teammates Andy Pettitte and Derek Jeter, he led the Yankees back to the playoffs.

They clawed their way through three playoff series where Rivera was as effective and important as ever. He pitched 14⅓ innings across eight appearances and allowed just one run. In the final game of the World Series, he pitched two scoreless innings, which held the Yankees' slim one-run lead as they won their first championship in 18 years. They likely would not have done so without Rivera: as catcher Joe Girardi would later say, "When I think of 1996, I think of Mariano Rivera."

Thanks to Rivera's overwhelming success, the Yankees named him the closer heading into 1997. He struggled to adjust to the role at first, but found his groove as the calendar turned to May. That June he was the beneficiary of another mysterious and sudden change to his bread and butter pitch. While playing catch before a game in Detroit, his throws had a sudden and late break. Rivera insisted he wasn't doing anything differently. When Mel Stottlemyre joined him for a bullpen session later they still couldn't explain the new phenomenon, but it was clear that his dominant fastball had transformed into a cutter. He was still a one-trick pony, but it was quite a trick. He finished the season with 43 saves and a minuscule 1.88 ERA as the Yankees returned to the playoffs. He locked down a save in Game 1 of the Division Series against the Cleveland Indians and was called on again in Game 4 to protect a one-run lead in the bottom of the eighth. The second batter he faced was Sandy Alomar Jr., who stroked a high, outside pitch over the right field wall in Jacobs Field to tie the game. The Yankees would go on to lose in the 10th inning and the series a game later. The first major failure of Rivera's career also meant failure for the Yankees.

The continued success of Rivera was no sure thing heading into 1998. Relief pitchers can be a fickle sort, and it didn't help that Rivera hit the disabled list with a strained groin after his first appearance of the season. But when he returned to the mound he was back to being a lights-out closer for a Yankee team that won a whopping 114 games. Having mastered his new cutter, he relied less on strikeouts and more on weak contact off broken bats.

In the playoffs Rivera was even better. He pitched 13⅓ innings over 10 appearances, earning six saves and never allowing a run. During the World Series, the San Diego Padres had their best chance to win in Game 3 as they carried a 3–2 lead into the eighth inning until San Diego's star closer, Trevor Hoffman, surrendered a two-run home run to Yankee third baseman Scott Brosius. Rivera quietly took care of business to close it out as the Yankees swept their way to another World Series.

In 1999 it was more of the same. Rivera dominated with a 1.83 ERA, which yielded an almost unheard of 257 ERA+, and led the major leagues with 45 saves. He continued his dominance in the playoffs, this time making eight scoreless appearances with six saves, including an MVP-performance in a World Series sweep over the Atlanta Braves.

By 2000 a World Series win for the Yankees and Rivera was almost a given, and they didn't disappoint. Despite a rocky regular season and an even rockier road than usual in the playoffs, the Yankees ended the season by beating the New York Mets in the Subway Series, sealing a World Series three-peat. After the series Mets infielder Joe McEwing incredulously said, "You sit there on the bench thinking, 'What's the problem? This guy's a one-pitch pitcher. We all know what's coming. Why aren't we hitting him?' Then guys come back to the bench shaking their head. . . ."

Four straight World Series wins, and five in six years, seemed to be at hand for the Yankees right up until Game 7 in 2001 against the Arizona Diamondbacks. Handed a 2–1 lead heading into the bottom of the eighth inning, it was a foregone conclusion that Rivera would shut the door, just as he always had. Yet in the ninth inning Mark Grace led off with a single and Damian Miller bunted a weak groundball back to the pitcher. Rivera shockingly made an errant throw on what should have been a double play ball. A few plays later, the Diamondbacks had beaten the best closer in baseball to win the World Series. Since 1996 the Yankees had failed to win the World Series only twice, and both times were a result of a Rivera misstep. But his importance to the Yankees' dominance could not be overstated.

In 2002, Rivera's title of baseball's best closer was in jeopardy due to injuries more so than his World Series failure the year before. At 32 he made three separate trips to the disabled list with groin and shoulder injuries, and although he pitched well when healthy, it wasn't up to his usual standard.

The following season Rivera came back better than ever and embarked on an unprecedented run of dominance for a closer. From 2003 through 2006 he pitched to an ERA below 2.00 every year and averaged 42 saves per season. His ERA+ over this time was an astonishing 261 and during the 2004 campaign he set a career high with a major-league-leading 53 saves. After a subpar 2007, he went on another four-year tear that saw him go from his late 30s into his early 40s. His 2008 through 2011 seasons were almost a mirror image of his stretch from 2003 through 2006. He averaged 40 saves a year, posting an ERA below 2.00 each year again while his ERA+ during this period was 259. Rivera recorded his 600th career save in September of 2011, and a week later he recorded number 602, which surpassed Trevor Hoffman for the all-time record.

The Yankees enjoyed far less success in the playoffs during this time than they had at the beginning of Rivera's career, despite his continued brilliance. The only bad playoff outings that Rivera had in this period were back-to-back blown saves in Games 4 and 5 of the 2004 American League Championship Series. All told he posted an ERA of 0.58 in 62 playoff innings pitched from 2002 through 2011, which included another World Series win. It's safe to say that the 2001 World Series didn't break his confidence.

In early May of 2012 Rivera was shagging flyballs in the outfield before a game in Kansas City. Chasing one down, he felt his right knee buckle. He'd torn his ACL and would require season-ending knee surgery. At 42 years old, most fans feared that would be the end of his career, but the normally reserved Rivera insisted a day later that he would be back. He kept his word and in 2013 posted 44 saves with a 2.11 ERA.

Having announced that 2013 would be his last season, the Yankees held Mariano Rivera Day on September 22 at Yankee Stadium. The pregame festivities included a host of former teammates and coaches showering him with kind words and gifts. Metallica even showed up to play a live rendition of "Enter Sandman," his entrance music since 1999, in center field as he walked out from the bullpen for the ceremony. Four days later he pitched in his final game. After entering in the eighth, manager Joe Girardi decided to remove him with two outs in the ninth to ensure a proper ovation from the Yankee Stadium crowd. He surprised Rivera by sending Andy Pettitte and Derek Jeter out to take the ball from him. The sight of two teammates he had been through so many ups and downs with for over 20 years during the final moment of his career got the best of him. The man who spent a career holding back any semblance of emotion even in the most pressure-packed situation opened the floodgates, and he embraced his former teammates with tears in his eyes for what seemed an eternity. As Rivera put it, "I was sobbing in Andy's arms. I had held in my emotions for a long, long time. I was ready to let them go."

Not only did Rivera retire as the greatest closer of all time, but you can make the case that he is the greatest pitcher of any kind in Yankee history. Advanced metrics back this up, as his 56.6 career pitcher WAR is the highest mark for any Yankee. This is especially noteworthy because as a reliever he pitched in less than half the innings of some starting pitchers on this All-Star team. Furthermore, his career ERA+ of 205 is the best mark in major-league history.

As if that wasn't enough to make him a legend, he was even better in the playoffs where his career 0.70 ERA, 42 saves, and 33⅓ consecutive scoreless innings streak are records not likely to be broken. He played a major role in every one of the five World Series rings he owns, and throughout his career gained the respect of even his most heated playoff rivals. David Ortiz, of all people, once said of Rivera, "I have respect for Mariano like I have for my father. . . . To him everybody else is the best." Thanks to a never-ending reservoir of skill, mental fortitude, and humility, it's safe to say that there never has been nor ever will be another one like Mariano Rivera.

RELIEF PITCHER—DAVE RIGHETTI

A phenomenal left-hander. People like him don't come around very often—as far as talent and ability to pitch. And the command of four pitches. Fresh face out of California. I mean, this was a great, great pitcher.

—George Frazier

Dave Righetti is in rare company as a Yankee who flourished in two distinct roles in pinstripes. First, he was a promising young starting pitcher pegged to be the next great Yankee lefty after Ron Guidry. He made good on that promise, which culminated with the signature moment of his career against the Boston Red Sox in 1983. When the Yankees suddenly needed a closer the following year, his second career began. He seamlessly transitioned to a role forced upon him by becoming one of the premier closers in the major leagues. Unfortunately, he was never able to earn a World Series ring, but his team-first attitude and pristine reputation with his teammates makes him a great one nonetheless.

Hailing from San Jose, California, Righetti already had ties to the Yankees on the day he was born. His father, Leo, was a Yankee farmhand in the 1940s but was never called up to the big leagues. Leo imparted his baseball wisdom on a young Dave, who joined his high school team as an outfielder. When a local scout for the Texas Rangers observed Dave's throws from the outfield, he suggested he try pitching and by his senior year he won every start he made. For one season he pitched at San Jose City College before being selected 10th overall in the 1977 amateur draft by the Rangers. He displayed excellent command of his fastball, slider, and changeup over two years in their minor-league system. During one game, he even struck out 21 batters. In the fall of 1978 he was dealt to the Yankees as part of a massive 10-player trade that centered on Sparky Lyle going to Texas.

During his first two years with the Yankees, he showed flashes of brilliance in the higher levels of their farm system and spent a brief stint in the big leagues to close the 1979 season. In 1981 he dominated over his first seven starts at Triple-A Columbus and was recalled by the Yankees that May. Yankee first baseman Bob Watson saw something special in Righetti right away: "You knew Dave Righetti was going to be a good pitcher—he was left-handed and had good stuff. For a youngster, he pitched beyond his years."

Still baby-faced at 22 years old, he was a breath of fresh air for a Yankee team chasing after the championship glory of just a few years prior. During the strike-shortened season,

Righetti was superb over his 15 starts, going 8-4 with a 2.05 ERA and an American League leading 174 ERA+. He was named the Rookie of the Year and his 3.5 WAR led a Yankee team that snuck into the playoffs. In the specially designed format, the Yankees took on the Milwaukee Brewers in the best-of-five Division Series. Righetti started Game 2 and pitched six shutout innings while striking out 10 in a 3–0 Yankee victory. In the decisive Game 5, he pitched three innings in relief of Ron Guidry, who was pulled after the fourth, and allowed just one run as the Yankees outlasted the Brewers by a 7–3 margin.

The Yankees moved on to battle the Oakland Athletics in the American League Championship Series. With a 2–0 lead in another best-of-five series, Righetti got the start in Game 3. He hurled another six shutout innings and allowed just four hits as the Yankees advanced to their third Fall Classic matchup with the Los Angeles Dodgers in five years. Staked to another 2–0 series lead, Righetti faced off against fellow rookie sensation Fernando Valenzuela. The magic ran out for Righetti, and he was pulled from the game after just two innings. The Yankees would lose that game and the next three to give the Dodgers the series. Despite the disappointment it had been a sensational rookie campaign, yet Righetti would have none of it. He said after earning the Rookie of the Year Award, "It's a nice honor, but it's an individual honor. I was hoping to do better in the World Series." For the next decade he'd be one of the few Yankees with such a selfless attitude.

Righetti suffered a sophomore slump in 1982. He remained in the starting rotation for most of the year and led the American League in strikeout rate, but also issued a league-high

108 walks. Meanwhile, the Yankees slipped below .500 for the first time in nearly 10 years. He regained his command in 1983, and as the summer sun got hotter, so did his left arm. On June 29 Righetti stifled the Baltimore Orioles for his first career shutout, and his next turn in the rotation would be on Independence Day against the Boston Red Sox.

In sweltering 94-degree heat at Yankee Stadium, the Boston bats couldn't touch the man affectionately known as "Rags." After eight innings he had a 4–0 lead and the only baserunners he had allowed were via three walks. He received a standing ovation when taking the mound for the ninth inning. After the game Righetti would say, "They were making me nervous. I didn't look in the dugout because I didn't want to get more nervous. But I calmed down. I was enjoying the fans. I was enjoying being a Yankee." He quickly induced back-to-back groundouts and all that stood between Righetti and the first Yankee no-hitter since Don Larsen's perfect game in the 1956 World Series was future Hall of Famer Wade Boggs. He worked the count to 2-2 before Righetti uncorked a nasty slider that Boggs offered at but couldn't get a piece of. The crowd erupted as George Steinbrenner got the best birthday present he could ask for. For the season Righetti finished 14-8 with 3.6 WAR, behind only Ron Guidry for the team lead. The Yankees finished with 91 wins, albeit well out of first place.

Yankee relief ace Rich "Goose" Gossage departed as a free agent after the 1983 season, leaving a giant hole in the bullpen. Manager Yogi Berra saw the 25-year-old Righetti as his ideal replacement due to his superb strikeout ability. Righetti wasn't keen on the role change, but would do whatever was best for the team. In the face of more intense scrutiny among fans and the press as a closer than he was used to as a starter, his low-key, quiet nature served him well.

From 1984 through 1986 one could make the argument that he was the best closer in baseball. During that period, he pitched to a sparkling 2.53 ERA and 158 ERA+ while leading all major-league closers with 106 saves and 9.7 WAR. In both 1984 and 1985 he ranked in the top five of the American League in saves, but 1986 was his career year. Righetti led the major leagues with 46 saves, which also set the all-time record. He finished the season with a career-high 3.8 WAR, made his first All-Star team, finished fourth in the Cy Young Award vote, and 10th in the vote for American League MVP. He also remained the stand-up guy that the Yankees knew as a starter. Righetti's former teammate Steve Kemp, a Yankee outfielder in 1983 and 1984, confirmed as much years later when he noted, "Dave was an awesome teammate. He was just great to play for. . . . If you made a mistake, [he] didn't sit out there and glare at you. [He] just went from there and tried to bail you out if you made an error."

During Righetti's dominance the Yankees were one of the best teams in the American League, averaging 91 wins per season, but failed to qualify for the playoffs each year. Over the next four years, they would regress to the bottom of the American League as Righetti's production tapered off as well. In 1987 his ERA ballooned to 3.51, but he was named an All-Star again thanks to his 31 saves. Soreness in his throwing arm plagued him over the next two seasons. Wanting to help the team at any and all cost, he didn't let on and trudged through at less than 100 percent. He was still able to save 25 games in each season, the latter of which saw the Yankees fall below .500 for just the second time of his career.

At 31 years old Righetti entered the final season of his contract in 1990. He was a rare bright spot for a Yankee team that would hit rock bottom. He saved 36 games in 39 opportunities, or more than half of the last-place Yankees' 67 wins. It was by far the best save conversion rate of his career. After the season the Yankees entered full rebuild mode, and Righetti was collateral damage. Now a family man, he returned home to California on a three-year deal with the San Francisco Giants. He then made brief stops in Oakland, Toronto, and Chicago with the White Sox before calling it a career at age 36. In 2000 he was named the Giants' pitching coach and spent a successful 18-year run managing their staff, highlighted by three World Series wins in 2010, 2012, and 2014.

When Righetti left the Yankees after the 1990 season, his 224 saves were the most in franchise history by a wide margin over Goose Gossage. That record stood until Mariano Rivera surpassed him in 2002, but putting Righetti's Yankee career in the context of personal accomplishments would be missing the point. He's best remembered as a selfless player who put team success above all else. Whether it was a lights-out performance in a playoff game, a no-hitter over the hated Boston Red Sox, or serving as one of the best closers in baseball, he was indispensable to Yankee teams that came tantalizingly close to glory in the 1980s, only to fall short each year. Still, he has no regrets about those days, once reflecting, "I wouldn't trade it, playing with Donnie, Willie, Winfield, Baylor, Rickey Henderson, and the pitchers, the players, the Hall of Famers. We were just in the wrong place at the wrong time." Rags may not have gone to riches as a Yankee, but he pitched his heart out while others took the money and ran.

RELIEF PITCHER—GOOSE GOSSAGE

*You either eat or you get eaten. And I'm going to eat. And
I hated hitters.*

—Goose Gossage

By the late 1970s the "fireman" reliever was all the rage before
the term "closer" was a part of baseball's lexicon. Pitchers
throwing heat to seal victories were so fashionable that they
were often escorted from the bullpen to the pitcher's mound
in outlandishly decorated golf carts. After winning the World
Series in 1977, the Yankees made a splash by signing Rich
"Goose" Gossage, arguably the best fireman in baseball, to take
periodic rides in their very own pinstriped bullpen cart. For the
next six seasons he made one of the best bullpens in baseball
even better. He backed up his violent windup with scorching
fastballs as the most dominant closer of his era and was a positive influence on his teammates, if not the Yankee front office,
during that time.

Rich Gossage was born in Colorado Springs, Colorado,
and grew strong by hunting and fishing in the Rocky Moun-
tains when he wasn't talking baseball with his father. He quickly
developed a reputation as a flamethrower and was drafted by
the Chicago White Sox out of high school in the 1970 draft.
Early on he struggled with his command and never settled into
a clear role with Chicago. In 1975 he was a dominant closer,
leading the major leagues with 26 saves. The next season he
was sent to the starting rotation where he posted an ugly 9-17
record with a below-average ERA. His time with the White
Sox wasn't a complete wash, though. A minor-league teammate
once observed how he stuck his neck out like a goose when

looking for his signs, and with that his nickname was born. He also learned an offspeed slurve from White Sox pitching coach Johnny Sain that complemented his blazing fastball.

In 1976 Gossage was traded to the Pittsburgh Pirates where they decided he was best suited as a closer. It was the right move as he posted 26 saves with a 1.62 ERA and 244 ERA+. A free agent at season's end, the Yankees offered a massive contract worth $3.6 million over six years that Gossage couldn't refuse. The defending World Series champs signed him to replace their incumbent closer and reigning Cy Young Award winner, Sparky Lyle. Gossage got off to a shaky start in New York. He surrendered runs in his first three appearances and didn't earn a save until May. However, he was at his best when the Yankees needed him most in the pennant race.

In regular-season game 163 against Boston to determine the winner of the American League East, Gossage worked the final 2⅔ innings and while he gave up two runs, he did enough to nail down his league-leading 27th save and bring the Yankees back to the playoffs. For the season he pitched to a 2.01 ERA over 134⅓ innings, which was good for a fifth-place finish in the Cy Young Award vote and also garnered MVP consideration. His new teammate Ron Davis worked with Gossage in the bullpen every day and later reflected, "Rich is probably one of the greatest relief pitchers there ever was. He was so dominant." Davis added, "As far as a teammate, he was probably one of the most fantastic guys there is—as far as camaraderie." Gossage was equally effective in the playoffs, allowing just two runs over five appearances, and earned victories in both the League Championship Series over the Kansas City Royals and World Series over the Los Angeles Dodgers.

The Yankees had secured their second of back-to-back championships, and their gamble on the big righty had paid off.

Gossage pitched well in his second season with the Yankees
when healthy, but torn ligaments in his right thumb forced him
to sit out half the season. The rest of the Yankees also struggled with injuries, but Thurman Munson's tragic death sealed
their fate as they failed to return to the playoffs. Fully healthy
in 1980, Gossage returned to lights-out form. He struck out
over 100 batters and pitched to a 2.27 ERA while leading the
major leagues with a career-high 33 saves. He finished third in
both the Cy Young and MVP Award votes in the American
League as the Yankees took on the Kansas City Royals in the
playoffs. There, he was rocked in his only appearance in Game
3 thanks to a monster three-run home run from George Brett
that reached the third deck of Yankee Stadium. That blew the
save, the game, and effectively the series for the Yankees as the
Royals swept them.

A year later Gossage put up video game numbers in a
strike-shortened season. Sporting his now famous handlebar
moustache for the first time as a snub to George Steinbrenner
for his constant criticism, he gave up just four earned runs all
year, which translated to a 0.77 ERA and a ridiculous 465
ERA+. Reserve catcher Barry Foote later noted, "We had an
unbelievable record that year from the seventh inning. With
a lead in the seventh, I think we only lost one game all year."
This time, Gossage didn't falter come playoff time. With the
Yankees making a deep run to the World Series, Gossage was
unhittable throughout. In eight total appearances he pitched
14⅓ shutout innings, struck out 15, and allowed just six hits.
The Yankees may not have won the World Series, but their big
money pitcher came up huge.

For the next two years Gossage was good for near carbon copy performances of his stellar 1980 season. In 1982 he led a middling Yankee team in WAR with 4.5 and also made the last of three straight All-Star appearances. His 1983 season was notable for his central role in the infamous "Pine Tar Incident." When Gossage faced his old nemesis, George Brett, in a late July game he surrendered another monster home run that blew a one-run lead. Yankee manager Billy Martin argued that the pine tar on Brett's bat extended too far and the umpires called him out. After much drama the homer was reinstated, the game was replayed from that point, and the Yankees lost again anyway.

Despite improving to 91 wins in 1983, the Yankees would miss the playoffs again and Gossage, having grown weary of constant jarring with George Steinbrenner, decided not to return to New York. At 32 years old he signed another free agent deal, this time with the San Diego Padres, but by his mid-30s he was no longer a dominant closer. He finished his career as a serviceable reliever for a handful of teams, including a brief return to the Yankees at the end of the 1989 season.

Even if his career in pinstripes was relatively short, Gossage accomplished everything that was expected of him and then some. He was brought in to help capture back-to-back World Series championships in 1978 and he did just that. Over his six years in New York, his 18.8 WAR and 183 ERA+ were the best for any reliever, and the only one with more saves was fellow Hall of Famer Bruce Sutter. Furthermore, his only misstep in the playoffs was the home run he served up in 1980 to another fellow Hall of Famer in George Brett. Otherwise, he was untouchable in October.

The best evidence of Gossage's value to the Yankees came from his teammates. Barry Foote has said, "Obviously, Goose was at the top of the heap as a closer in those years with the Yankees." Meanwhile George Frazier, who spent three years in the Yankee bullpen with Gossage, offered, "When he started warming up, there was no joking around with Goose Gossage—he was getting locked in. And he was a tremendous, tremendous asset. A tremendous person. A heart the size of the Grand Canyon." When the Goose was loose, he did great things for the Yankees.

Chapter VIII

MANAGER

Manager—Joe McCarthy

*He was the complete general who ran the whole show.
Regardless of the situation, the problem, or the complexity
of the dilemma, on the baseball field or off, McCarthy knew
the right answer. And rarely was his advice inappropriate.*

—*Peter Golenbock*

When one thinks of baseball, they rarely conjure the image of
a short, stocky Irish-American with a grim face and grumpy
attitude. Yet, that's the package that Joe McCarthy came in, one
of the greatest baseball minds there ever was. McCarthy ate,
slept, and breathed the game, but he seemingly never enjoyed a
minute of it. A demanding hands-on manager, he left nothing
to chance. In the end, his grimace hid a resigned patience that
helped the Yankees set a new standard of success in baseball.

Born and raised in the Germantown section of Philadelphia, Joe McCarthy had a rough upbringing but took solace
in baseball. A limited player, he still showed enough promise
to earn a baseball scholarship at Niagara University. After two
years in the frigid climate of western New York, he embarked

on a 15-year minor-league career that stopped at seven different cities across the Northeast. He observed and absorbed everything he could from his teammates and managers during this time, knowing that coaching would be his best chance at a successful career. He started by serving as player-manager for the Louisville Colonels before removing the "player" tag at 35 years old.

The Chicago Cubs signed McCarthy as manager after a successful stint in Louisville. He took a team that finished in last place in 1925 to 10 games over .500 in 1926 and would manage a winning team each of his five seasons in Chicago. The Cubs even made it to the World Series in 1929 but were steamrolled by the powerhouse Philadelphia Athletics. Chicago cut a bitter McCarthy loose after the 1930 season and the Yankees pounced, beating out the Boston Red Sox for his services. In 1931 he led the Yankees to 94 wins, an eight-win improvement for the team, but they finished in second place behind the juggernaut in Philadelphia.

When McCarthy arrived in New York, he changed the entire Yankee culture. As Peter Golenbock wrote, "Under McCarthy a player had to hold his head high and act with decorum. There was no horseplay, joking, or tomfoolery in the Yankee clubhouse before a game under any circumstances." His no-nonsense style drove the Yankees to 107 wins and an easy World Series victory in 1932. Even better for the Yankee skipper, in that series he exacted revenge on the Chicago Cubs. For the next three seasons the Yankees would finish in second place as McCarthy struggled to find a replacement for Babe Ruth to complement Lou Gehrig's bat. In 1936 he found his man.

Joe DiMaggio was a hot prospect and McCarthy made the wise decision to plug him into the lineup every day. That move combined with an elegantly simple philosophy—he once summed up managing for announcer Red Barber in three words: "memory and patience"—sparked an unprecedented run of success for the Yankees. Each year between 1936 and 1939, the Yankees posted the American League's best record, winning at least 99 games all four years. During World Series play they went 16-3 to bring home four straight championships. An unemotional workhorse, McCarthy had an insatiable desire to teach the game and demanded nothing short of the best a player had to offer. Few could argue with the results.

McCarthy and the Yankees slipped to 88 wins and a third-place finish in 1940, but that was a blip on the radar. They subsequently reeled off another three straight pennants, winning the World Series twice, and averaged over 100 regular-season wins. For the eight-year period ending in 1943, McCarthy oversaw a team that won over 100 games five times, earned seven pennants, and won the World Series six times. No other manager had ever come close to that kind of success, but the stoic McCarthy never rested on his laurels.

In fact, the only emotional moment he had during these years was on Lou Gehrig Appreciation Day at Yankee Stadium in 1939. Just prior to Gehrig's address to the crowd, McCarthy introduced him and, fighting back tears, said, "it was a sad day in the life of everybody who knew you when you came to my hotel room that day in Detroit and told me you were quitting as a ballplayer because you felt yourself a hindrance to the team. My God, man, you were never that."

US involvement in World War II hit the Yankees hard as they lost the services of star players DiMaggio, Charlie Keller, and Joe Gordon. Those losses were too much for even McCarthy to handle as the Yankees finished no better than third in 1944 and 1945. Less than two months into the 1946 season, the 59-year-old McCarthy resigned as Yankee manager, citing a gall bladder issue as the reason. There were whispers, though, that his resignation was due to an icy relationship with new team president Larry MacPhail. Two years later McCarthy resurfaced to manage the hated Boston Red Sox and led them to back-to-back 96-win seasons. Before the All-Star break in 1950, he called it quits for good and retired to his farm in upstate New York.

When McCarthy left baseball he was firmly in the conversation for greatest manager in baseball history, and to this day, baseball historian Bill James insists there has never been a better one. He wasn't without his detractors though. Longtime Chicago White Sox manager Jimmy Dykes once said of McCarthy, "What do you mean he's a great manager? All's he's got [*sic*] to do is push a button and a better ballplayer comes off the bench. If I had a club like that, I wouldn't even go out to the ballpark." In his history of the 1939 Yankees, sportswriter Richard J. Tofel countered that the Yankees won because McCarthy "never let up, never stopped trying to find the perfect combination, never got far enough ahead to relax." There have been plenty of managers who were more player-friendly or had more colorful personalities, but no manager has ever been more dedicated to winning than Joe McCarthy.

Chapter IX

OPTIMIZATION OF BATTING ORDER

In 2006, baseball statisticians Tom Tango, Mitchel Lichtman, and Andrew Dolphin set out to test baseball's conventional wisdom via quantitative analysis. The results of their research were published in *The Book: Playing the Percentages in Baseball*, which included a section on optimizing a batting order. By calculating the run expectancy of each batting event, the number of expected plate appearances, the average number of runners on base, and average number of outs for each position in the batting order, they could identify the ideal spot for each type of hitter.

One of their more interesting findings was that, on average, a batter in the number five spot should be a better hitter than the one in the number three spot. This is counterintuitive, as most managers will deploy the best hitter third in the lineup. However, as they point out, the number three batter comes to bat more often with two outs compared to the number five hitter and therefore has fewer chances to do more damage. In general, they summed up their findings with the following principles:

Your three best hitters should bat somewhere in the #1, #2, and #4 slots. Your fourth- and fifth-best hitters should occupy the #3 and #5 slots. The #1 and #2 slots will have players

*with more walks than those in the #4 and #5 slots. From slot
#6 through #9, put the players in descending order of quality.*

It's worth pointing out that they make clear in their findings that optimizing a lineup using these principles compared
to conventional wisdom yields an almost negligible return.
Over the course of 162 games, they estimate that this type of
lineup would only be worth about 10 to 15 more runs than your
run-of-the-mill MLB lineup configuration. Still, in a tight
pennant race, or a pivotal game, every run counts.

Now that we have identified all of the starters on this all-
time Yankee All-Star team, we can use these principles to put
together the best lineup possible for this crew of superstars.
Since this is an All-Star team, we'll assume we're getting a
version of the player at the height of his powers, and will therefore use relevant offensive statistics from the best five-year run
of their Yankee career to make our decisions. Here are those
numbers for our starters:

Pos	Player	Bats	Years	AVG	OBP	SLG	OPS+	BB%	HR%
C	Yogi Berra	Left	1950–1954	.299	.365	.503	136	8.9%	4.4%
1B	Lou Gehrig	Left	1927–1931	.354	.458	.677	195	15.4%	5.6%
2B	Willie Randolph	Right	1976–1980	.277	.378	.371	111	13.7%	0.7%
3B	Graig Nettles	Left	1974–1978	.259	.328	.453	121	9.2%	4.3%
SS	Derek Jeter	Right	1998–2002	.324	.398	.483	129	9.8%	2.8%
LF	Babe Ruth	Left	1920–1924	.370	.511	.777	229	21.7%	7.4%
CF	Joe DiMaggio	Right	1937–1941	.350	.420	.638	168	10.2%	5.5%

Pos	Player	Bats	Years	AVG	OBP	SLG	OPS+	BB%	HR%
RF	Mickey Mantle	Switch	1954– 1958	.325	.451	.618	191	18.7%	6.0%
DH	Charlie Keller	Left	1941– 1946	.285	.409	.540	164	17.0%	4.7%

There are two quick observations to get out of the way here that have nothing to do with the batting order itself. First, the designated hitter was never explicitly identified in the earlier profiles found in this book. It should be obvious now that Charlie Keller was the big winner of that role. There were plenty of excellent options to fill that spot on this team, with Don Mattingly and Alex Rodriguez probably being Keller's closest competition. However, Keller's elite ability to draw walks gave him the edge here. The other observation that may be leaving fans scratching their heads is Babe Ruth in left field. More commonly known as a right fielder, Ruth actually played close to 40 percent of his games in left and was surprisingly effective there. Meanwhile, Mickey Mantle was no stranger to right field, having played there during his overlapping time with Joe DiMaggio. That's why the outfield configuration appears the way it does.

Getting back to the order, let's start with the easy part of how the bottom four spots will look. If one were to sort the table above on OPS+, there is a clear gap between the top five and bottom four hitters. The "worst" four hitters on this team, ranked from highest to lowest OPS+, are Yogi Berra, Derek Jeter, Graig Nettles, and Willie Randolph. Accordingly, those four players will occupy spots six through nine in the lineup.

Next up will be filling the number three and five spots, which should be occupied by the fourth and fifth best hitters on the team. As we already established, between these two spots, the better hitter should bat fifth, so Joe DiMaggio will get that honor and Charlie Keller will be penciled in at the number three spot. One would be hard-pressed to find a manager that would bat Keller third when given this lineup, but that is what the optimization logic dictates.

Last but not least, the first, second, and fourth spots will need to be filled by the best three hitters on the team. Inarguably, that means Babe Ruth, Lou Gehrig, and Mickey Mantle will get the call here. Based on the research in *The Book*, the run expectancy for each batting event across these three spots is very similar, with the main difference being that home runs are most valuable when batting fourth and walks are most valuable when batting first. Our conundrum then, is that Babe Ruth has both the best home-run rate and walk rate among this trio. Yet something would feel very wrong with Ruth, the crowned king of home runs, being a leadoff hitter. Therefore, he'll bat cleanup. Between Mantle and Gehrig, The Mick has the advantage in walk rate, which means that he'll leadoff and Gehrig will bat second. Here, then, is the optimized lineup card that manager Joe McCarthy should fill out:

Order	Pos	Bats	Player
1	RF	Switch	Mickey Mantle
2	1B	Left	Lou Gehrig
3	DH	Left	Charlie Keller
4	LF	Left	Babe Ruth
5	CF	Right	Joe DiMaggio
6	C	Left	Yogi Berra
7	SS	Right	Derek Jeter
8	3B	Left	Graig Nettles
9	2B	Right	Willie Randolph

While this is the lineup that would maximize the run potential of this mega-team, even if the players were scrambled in a random order, it's hard to believe that they would lose with any kind of frequency no matter who is pitching.

CHAPTER X

HONORABLE MENTIONS

In determining who should fill each roster spot on this team, some very close calls had to be made. The following players would offer no significant dropoff if they were to replace one of the players selected as reserves on the All-Star team.

CATCHERS
Elston Howard

The 1963 American League MVP was an excellent hitter in his prime and rock solid as a backstop. He was also versatile enough to be serviceable as a corner outfielder and first baseman during his years playing with Yogi Berra. He will forever be remembered as the first black player for the Yankees when he made his debut in 1955. Although that distinction was well overdue, by all accounts he was a mensch and continued with the Yankees as a coach for more than 10 years after his playing career.

Mike Stanley

For the first six years of his career, all spent with the Texas Rangers, he compiled a total of -0.3 WAR. The Yankees signed him as a free agent in 1992 and his career made a 180-degree turn. Across five seasons in New York he amassed nearly 13 WAR and helped bring the team back to respectability before leaving as a free agent. His 134 OPS+ in pinstripes is the best mark for a Yankee catcher with at least 1,000 plate appearances.

FIRST BASEMEN

Bill Skowron

He earned the nickname "Moose" as a child thanks to a haircut that resembled Benito Mussolini's. In his nine seasons with the Yankees, he was a key contributor to four World Series championships in the late 1950s and early 1960s as an excellent fielder and well-rounded hitter. He was a much-needed right-handed bat in lefty-dominant Yankee lineups. He enthusiastically shared stories of his playing days to any willing ears until the day he died.

Jason Giambi/Tino Martinez/Mark Teixeira

For 20 consecutive years this three-headed monster held down first base for the Yankees. They were all similarly productive, but in different ways. Giambi was a world-class slugger whose game was built almost entirely on patience and power. He never won a World Series in the Bronx, but the Yankees would never have won the dramatic 2003 American League Championship Series over the Red Sox without his two home runs in Game 7. Martinez had no overwhelming strengths, but also few weaknesses, as a player. He was a solid fielder who could also hit for a decent batting average with some power. The Yankees won four World Series in the late 1990s with him as a mainstay in the middle of the lineup. Teixeira was a Gold Glover at first base and a longball threat from either side of the plate. In his first year on a mega-deal with the Yankees in 2009, he helped them to a World Series win as he was runner-up for the American League MVP.

SECOND BASEMEN
Tony Lazzeri

One of the toughest decisions in deciding which players to include on this all-time Yankee roster was leaving Lazzeri off of it. As a young player he was part of the infamous Murderers' Row Yankees in 1927 and was often the third-best hitter on the team. That's no crime when your lineup includes Ruth and Gehrig. For his career he won five World Series in New York. The other Yankee second basemen that made the roster in front of him were all dual threats, whereas Lazzeri was average at best with the glove. Still, it was an extremely close call.

Gil McDougald

Due to his relatively short career and the fact that he never settled on one position, McDougald is quite possibly the most underrated Yankee of all time. Yet his versatility was his greatest asset. He rotated between second base, third base, and shortstop throughout his career and was certain death to groundballs no matter where he was deployed. Add to that an above average bat and it's no surprise that the Yankees won five World Series in his 10 years with the team. Bill James: "There are three men who made Casey Stengel a genius—Yogi Berra, Mickey Mantle, and Gil McDougald."

THIRD BASEMEN
Home Run Baker

John Franklin Baker earned the nickname "Home Run" during his days with the Philadelphia Athletics, where he won four consecutive home-run titles between 1911 and 1914, but never topped 12 in any season. Desperate for premium talent, the Yankees purchased his contract in 1916. He would never be a home-run king again, but spent the back end of his career with the Yankees as a solid hitter and consistently good fielder. His presence helped to finally bring respectability to the franchise in the late 1910s.

Red Rolfe

A favorite of Joe McCarthy in the late 1930s, he was a very useful player in non-obvious ways. He supplemented his light hitting with plenty of walks and brought the range and quickness of a middle infielder to the third base position. He held down the hot corner for a Yankee team that won five World Series championships in the six-year period from 1936 through 1941.

SHORTSTOPS

Roger Peckinpaugh

A classic slick-fielding shortstop with a weak bat, in 1914 he was named the Yankees' captain at just 23 years old. He held the position until 1921, which makes him the longest-tenured captain in Yankee history not named Derek Jeter. One can make the case that he was an effective one, too, as the Yankees went from laughingstocks to American League pennant winners under his watch.

Tony Kubek

In the same mold as Peckinpaugh, except he was a worse hitter and a better fielder, despite being 6-foot-3 with a strong build and a left-handed swing. Yet somehow he was never able to find his home run stroke consistently, even at Yankee Stadium. His career highlights include the 1957 American League Rookie of the Year Award and three World Series rings.

OUTFIELDERS

Roger Maris

Traded to the Yankees prior to the 1960 season, he promptly won back-to-back American League MVP Awards. This included a thrilling home-run chase with Mickey Mantle during which he broke Babe Ruth's record of 60 in a season amid an unfair and undue amount of pressure from media and fans. He had three more productive seasons in pinstripes before injuries took their toll on his career. The home-run record has and will always overshadow the fact that he was a great all-around ballplayer in his prime.

Rickey Henderson

As part of a nomadic Hall of Fame career he spent five seasons with the Yankees in the late 1980s. Over those five years he totaled 134 Batting Runs Above Average, 52 Baserunning Runs Above Average, and 46 Fielding Runs Above Average. No Yankee before or since has dominated so thoroughly in every facet of the game. Alas, he never played in a playoff game as a Yankee, and his time in New York is mostly seen as just a brief stop on his express route to Cooperstown.

Hank Bauer

Whether it was patrolling Yankee Stadium's outfield, stepping into the batter's box, or carousing in Midtown Manhattan, he always played second fiddle to Mickey Mantle. He played the role well. Bauer was a solid hitter, solid fielder, solid baserunner, and a former marine who could hold his own in a fight. As a right-handed hitter, Yankee Stadium robbed him of much of his power, but he still hit 20 or more home runs in a season twice. In his 12 years in pinstripes, he earned seven World Series rings.

Brett Gardner

Per Fielding Runs Above Average, he's the best fielding out-fielder in Yankee history by a very wide margin. As he entered his prime, he was also an elite base stealer and capable leadoff hitter and has served as a much-needed veteran leader of the Baby Bombers in the latter part of the 2010s. Gardner is a workmanlike player in the vein of Roy White and Willie Randolph, the latter of whom he shares a hometown with in Holly Hill, South Carolina.

Dave Winfield

In 1981 Steinbrenner made him the highest paid player in baseball and spent the next 10 years resenting him for it. With a tall, athletic physique equally at home on the basketball court or gridiron, all Winfield did was consistently produce on the baseball diamond. He spent the plurality of his Hall of Fame career with the Yankees but never won a World Series in New York.

Paul O'Neill

From George Steinbrenner's viewpoint, O'Neill was the antithesis of Dave Winfield thanks to his hypercompetitive attitude and ability to play through pain. Dubbed "The Warrior" by The Boss, it seemed that every year he would hit .300 with 20 home runs and 100 RBIs while the Yankees won the World Series. In reality, those stars aligned just once, in 1998. Across nine years in New York, he averaged .303 with 21 home runs and 95 RBIs. Still a fan favorite.

Bobby Murcer

A shortstop turned center fielder from Oklahoma with power and speed, he drew comparisons early in his career to Mickey

Mantle, although he never lived up to that hype. The comparison unfortunately undermined his fine playing career. Spending his playing days mostly with the Yankees in the 1970s and early 1980s, he amassed 252 home runs and was a perennial All-Star in his prime. He then spent over 20 years in the broadcast booth for the Yankees and was by all accounts an even better person than he was a baseball player.

PITCHERS
Herb Pennock

Pennock was one of many players to leave Boston and find great success with the Yankees in the early 1920s. In a career that spanned 22 years, nearly 75 percent of his total career value was concentrated in his first six seasons in New York. Not coincidentally, the Yankees won three World Series in that time period. He was the first in a long line of left-handed star pitchers to call Yankee Stadium home.

Spud Chandler

Chandler was the MVP of the American League in 1943, although many of baseball's best players had joined the war effort by then. In an era where pitch counts and innings limits were unheard of, Chandler still only topped 200 innings three times in his career, although his 132 career ERA+ is the best for any Yankee pitcher who made at least 150 starts and is not named Whitey Ford (133 career ERA+).

Bob Shawkey

Shawkey joined the Yankees in 1915 and was soon the ace of a pitching staff that helped slowly bring respectability to the franchise. By the time the Yankees were winning the World

Series, he was pitching at the back-end of the rotation or mostly in relief. In 1923 he became the first pitcher to record a win at Yankee Stadium. In 1930 he was called on to replace Miller Huggins as manager, but lasted only that one disappointing season.

Allie Reynolds/Eddie Lopat/Vic Raschi

Another three-headed monster, this one served as the Yankees' pitching ace from 1948 to 1953, just before Whitey Ford hit his stride. Like the three-headed monster described at first base, this group is also comprised of similarly effective guys who went about it in different ways. Reynolds was an aggressive gamer who became the first pitcher in American League history to throw two no-hitters in the same season in 1951. Though primarily used as a starter, he also happily took the ball in relief, where he was lights out. Lopat was a junkballing lefty who survived with a weak fastball by consistently inducing weak contact and trusting his fielders. Raschi was a flame-throwing right-hander whose quiet, reserved attitude stood in stark contrast to Reynolds'. Together, the trio was nearly unstoppable. In their six years as teammates, the Yankees won five World Series. Reynolds, Lopat, and Raschi accounted for 15 of the 20 Yankee victories in those series.

Sparky Lyle

Another player who left the Red Sox to enjoy great success in New York, the left-handed relief ace was among the best closers in baseball for his first six years in pinstripes. This culminated with the American League Cy Young Award and a World Series championship in 1977. When the Yankees acquired Goose Gossage a season later, he lost his closer role and was deemed expendable.

Johnny Murphy

Joe Page is often given credit for being the first "closer" in Yankee history, but it's simply not true. Ten years before Page, Johnny Murphy was a dominant relief ace for the Yankees. From 1938 through 1942 he led the American League in saves four times. Overall in his Yankee career he won six World Series rings and pitched to a 1.10 ERA during those games. After his playing days he served as general manager of the Mets and was the architect of their 1969 World Series win. The case can be made that he belongs in the Hall of Fame.

MANAGER

Casey Stengel

After a distinguished playing career, he was a subpar major-league manager when hired by the Yankees in 1949. With a surplus of talent on the Yankee roster, he deployed platoons to perfection and with his quirky charm he won over the New York fans and press. In 12 seasons under his watch, the Yankees won 10 pennants and seven World Series, including a record five straight from 1949 through 1953.

ACKNOWLEDGMENTS

Writing this book has been a humbling experience and wouldn't have been possible without the good fortune of support and inspiration at every turn. I could fill another book with the thanks I *should* dole out. Instead, here are the most important bits of gratitude.

To Mary Griffin, for surrounding me with books since birth and being my biggest fan.

To Sean Griffin, for showing your little brother that baseball was the best way to dream big in a small backyard on Long Island.

To Brian Griffin, for making my first trip to Yankee Stadium happen in 1987, and Keith Griffin for keeping that tradition alive.

To Mike McCormack, Connor McCormack, Joyce Griffin, and Pat Sullivan, for sage advice and much needed technical support on all things book-related.

To Josephine and Seamus, for turning every day into an adventure.

To *Earl Weaver Baseball*, an ancient computer game in which I built my first All-Star team.

To Niels Aaboe, for taking a chance on and being patient with a rookie author.

To the *Pinstripe Alley* community and Sensei John Kreese at NoMaas.org, for giving me my first opportunities to write about the Yankees.

To the Society for American Baseball Research and Baseball-Reference.com, for being indispensable resources for background information and statistics.

To Amanda DiGrazia, for encouragement, love, and respect beyond reason. I couldn't have done this without you.

APPENDIX I

Statistics and Supplemental Factors Used for Rankings

Statistics are the lifeblood of baseball. In no other sport are so many available, and studied so assiduously by participants and fans.

—*Leonard Koppett*

The first step in selecting the all-time Yankee roster was to rank all historical Yankee players by position using a treasure trove of data. Home runs, batting average, runs scored, runs batted in, and ERA are the most widely used numbers available for players going back to major-league baseball's birth. Those numbers were considered, but there have been major advancements, especially over the past 10 to 15 years, in the development of more meaningful baseball metrics. Many of these are available on the Baseball-Reference.com website and those described below were the main factors in the rankings.

The key attribute of the advanced metrics is that, with one exception, they are context-neutral. That is, they are adjusted for the run-scoring environment, time period, and ballpark in which they occurred so they can be compared without bias across eras. Take for example the individual seasons that Carl Yastrzemski and Mo Vaughn had for the Boston Red Sox in

1967 and 1996, respectively. On the surface, they both hit 44 home runs with a .326 batting average. Vaughn has the edge in RBIs with 143 to Yastrzemski's 121. Given just these numbers, most people would say Vaughn had a slightly better year in 1996 than Yaz did in 1967.

However, context is everything. In 1967 scoring rates were plummeting as pitchers ruled baseball, but in 1996 offense was soaring and teams were averaging over five runs per game for the first time since the 1930s. Given those circumstances and accounting for defense and baserunning, context-neutral metrics measure Yastrzemski's season as more than twice as valuable as Vaughn's. To take it a step further, Yaz's efforts in 1967 earned him the American League Triple Crown, whereas Vaughn's campaign in 1996, fine as it was, didn't see him lead the league in any major category. Understanding context in situations like this is imperative if we're to compare players in a fair, unbiased way.

DESCRIPTION OF CONTEXT-NEUTRAL METRICS— POSITIONAL

OPS+—An indexed version of on-base percentage plus slugging percentage (OPS) for the player compared to his league's average, adjusted for the ballpark in which the player played. A value over 100 indicates that the player had an OPS above average. Subtracting 100 from a player's OPS+ yields the percentage above or below league average that the player's OPS was. (Ex: An OPS+ of 120 means that the player had an OPS 20 percent above average).

WAA (Wins Above Average)—Number of wins added by the player above that of an average player. The first step is finding runs above average. At Baseball-Reference.com, the four major components to calculating runs above average are those coming from hitting, fielding, baserunning, and a positional adjustment where designated hitters and first basemen get the stiffest penalty while shortstops and catchers get the largest bonus. The run components are calculated based on actual events and are adjusted for the run-scoring environment in which they took place. In general, the conversion of runs above average to WAA is roughly 10 runs per win.

WAR (Wins Above Replacement)—A single number representing the wins a player adds to the team above what a replacement player would add. The key difference between this and WAA is the concept of "replacement." In real life, average major-league players are difficult to acquire when a starter goes down. Usually, a starter is replaced by a veteran past his prime or a minor leaguer who is not good enough to play every day in the majors. Those replacement players are well below average, and comparing a player to that baseline more accurately quantifies his value compared to the alternative.

DESCRIPTION OF CONTEXT-NEUTRAL METRICS— PITCHING

ERA+—An indexed version of earned run average (ERA) for the pitcher compared to the league average, adjusted for the ballpark in which the pitcher played. A value over 100 indicates that the pitcher had an ERA above average when adjusted for ballpark. An above average ERA means that the value was below the league average, since with ERA the lower the number the better the performance.

WAA (Wins Above Average)—Number of wins added by the pitcher above that of an average pitcher. To get runs above average for pitchers, the total runs they surrendered (both earned and unearned) are compared to the number of runs an average pitcher would have surrendered in the same situation after adjusting for the parks in which they played, the fielders behind them, and whether they were a starter or reliever. Just as for position players, roughly 10 runs equal a win.

WAR (Wins Above Replacement)—A single number that represents the wins the pitcher added to the team above what a replacement pitcher would add. The WAR calculation for pitchers is no different than the calculation laid out above for position players.

DESCRIPTION OF CONTEXT-BIASED METRICS
Batting WPA (Win Probability Added, available only for seasons since 1925)—The change in win probability for his team caused by a batter during a game. The sum of all those changes over a given time period results in WPA. The number itself represents the number of wins above average the player added where 0 indicates that a player had an exactly average impact. This metric is not context-neutral but roughly captures how "clutch" a player was because tight situations will have much larger impacts on win probability.

Pitching WPA (Win Probability Added, available only for seasons since 1925)—This is calculated exactly as described above for position players, except it's from the pitcher's perspective. WPA has the interesting effect of putting the best starting pitchers and best relievers on a level playing field. Starting pitchers compile more innings than relievers, but many are at the beginning of games when each event has a relatively small effect on the game's outcome. The best relievers usually enter the late innings in a tight situation where the game is on the line and can have just as much impact as a starter.

DESCRIPTION OF SUPPLEMENTAL FACTORS

Advanced metrics weren't the only tools used for selecting this All-Star team. The following factors, some of them highly subjective, were also taken into account.

Captaincy—Despite its inconsistencies over the years, being named captain of the Yankees is a significant honor.

Rookie of the Year Award (since 1947)—Awarded to the top rookie-eligible player as voted on by the Baseball Writers' Association of America (BBWAA).

All-Star Game Appearances (since 1933)—Player was selected to play in MLB's annual All-Star Game. The rules for selecting All-Stars and the size of rosters have changed over time, but it is generally some form of fan voting and manager selection. There was no game played in 1945.

MVP Award (since 1911)—Awarded to the most valuable player in each league each season. In the 1920s a player could win only once. Since 1931, the MVP award has been voted on by the BBWAA and the rules have been relatively stable, with players able to win multiple awards.

Gold Glove Award (since 1957)—Given to players who have exhibited overall excellence in the field at each position in both leagues as voted on by managers and coaches each season. Since 2013 there has also been a component based on advanced defensive metrics developed by the Society for American Baseball Research (SABR), which accounts for 25 percent of the vote.

Home-Run Title—Player who hit the most home runs in each league each season.

Batting Title—Player with the highest batting average in each league each season. To qualify, a player must have at least 3.1 plate appearances per team game.

Silver Slugger Award (since 1980)—Awarded to players who were the best hitters at each position in both leagues as voted on by managers and coaches each season.

Wins Leader—Pitcher who won the most games in each league each season.

ERA Title—Pitcher with the lowest earned run average in each league each season. To qualify, a pitcher must have at least one inning pitched per team game.

Strikeout Title—Pitcher who struck out the most batters in each league each season.

Playoff Performance—A player's performance in the postseason was taken into account. The League Championship Series has only been played since 1969 and the Division Series since 1995. Therefore, World Series performance was given the highest consideration. World Series MVP wins, awarded since 1955, were also taken into account.

APPENDIX II

Detailed Rankings

DEFINITIONS OF ABBREVIATED STATISTICS
BA/OBP/SLG—Batting Average/On-base Percentage/Slugging Percentage. Also referred to as a "slash line."
R—Runs scored.
HR—Home-runs hit.
RBI—Runs batted in.
OPS+—Park adjusted On-base Percentage plus Slugging Percentage.
WAA—Wins Above Average.
WAR—Wins Above Replacement.
WPA—Win Probability Added.
IP—Innings Pitched.
W-L—Won/Lost record.
SV—Saves.
ERA—Earned Run Average.
ERA+—Park adjusted Earned Run Average.
SO—Strikeouts.

DEFINITIONS OF ABBREVIATED AWARDS
Cpt—Yankee captain.
ROY—Rookie of the Year.

AS—All-Star.
MVP—Most Valuable Player.
GG—Gold Glove.
HR—Home-Run Title.
BA—Batting Title.
SS—Silver Slugger.
W—Wins leader.
ERA—ERA Title.
K—Strikeout Title.
WS—World Series won.
WS MVP—World Series MVP.

Catchers

Rank	Player	Years	Games	BA/OBP/SLG	R	HR	RBI	OPS+	WAA	WAR	WPA	Awards
1	Yogi Berra	1946–1963	2116	.285/.348/.483	1174	358	1430	125	34.1	59.5	39.2	15x AS, 3x MVP, 10x WS
2	Bill Dickey	1928–1946	1789	.313/.382/.486	930	202	1209	127	31.6	55.8	24.5	11x AS, 7x WS
3	Thurman Munson	1969–1979	1423	.292/.346/.410	696	113	701	116	25.5	46.1	15.4	Cpt, ROY, 7x AS, MVP, 3x GG, 2x WS
4	Jorge Posada	1995–2011	1829	.273/.374/.474	900	275	1065	121	17.4	42.8	12.9	5x AS, 5x SS, 4x WS
5	Elston Howard	1955–1967	1492	.279/.324/.436	588	161	733	110	10.6	27.6	6.4	9x AS, MVP, 2x GG, 4x WS
6	Mike Stanley	1992–1995, 1997	426	.285/.377/.504	227	72	263	134	7.2	12.8	6.7	AS, SS
7	Butch Wynegar	1982–1986	449	.259/.368/.363	161	27	168	105	5.3	10.7	1.7	
8	Pat Collins	1926–1928	264	.269/.413/.412	97	20	85	117	3.0	6.2	0.0	2x WS
9	Wally Schang	1921–1925	529	.297/.390/.406	225	16	209	105	3.5	10.7	-0.2	WS
10	Jake Gibbs	1962–1971	538	.233/.289/.321	157	25	146	81	0.5	6.7	-2.3	

First Basemen

Rank	Player	Years	Games	BA/OBP/SLG	R	HR	RBI	OPS+	WAA	WAR	WPA	Awards
1	Lou Gehrig	1923–1939	2164	.340/.447/.632	1888	493	1995	179	78.5	112.4	79.1	Cpt, 7x AS, 2x MVP, 3x HR, BA, 6x WS
2	Don Mattingly	1982–1995	1785	.307/.358/.471	1007	222	1099	127	17.6	42.4	23.1	Cpt, 6x AS, MVP, BA, 3x SS, 9x GG
3	Bill Skowron	1954–1962	1087	.294/.346/.496	518	165	672	129	11.1	23.6	14.4	5x AS, 4x WS
4	Jason Giambi	2002–2008	897	.260/.404/.521	515	209	604	143	9	22.1	20.7	3x AS, SS
5	Tino Martinez	1996–2001, 2005	1054	.276/.347/.484	566	192	739	113	1.8	16.7	11.6	AS, SS, 4x WS
6	Mark Teixeira	2009–2016	958	.248/.343/.479	533	206	622	118	6.3	20.5	8.2	2x AS, HR, SS, 3x GG, WS
7	Wally Pipp	1915–1925	1488	.282/.343/.414	820	80	833	107	5	29.1	-1.0	2x HR, WS
8	Chris Chambliss	1974–1979, 1988	885	.282/.323/.417	415	79	454	108	2.9	15.4	5.7	AS, GG, 2x WS
9	Joe Collins	1948–1957	908	.256/.350/.421	404	86	329	111	3.9	12.2	4.0	5x WS
10	Joe Pepitone	1962–1969	1051	.252/.294/.423	435	166	541	105	-6	7.4	2.4	3x AS, 3x GG

Second Basemen

Rank	Player	Years	Games	BA/OBP/SLG	R	HR	RBI	OPS+	WAA	WAR	WPA	Awards
1	Willie Randolph	1976–1988	1694	.275/.374/.357	1027	48	549	105	30.6	54	5.3	Cpt, 5x AS, 1x SS, 2x WS
2	Joe Gordon	1938–1946	1000	.271/.358/.467	596	153	617	120	24.3	37.5	8.5	6x AS, MVP, 4x WS
3	Robinson Canó	2005–2013	1374	.309/.355/.504	799	204	822	126	24.9	45.5	11.9	5x AS, 5x SS, 2x GG, WS
4	Tony Lazzeri	1926–1937	1659	.293/.379/.467	952	169	1157	120	22.8	48.3	15.4	AS, 5x WS
5	Gil McDougald	1951–1960	1336	.276/.356/.410	697	112	576	111	24.1	40.7	10.3	ROY, 5x AS, 5x WS
6	Snuffy Stirnweiss	1943–1950	884	.274/.366/.382	562	27	253	108	16.9	27.7	3.8	2x AS, BA, 3x WS
7	Bobby Richardson	1955–1966	1412	.266/.299/.335	643	34	390	77	-9	8.2	-12.4	7x AS, 5x GG, 3x WS, WS MVP
8	Del Pratt	1918–1920	420	.295/.348/.394	218	10	219	106	6.4	13.1	NA	
9	Alfonso Soriano	1999–2003, 2013–2014	626	.276/.315/.492	385	121	343	112	1.6	10.4	0.4	2x AS, SS
10	Horace Clarke	1965–1974	1230	.257/.309/.315	543	27	300	84	-1.4	16	-9.4	

Third Basemen

Rank	Player	Years	Games	BA/OBP/SLG	R	HR	RBI	OPS+	WAA	WAR	WPA	Awards
1	Graig Nettles	1973–1983	1535	.253/.329/.433	750	250	834	114	23.2	44.4	12.8	Cpt, 5x AS, HR, 2x GG, 2x WS
2	Alex Rodriguez	2004–2016	1509	.283/.378/.523	1012	351	1096	136	31.6	54.2	27.9	7x AS, 2x MVP, 2x HR, 3x SS, WS
3	Home Run Baker	1916–1922	676	.288/.347/.404	314	48	379	113	9.7	20.5	NA	
4	Red Rolfe	1931–1942	1175	.289/.360/.413	942	69	497	99	6.4	23.5	7.7	4x AS, 5x WS
5	Wade Boggs	1993–1997	602	.313/.396/.407	355	24	246	112	9.4	18.3	2.0	4x AS, 2x SS, 2x GG, WS
6	Clete Boyer	1959–1966	1068	.241/.298/.371	434	95	393	86	7.1	19.6	–6.9	2x WS
7	Scott Brosius	1998–2001	540	.267/.331/.428	264	65	282	96	0.8	8.3	–2.5	AS, GG, 3x WS, WS MVP
8	Bobby Brown	1946–1954	548	.279/.367/.376	233	22	237	100	1.2	6.6	4.2	4x WS
9	Billy Johnson	1943–1951	735	.275/.349/.395	344	45	388	104	1.6	10	5.8	AS, 4x WS
10	Andy Carey	1952–1960	688	.266/.332/.397	288	47	259	99	1.7	9.2	1.6	2x WS

Shortstops

Rank	Player	Years	Games	BA/OBP/SLG	R	HR	RBI	OFS+	WAA	WAR	WPA	Awards
1	Derek Jeter	1995–2014	2747	.310/.377/.440	1923	260	1311	115	31	72.4	30.9	Cpt, ROY, 14x AS, 5x SS, 5x GG, 5x WS, WS MVP
2	Phil Rizzuto	1941–1956	1661	.273/.351/.355	877	38	563	93	21	40.8	-5.9	5x AS, MVP, 7x WS
3	Roger Peckinpaugh	1913–1921	1219	.257/.334/.342	670	36	428	93	11.9	32	NA	Cpt
4	Tony Kubek	1957–1965	1092	.266/.303/.364	522	57	373	85	4.7	18.7	-2.8	ROY, 3x AS, 3x WS
5	Bucky Dent	1977–1982	695	.239/.295/.324	229	27	209	72	4.4	12.5	-6.4	2x AS, 2x WS, WS MVP
6	Frankie Crosetti	1932–1948	1683	.245/.341/.354	1006	98	649	83	0.7	23.9	-10.3	2x AS, 6x WS
7	Kid Elberfeld	1903–1909	667	.268/.340/.333	330	4	257	106	8.2	18.9	NA	Cpt
8	Didi Gregorius	2015–2018	578	.274/.319/.447	287	81	299	103	5.3	13.3	-1.5	
9	Lyn Lary	1929–1934	496	.274/.368/.388	322	21	237	100	3.3	10.5	0.7	WS
10	Everett Scott	1922–1925	481	.254/.282/.324	171	13	174	57	-6	1	NA	Cpt, WS

Outfielders

Rank	Player	Years	Games	BA/OBP/SLG	R	HR	RBI	OPS+	WAA	WAR	WPA	Awards
1	Babe Ruth	1920–1934	2084	.349/.484/.711	1959	659	1978	209	109.4	142.6	55.4	Cpt, 2x AS, MVP, 10x HR, BA, 4x WS
2	Mickey Mantle	1951–1968	2401	.298/.421/.557	1676	536	1509	172	79.5	110.3	93.5	16x AS, 3x MVP, 4x HR, BA, GG, 7x WS
3	Joe DiMaggio	1936–1951	1736	.325/.398/.579	1390	361	1537	155	54.5	78.1	54.2	13x AS, 3x MVP, 2x HR, 2x BA, 9x WS
4	Charlie Keller	1939–1949, 1952	1066	.286/.410/.518	712	184	723	152	28.3	41.9	31.6	5x AS, 3x WS
5	Bernie Williams	1991–2006	2076	.297/.381/.477	1366	287	1257	125	18.7	49.6	23.9	5x AS, BA, SS, 4x GG, 4x WS
6	Roy White	1965–1979	1881	.271/.360/.404	964	160	758	121	20.4	46.8	27.9	2x AS, 2x WS
7	Earle Combs	1924–1935	1455	.325/.397/.462	1186	58	633	125	19.6	42.5	20.3	3x WS
8	Tommy Henrich	1937–1950	1284	.282/.382/.491	901	183	795	132	19.4	35.7	30.4	5x AS, 4x WS
9	Reggie Jackson	1977–1981	653	.281/.371/.526	380	144	461	148	8.1	17.2	14.9	5x AS, HR, SS, 2x WS, WS MVP
10	Roger Maris	1960–1966	850	.265/.356/.515	520	203	547	139	15.6	26.3	19.9	3x AS, 2x MVP, HR, GG, 2x WS
11	Rickey Henderson	1985–1989	596	.288/.395/.455	513	78	255	135	22.8	30.9	18.7	4x AS, SS

	Name	Years	G	AVG/OBP/SLG								
12	Hank Bauer	1948–1959	1406	.277/.347/.444	792	158	654	115	12.9	29.3	9.6	3x AS, 7x WS
13	Brett Gardner	2008–2018	1358	.261/.344/.390	790	96	450	99	18.7	37.5	10.0	AS, GG, WS
14	Dave Winfield	1981–1990	1172	.290/.356/.495	722	205	818	134	11.2	27.1	19.6	8x AS, 5x SS, 5x GG
15	Paul O'Neill	1993–2001	1254	.303/.377/.492	720	185	858	125	8.1	26.7	15.7	4x AS, BA, 4x WS
16	Bobby Murcer	1965–1974, 1979–1983	1256	.278/.349/.453	641	175	687	129	10.4	27.7	22.6	4x AS, GG
17	George Selkirk	1934–1942	846	.290/.400/.483	503	108	576	127	10.9	22.1	10.5	2x AS, 5x WS
18	Mickey Rivers	1976–1979	490	.299/.324/.422	289	34	209	110	8	15.1	5.9	AS, 2x WS
19	Ben Chapman	1930–1936	910	.305/.379/.451	626	60	589	119	11	25.3	9.2	3x AS, WS
20	Gene Woodling	1949–1954	698	.285/.388/.434	361	51	336	124	8.2	16.4	9.0	5x WS
21	Bob Meusel	1920–1929	1294	.311/.358/.500	764	146	1009	121	7	27.6	7.7	HR, 3x WS
22	Hideki Matsui	2003–2009	916	.292/.370/.482	536	140	597	123	7	20.4	11.0	2x AS, WS, WS MVP
23	Tom Tresh	1961–1969	1098	.247/.337/.413	549	140	493	115	6.9	21.4	12.1	ROY, 2x AS, GG, WS

Rank	Player	Years	Games	BA/OBP/SLG	R	HR	RBI	OPS+	WAA	WAR	WPA	Awards
24	Curtis Granderson	2010–2013	513	.245/.335/.495	345	115	307	120	7.4	15.0	4.8	2x AS, SS
25	Johnny Damon	2006–2009	576	.285/.363/.458	410	77	296	112	5.7	14.4	6.9	WS
26	Oscar Gamble	1976, 1979–1984	540	.259/.361/.496	220	87	276	141	5.7	11.3	8.7	
27	Johnny Lindell	1941–1950	742	.275/.343/.428	371	63	369	114	4.4	12.8	4.6	AS, 3x WS
28	Nick Swisher	2009–2012	598	.268/.367/.483	331	105	349	124	2.9	11.9	6.1	AS, WS
29	Gary Sheffield	2004–2006	347	.291/.383/.515	243	76	269	135	3.5	8.7	9.1	2x AS, 2x SS
30	Lou Piniella	1974–1984	1037	.295/.338/.413	392	57	417	111	-2.8	9.3	2.9	2x WS

Pitchers

Rank	Player	Years	IP	W-L	SV	ERA	ERA+	SO	WAA	WAR	WPA	Awards
1	Mariano Rivera	1995–2013	1283.2	82-60	652	2.21	205	1173	32.5	56.3	56.6	13x AS, 5x WS, WS MVP
2	Whitey Ford	1950–1967	3170.1	236-106	11	2.75	133	1956	28.7	53.5	37.0	8x AS, CY, 3x W, 2x ERA, 6x WS, WS MVP
3	Ron Guidry	1975–1988	2392	170-91	4	3.29	119	1778	26.6	48.2	23.5	Cpt, 4x AS, 5x GG, CY, 2x W, 2x ERA, 2x WS
4	Lefty Gomez	1930–1942	2498.1	189-101	10	3.34	125	1468	19.8	43.3	22.2	7x AS, 2x W, 2x ERA, 3x K, 5x WS
5	Andy Pettitte	1995–2003, 2007–2013	2796.1	219-127	0	3.94	115	2020	24.7	51.4	18.2	3x AS, W, 5x WS
6	Red Ruffing	1930–1946	3168.2	231-124	9	3.47	119	1526	17.8	46.6	34.9	6x AS, W, K, 6x WS
7	Waite Hoyt	1921–1930	2272.1	157-98	29	3.48	115	713	13.5	35.8	10.9	W, 3x WS
8	Mel Stottlemyre	1964–1974	2661.1	164-139	1	2.97	112	1257	17.9	40.8	13.3	5x AS
9	David Cone	1995–2000	922	64-40	0	3.91	118	388	11.5	20.3	8.9	2x AS, W, 4x WS
10	Mike Mussina	2001–2008	1553	123-72	0	3.88	114	1278	20.3	35.2	12.3	3x GG
11	Dave Righetti	1979–1990	1136.2	74-61	224	3.11	127	940	10.8	23	16.4	ROY, 2x AS

Rank	Player	Years	IP	W-L	SV	ERA	ERA+	SO	WAA	WAR	WPA	Awards
12	Goose Gossage	1978–1983, 1989	533	42-28	151	2.14	179	512	9.3	18.9	19.1	4x AS, WS
13	Herb Pennock	1923–1933	2203.1	162-90	23	3.54	114	700	11.8	32.9	11.5	3x WS
14	Spud Chandler	1937–1947	1485	109-43	6	2.84	132	614	11.5	23.2	19.7	4x AS, MVP, W, 2x ERA, 3x WS
15	Bob Shawkey	1915–1927	2488.2	168-131	27	3.12	117	1163	19.5	43.3	1.0	ERA, 2x WS
16	Allie Reynolds	1947–1954	1700	131-60	40	3.30	115	967	6.6	19.6	16.1	5x AS, ERA, K, 6x WS
17	Eddie Lopat	1948–1955	1497.1	113-59	2	3.19	121	502	5.9	17.5	13.8	AS, ERA, 5x WS
18	Vic Raschi	1946–1953	1537	120-50	3	3.47	111	832	3.7	15.5	17.3	4x AS, K, 6x WS
19	CC Sabathia	2009–2018	1810.2	129-80	0	3.74	115	1593	12.8	29.7	6.9	3x AS, 2x W, WS
20	Russ Ford	1909–1913	1112.2	73-56	3	2.54	127	553	16.5	26.7	NA	
21	Roger Clemens	1999–2003, 2007	1103	83-42	0	4.01	114	1014	10.6	21.2	10.2	2x AS, CY, 2x WS

22	Orlando Hernandez	1998–2004	876.1	61-40	1	3.96	116	703	10.7	19.1	10.2	3x WS
23	David Wells	1997–1998, 2002–2003	851.2	68-28	0	3.90	114	557	9	17.1	7.9	AS, WS
24	Jack Chesbro	1903–1909	1952	128-93	2	2.58	109	313	11.2	28.8	NA	W
25	Tiny Bonham	1940–1946	1176.2	79-50	6	2.73	129	348	10.6	19.4	15.7	2x AS, 2x WS
26	Jimmy Key	1993–1996	604.1	48-23	0	3.68	123	400	7.7	13.5	7.3	2x AS, W, WS
27	Tommy John	1979–1982, 1986–1989	1367	91-60	0	3.59	112	483	7.8	20	9.2	2x AS
28	Sparky Lyle	1972–1978	745.2	57-40	141	2.41	148	454	5.9	15	12.9	3x AS, CY, 2x WS
29	Dellin Betances	2011–2018	381	21-22	36	2.36	178	519	6.8	11.6	10.8	4x AS
30	David Robertson	2008–2014, 2017–2018	498	38-22	53	2.75	155	666	7.3	13.1	15.0	AS, WS

Managers

Rank	Name	Years	Games	Wins	Losses	Win %	Ties	BestFin	WorstFin	Pennants	World Series
1	Joe McCarthy	1931–1946	2348	1460	867	.627	21	1	4	8	7
2	Casey Stengel	1949–1960	1851	1149	696	.623	6	1	3	10	7
3	Miller Huggins	1918–1929	1796	1067	719	.597	10	1	7	6	3
4	Joe Torre	1996–2007	1942	1173	767	.605	2	1	2	6	4
5	Billy Martin	1975–1978, 1979, 1983, 1985, 1988	941	556	385	.591	0	1	5	2	1
6	Joe Girardi	2008–2017	1620	910	710	.562	0	1	4	1	1
7	Ralph Houk	1961–1963, 1966–1973	1757	944	806	.539	7	1	10	3	2
8	Buck Showalter	1992–1995	582	313	268	.539	1	1	4	0	0
9	Bucky Harris	1947–1948	309	191	117	.620	1	1	3	1	1
10	Clark Griffith	1903–1908	807	419	370	.531	18	2	8	0	0

BIBLIOGRAPHY

Amernic, Jerry. *Babe Ruth—A Superstar's Legacy.* Toronto: Wordcraft Communications, 2018.

Anderson, Dave. "Earn Those Pinstripes, Reggie." *New York Times*, May 26, 1977. https://www.nytimes.com/1977/05/26/archives/earn-those-pinstripes-reggie.html.

Anderson, Dave. "Gordon, Overlooked Yankee, Gets His Due." *New York Times*, December 13, 2008. https://www.nytimes.com/2008/12/14/sports/baseball/14anderson.html.

Arangure Jr., Jorge. "Cano Carrying Injury-Riddled Yankees." *New York Times*, April 26, 2013. https://bats.blogs.nytimes.com/2013/04/26/cano-carrying-injury-riddled-yankees.

Araton, Harvey. *Driving Mr. Yogi: Yogi Berra, Ron Guidry, and Baseball's Greatest Gift.* New York: Houghton Mifflin Harcourt, 2012.

Araton, Harvey. "A Fearless Prediction by Yanks' Cano." *New York Times*, October 9, 2010. https://www.nytimes.com/2010/10/10/sports/baseball/10cano.html.

Araton, Harvey. "Jeter's Leadership Carries the Yankees Back Where They Belong." *New York Times*, October 15, 2001. https://www.nytimes.com/2001/10/15/sports/sports-times-jeter-s-leadership-carries-yankees-back-where-they-belong.html.

Axisa, Mike. "A-Rod's Final Game, from a Rain-Soaked Ceremony to 'Overwhelming' Love from Fans." CBS Sports, August 13, 2016. https://www.cbssports.com/mlb/news/a-rods-final-game-from-a-rain-soaked-ceremony-to-overwhelming-love-from-fans.

Baker, Kevin. "The Day It Rained Candy Bars." *New York Times*,
April 12, 1998. https://www.nytimes.com/1998/04/12/sports/
backtalk-the-day-it-rained-candy-bars.html.

Baldassaro, Lawrence. "Joe DiMaggio." SABR Baseball Biography
Project. Accessed September 12, 2018. https://sabr.org/bio
proj/person/a48f1830.

Baldassaro, Lawrence. "Phil Rizzuto." SABR Baseball Biography
Project. Accessed August 13, 2018. https://sabr.org/bioproj/
person/ae85268a.

Baseball Almanac. "Andy Pettitte Quotes." Accessed October 27,
2018. www.baseball-almanac.com/quotes/andy_pettitte_
quotes.shtml.

Baseball Almanac. "Babe Ruth Quotes." Accessed August 23, 2018.
www.baseball-almanac.com/quotes/quoruth.shtml.

Baseball Almanac. "Bill Dickey Quotes." Accessed May 3, 2018.
www.baseball-almanac.com/quotes/quodicky.shtml.

Baseball Almanac. "Joe DiMaggio Quotes." Accessed September 12,
2018. www.baseball-almanac.com/quotes/quodimg.shtml.

Baseball Almanac. "Jorge Posada Quotes." Accessed May 1, 2018.
www.baseball-almanac.com/quotes/jorge_posada_quotes.shtml.

Baseball Almanac. "Lou Gehrig Quotes." Accessed May 16, 2018.
www.baseball-almanac.com/quotes/quogehr.shtml.

Baseball Almanac. "Mickey Mantle Quotes." Accessed September 4,
2018. www.baseball-almanac.com/quotes/quomant.shtml.

Baseball Almanac. "Phil Rizzuto Quotes." Accessed August 14,
2018. www.baseball-almanac.com/quotes/quorizz.shtml.

Baseball Almanac. "Reggie Jackson Quotes." Accessed October 12,
2018. www.baseball-almanac.com/quotes/quojackr.shtml.

Baseball Almanac. "Whitey Ford Quotes." Accessed October 16,
2018. www.baseball-almanac.com/quotes/quoford.shtml.

Baseball Almanac. "Yogi Berra Quotes." Accessed May 3, 2018.
www.baseball-almanac.com/quotes/quoberra.shtml.

Berger, Ralph. "Earle Combs." SABR Baseball Biography Project.
Accessed October 6, 2018. https://sabr.org/bioproj/person/
62bcbcbd.

Berra, Yogi. *The Yogi Book*. New York: Workman Publishing, 1998.

Bishop, Bill. "Casey Stengel." SABR Baseball Biography Project. Accessed November 28, 2018. https://sabr.org/bioproj/person/bd6a83d8.

Borzi, Pat. "In Victory, Rodriguez Hits Home Run No. 400." *New York Times*, June 9, 2005. https://www.nytimes.com/2005/06/09/sports/baseball/in-victory-rodriguez-hits-home-run-no-400.html.

Borzi, Pat. "Rodriguez's 50th and 51st Sustain the Yankees." *New York Times*, September 9, 2007. https://www.nytimes.com/2007/09/09/sports/baseball/09yankees.html.

Brecker, Ryan. "Mike Mussina." SABR Baseball Biography Project. Accessed November 11, 2018. https://sabr.org/bioproj/person/d79f7a98.

Cady, Steve. "Nettles: Fielding Everything but More Pay." *New York Times*, March 11, 1979. https://www.nytimes.com/1979/03/11/archives/nettles-making-case-for-more-pay-nettles-fielding-everything-but.html.

Caldwell, Dave. "Rodriguez's Slap and Run Called a Foul." *New York Times*, October 20, 2004. https://www.nytimes.com/2004/10/20/sports/baseball/rodriguezs-slap-and-run-called-a-foul.html.

Chass, Murray. "Guidry Fans 18 Angels for Yank Mark and Wins No. 11 Without Loss, 4-0." *New York Times*, June 18, 1978. https://www.nytimes.com/1978/06/18/archives/guidry-fans-18-angels-for-yank-mark-and-wins-no-11-without-loss-40.html.

Chass, Murray. "Guidry to Retire As Yanks Spurn Bid." *New York Times*, July 11, 1989. https://www.nytimes.com/1989/07/11/sports/guidry-to-retire-as-yanks-spurn-bid.html.

Chass, Murray. "Guidry to Undergo Shoulder Surgery." *New York Times*, December 2, 1987. https://www.nytimes.com/1987/12/02/sports/guidry-to-undergo-shoulder-surgery.html.

Chass, Murray. "Righetti Pitches First Yankee No-Hitter Since 1956." *New York Times*, July 5, 1983. https://www.nytimes.com/1983/07/05/sports/righetti-pitches-first-yankee-no-hitter-since-1956.html.

Chass, Murray. "Yankees and Rodriguez Receive Approval for Deal." *New York Times*, November 25, 2007. https://www.nytimes .com/2007/11/25/sports/baseball/25arod.html.

Cohen, Alan. "Derek Jeter." In *From Spring Training to Screen Test: Baseball Players Turned Actors*, Bill Nowlin and Rob Edelman, eds., 127–36. Phoenix: Society for American Baseball Research, 2018.

Cohen, Alan. "Joe Torre." SABR Baseball Biography Project. Accessed December 4, 2018. https://sabr.org/bioproj/ person/09351408.

Corbett, Warren. "Red Ruffing." SABR Baseball Biography Project. Accessed October 29, 2018. https://sabr.org/bioproj/person/ 7111866b.

Cramer, Richard Ben. *Joe DiMaggio: The Hero's Life*. New York: Simon & Schuster, 2000.

Curry, Jack. "Friendship of 2 Stars Is Safe After They Were on the Outs." *New York Times*, February 16, 2004. https://www.ny times.com/2004/02/16/sports/baseball-friendship-of-2-stars -is-safe-after-they-were-on-the-outs.html.

Curry, Jack. "Jeter Says the Rodriguez Issue Is Resolved." *New York Times*, February 24, 2004. https://www.nytimes.com/2004/ 02/24/sports/baseball-jeter-says-the-rodriguez-issue-is-re solved.html.

Curry, Jack. "Move to 8th Spot Fails to Wake Up Rodriguez or Shake Up His Teammates." *New York Times*, October 8, 2006. https:// www.nytimes.com/2006/10/08/sports/baseball/08curry.html.

Curry, Jack. "On a Starry Night, Jeter Delivers a 4-for-4 Sparkler." *New York Times*, July 3, 1996. https://www.nytimes.com/1996/ 07/03/sports/baseball-on-a-starry-night-jeter-delivers-a-4-for -4-sparkler.html.

Curry, Jack. "What Yankees Knew About Rodriguez's Injury, and When They Knew It." *New York Times*, March 5, 2009. https:// www.nytimes.com/2009/03/06/sports/baseball/06curry.html.

Curry, Jack. "Williams Passes Mentor." *New York Times*, August 15, 2002. https://www.nytimes.com/2002/08/15/sports/baseball -williams-passes-mentor.html.

Curry, Jack, and Tyler Kepner. "For Rodriguez and Yankees, It's All but Over." *New York Times*, October 29, 2007. https://www.ny times.com/2007/10/29/sports/baseball/29arod.html.

Daley, Arthur. "Down Memory Lane with the Babe." *New York Times*, August 18, 1948. https://www.nytimes.com/1948/08/ 18/archives/sports-of-the-times-down-memory-lane-with -the-babe.html.

Daley, Arthur. "End of a Career." *New York Times*, December 20, 1950. https://www.nytimes.com/1950/12/20/archives/sports -of-the-times-end-of-a-career-final-flourish-the-first.html.

Daley, Arthur. "The Rediscovery of Tommy Henrich." *New York Times*, November 3, 1971. https://www.nytimes.com/1971/ 11/03/archives/the-rediscovery-of-tommy-henrich.html.

Dicker, Ron. "Rodriguez and Varitek Lead List Of Eight Suspended for Fight." *New York Times*, July 30, 2004. https://www.nytimes .com/2004/07/30/sports/baseball-rodriguez-and-varitek-lead -list-of-eight-suspended-for-fight.html.

Dominiak, Scott. "Jorge Posada." In *Puerto Rico and Baseball*, Bill Nowlin and Edwin Fernandez, eds., 288–92. Phoenix: Society for American Baseball Research, 2017.

Durso, Joseph. "Yanks 4-2 Victors on Guidry's 5-Hitter." *New York Times*, September 14, 1977. https://www.nytimes.com/1977/ 09/14/archives/yanks-42-victors-on-guidrys-5hitter-55269 -see-rivers-beat-red-sox.html.

Edelman, Rob. "Bernie Williams." In *Puerto Rico and Baseball*, Bill Nowlin and Edwin Fernandez, eds., 372–80. Phoenix: Society for American Baseball Research, 2017.

Edelman, Rob. "Tommy Henrich." SABR Baseball Biography Project. Accessed October 8, 2018. https://sabr.org/bioproj/ person/165bef13.

Eder, Steve. "Rodriguez Walks Out of Hearing and Pleads Case on Radio." *New York Times*, November 20, 2013. https://www.ny times.com/2013/11/21/sports/baseball/rodriguez-walks-out -of-grievance-hearing.html.

Feinstein, John. *Living on the Black: Two Pitchers, Two Teams, One Season to Remember*. New York: Little, Brown, 2008.

Frommer, Harvey. *Five O'Clock Lightning: Babe Ruth, Lou Gehrig and the Greatest Team in Baseball, the 1927 New York Yankees*. Hoboken, NJ: John Wiley & Sons, 2008.

Gallagher, Mark, and Walter LeConte. *The Yankee Encyclopedia*. 5th ed. New York: Sports Publishing, 2001.

Golenbock, Peter. *Dynasty: The New York Yankees, 1949–1964*. New York: Dover Publications, 2010.

Gomez, Verona, and Lawrence Goldstone. *Lefty: An American Odyssey*. New York: Ballantine Books, 2012.

Greene, Nelson "Chip." "Charlie Keller." SABR Baseball Biography Project. Accessed September 20, 2018. https://sabr.org/bio proj/person/56ec907f.

Griffith, Nancy Snell. "Willie Randolph." SABR Baseball Biography Project. Accessed June 12, 2018. https://sabr.org/bioproj/ person/efd87953.

Gross, Jane. "Yanks Won't Start Mattingly." *New York Times*, March 13, 1984. https://www.nytimes.com/1984/03/13/sports/yanks -won-t-start-mattingly.html.

Hanlon, Greg. "The Many Crimes of Mel Hall." SB Nation, July 15, 2014. https://www.sbnation.com/2014/7/15/5883593/the-many -crimes-of-mel-hall.

Hoch, Bryan. "Jeter Makes Long Strides at Shortstop." MLB.com, July 28, 2009. http://mlb.mlb.com/players/jeter_derek/news/ article.jsp?story=07282009_news.

Jaffe, Jay. "Mike Mussina Won't Get Into the Hall of Fame in 2018, but He's Building Toward Election." *Sports Illustrated*, December 5, 2017. https://www.si.com/mlb/2017/12/05/ mike-mussina-hall-of-fame-election-2018.

James, Bill. *The New Bill James Historical Baseball Abstract*. New York: Free Press, 2001.

James, Bill. *The Politics of Glory*. New York: Macmillan, 1994.

James, Bill, and Rob Neyer. *The Neyer/James Guide to Pitchers: An Historical Compendium of Pitching, Pitchers, and Pitches*. New York: Simon & Schuster, 2004.

Keenan, Jimmy, and Frank Russo. "Billy Martin." SABR Baseball Biography Project. Accessed December 7, 2018. https://sabr .org/bioproj/person/59c5010b.

Keenan, Jimmy, and Frank Russo. "Thurman Munson." SABR Baseball Biography Project. Accessed May 3, 2018. https://sabr.org/ bioproj/person/53cf0c87.

Kepner, Tyler. "An Appreciation of Mike Mussina." *New York Times*, November 19, 2008. https://bats.blogs.nytimes.com/2008/11/ 19/an-appreciation-of-mike-mussina.

Kepner, Tyler. "Bowa Hopes Canó's Errors Are Part of Maturing." *New York Times*, May 20, 2007. https://www.nytimes.com/ 2007/05/20/sports/baseball/20yankees.html.

Kepner, Tyler. "Day Honoring Yankees Stars of Past Ends with an Old-Fashioned Rout." *New York Times*, June 20, 2015. https:// www.nytimes.com/2015/06/21/sports/baseball/day-honoring -yankees-stars-of-past-ends-with-an-old-fashioned-rout.html.

Kepner, Tyler. "Derek Jeter Takes In, and Provides, a Memorable Final View at Shortstop." *New York Times*, September 27, 2014. https://www.nytimes.com/2014/09/27/sports/baseball/ derek-jeters-home-farewell-a-sight-to-behold.html.

Kepner, Tyler. "Girardi Wants to Make Sure That He Teaches Canó a Lesson." *New York Times*, September 15, 2008. https://www .nytimes.com/2008/09/16/sports/baseball/16pins.html.

Kepner, Tyler. "Jeter Gives Another Clinic in Leadership." *New York Times*, July 3, 2004. https://www.nytimes.com/2004/07/03/ sports/baseball-jeter-gives-another-clinic-in-leadership.html.

Kepner, Tyler. "A Magic Number by Rodriguez: 10 R.B.I." *New York Times*, April 27, 2005. https://www.nytimes.com/2005/04/27/ sports/baseball/a-magic-number-by-rodriguez-10-rbi.html.

Kepner, Tyler. "Now Batting, the Best Deal the Yankees Never Made." *New York Times*, March 2, 2008. https://www.nytimes.com/2008/03/02/sports/baseball/02yankees.html.

Kepner, Tyler. "Rodriguez Is Thriving in Second Season with Yanks." *New York Times*, September 6, 2005. https://www.nytimes.com/2005/09/06/sports/baseball/rodriguez-is-thriving-in-second-season-with-yanks.html.

Kepner, Tyler. "Yankees Said to Be Closing Deal to Obtain Rangers' Rodriguez." *New York Times*, February 15, 2004. https://www.nytimes.com/2004/02/15/nyregion/yankees-said-to-be-closing-deal-to-obtain-rangers-rodriguez.html.

Kepner, Tyler. "Yanks' Cano Playing as If He Belongs." *New York Times*, July 24, 2005. https://www.nytimes.com/2005/07/24/sports/baseball/yanks-cano-playing-as-if-he-belongs.html.

Klopsis, Nick. "56 Years Later, Don Larsen and Yogi Berra Reminisce About Perfect Game." *Newsday*, October 8, 2012. https://www.newsday.com/sports/baseball/yankees/56-years-later-don-larsen-and-yogi-berra-reminisce-about-perfect-game-1.4089156.

Koppett, Leonard. *A Thinking Man's Guide to Baseball*. New York: Dutton, 1967.

Krieger, Tara. "David Cone." SABR Baseball Biography Project. Accessed November 8, 2018. https://sabr.org/bioproj/person/191828e7.

Lally, Richard. *Bombers: An Oral History of the New York Yankees*. New York: Crown Publishers, 2002.

Leavengood, Ted. "Reggie Jackson." SABR Baseball Biography Project. Accessed October 11, 2018. https://sabr.org/bioproj/person/365acf13.

Levitt, Daniel R. "Ed Barrow." SABR Baseball Biography Project. Accessed December 12, 2018. https://sabr.org/bioproj/person/c9fdbace.

Madden, Bill, Michael O'Keeffe, Christian Red, and Teri Thompson. "Yankees' Alex Rodriguez Refuses to Pay Anthony Bosch, Who Then Cuts Deal to Help MLB." *New York Daily News*,

June 5, 2013. www.nydailynews.com/sports/i-team/a-rod
-refuses-pay-bosch-cuts-deal-mlb-article-1.1364586#.

Mahler, Jonathan. *Ladies and Gentlemen, The Bronx is Burning: 1977,
Baseball, Politics, and the Battle for the Soul of a City*. New York:
Picador, 2005.

Martinez, Pedro. "Pedro Martinez Talks Jorge Posada." YouTube
video, 1:34. Posted by user "SNY," January 8, 2015. https://
www.youtube.com/watch?v=W6dhhceBY-4.

McMurray, John. "Joe McCarthy." SABR Baseball Biography Project.
Accessed November 26, 2018. https://sabr.org/bioproj/person/
2c77f933.

Olney, Buster. "All-Star? Jeter Stats Are All-World." *New York
Times*, July 5, 1999. https://www.nytimes.com/1999/07/05/
sports/baseball-all-star-jeter-stats-are-all-world.html.

Pepe, Phil. *The Yankees: An Authorized History of the New York Yankees*. 3rd ed. Dallas: Taylor Publishing, 1998.

Petchesky, Barry. "10 Years of Newspapers Declaring That Mariano
Rivera Is Too Old." *Deadspin*, April 12, 2012. https://deadspin
.com/5901123/10-years-of-newspapers-declaring-that-mariano
-rivera-is-too-old.

Picker, David. "Young Yankee Has a Night to Remember." *New York
Times*, May 28, 2005. https://www.nytimes.com/2005/05/28/
sports/baseball/young-yankee-has-a-night-to-remember.html.

Posnanski, Joe. "Talkin' Matt Wieters and the Concept of Hype,
with Bill James." *Sports Illustrated*, June 1, 2009. https://www
.si.com/more-sports/2009/06/01/james-wieters.

Prato, Greg. *Just Out of Reach: The 1980s New York Yankees*. New
York: CreateSpace Independent Publishing Platform, 2014.

Ray, James Lincoln. "Don Mattingly." SABR Baseball Biography
Project. Accessed May 30, 2018. https://sabr.org/bioproj/
person/2242d2ed.

Ray, James Lincoln. "Lou Gehrig." SABR Baseball Biography Project. Accessed May 18, 2018. https://sabr.org/bioproj/person/
ccdffd4c.

Ray, James Lincoln. "Mickey Mantle." SABR Baseball Biography Project. Accessed September 5, 2018. https://sabr.org/bioproj/person/61e4590a.

Ray, James Lincoln. "Roy White." SABR Baseball Biography Project. Accessed October 4, 2018. https://sabr.org/bioproj/person/b0667516.

Rivera, Mariano, and Wayne Coffey. *The Closer: My Story*. New York: Little, Brown, 2014.

Roberts, Randy, and Johnny Smith. *A Season in the Sun: The Rise of Mickey Mantle*. New York: Basic Books, 2018.

Rogers III, C. Paul. "Lefty Gomez." SABR Baseball Biography Project. Accessed October 21, 2018. https://sabr.org/bioproj/person/94f0b0a4#sdendnote65anc.

Rogers III, C. Paul. "Whitey Ford." SABR Baseball Biography Project. Accessed October 15, 2018. https://sabr.org/bioproj/person/fca49b7c.

Rogers, Thomas. "Bill Dickey, the Yankee Catcher and Hall of Famer, Dies at 86." *New York Times*, November 13, 1993. https://www.nytimes.com/1993/11/13/obituaries/bill-dickey-the-yankee-catcher-and-hall-of-famer-dies-at-86.html.

Sandomir, Richard. "Phil Rizzuto, Yankees Shortstop, Dies at 89." *New York Times*, August 14, 2007. https://www.nytimes.com/2007/08/14/sports/baseball/14cnd-rizzuto.html.

Schmidt, Michael S. "Rodriguez Said to Test Positive in 2003." *New York Times*, February 7, 2009. https://www.nytimes.com/2009/02/08/sports/baseball/08arod.html.

Sherman, Joel. *Birth of a Dynasty: Behind the Pinstripes with the 1996 Yankees*. Emmaus, PA: Rodale, 2006.

Smith, Claire. "Rivera Completes 'No-Hitter' in Victory." *New York Times*, April 29, 1996. https://www.nytimes.com/1996/04/29/sports/baseball-rivera-completes-no-hitter-in-victory.html.

Sports Reference LLC. Baseball-Reference.com—Major League Statistics and Information. https://www.baseball-reference.com/. 2018.

Steinberg, Steve. "Miller Huggins." SABR Baseball Biography Project. Accessed December 1, 2018. https://sabr.org/bioproj/person/7b65e9fa.

Tango, Tom M., Mitchel G. Lichtman, and Andrew E. Dolphin. *The Book: Playing the Percentages in Baseball.* TMA Press, 2006.

Tofel, Richard J. *A Legend in the Making: The New York Yankees in 1939.* Chicago: Ivan R. Dee, 2002.

Torre, Joe, and Tom Verducci. *The Yankee Years.* New York: Doubleday, 2009.

Tusa C, Alfonso L. "Rich Gossage." SABR Baseball Biography Project. Accessed November 22, 2018. https://sabr.org/bioproj/person/0871f3e2.

Vecsey, George. "Rodriguez Offers Apology, but Is It the Whole Truth?" *New York Times,* February 9, 2009. https://www.nytimes.com/2009/02/10/sports/baseball/10george.html.

Verducci, Tom. "Mariano Saves." *Sports Illustrated,* October 5, 2009. https://www.si.com/vault/2009/10/05/105863331/mariano-saves.

Verducci, Tom. "The M&M Boys: Plain and Peanut." *Sports Illustrated,* July 18, 1994. https://www.si.com/vault/1994/07/18/106786720/the-mm-boys-plain-and-peanut.

Waldstein, David. "Alex Rodriguez Offers Apology in Meeting with Yankees." *New York Times,* February 10, 2015. https://www.nytimes.com/2015/02/11/sports/baseball/alex-rodriguez-meets-with-yankees-executives-to-clear-the-air.html.

Waldstein, David. "A Graceful Swing That Bears Resemblance to Federer's." *New York Times,* October 6, 2012. https://www.nytimes.com/2012/10/07/sports/baseball/swing-of-yankees-cano-bears-resemblance-to-federers.html.

Waldstein, David. "Rodriguez Is Expected to Play While Appealing Suspension." *New York Times,* August 4, 2013. https://www.nytimes.com/2013/08/05/sports/baseball/rodriguez-is-expected-to-play-while-appealing-suspension.html.

Wancho, Joseph. "Bill Dickey." SABR Baseball Biography Project. Accessed May 3, 2018. https://sabr.org/bioproj/person/25ce33d8.

Wancho, Joseph. "Dave Righetti." SABR Baseball Biography Project. Accessed November 18, 2018. https://sabr.org/bioproj/person/a699d5f8.

Wancho, Joseph. "Graig Nettles." SABR Baseball Biography Project. Accessed July 11, 2018. https://sabr.org/bioproj/person/516e763c.

Wancho, Joseph. "Joe Gordon." SABR Baseball Biography Project. Accessed June 25, 2018. https://sabr.org/bioproj/person/4d6bb7cb.

Williams, Dave. "Yogi Berra." SABR Baseball Biography Project. Accessed May 3, 2018. https://sabr.org/bioproj/person/a4d43fa1.

Wolf, Gregory H. "Mel Stottlemyre." SABR Baseball Biography Project. Accessed November 3, 2018. https://sabr.org/bioproj/person/b3f6e8d6.

Wolf, Gregory H. "Waite Hoyt." SABR Baseball Biography Project. Accessed November 2, 2018. https://sabr.org/bioproj/person/5fca5ae6.

Wood, Allan. "Babe Ruth." SABR Baseball Biography Project. Accessed August 23, 2018. https://sabr.org/bioproj/person/9dcdd01c.

Zinser, Lynn. "Rodriguez Is Youngest to Reach 500 Home Runs." *New York Times*, August 4, 2007. https://www.nytimes.com/2007/08/04/sports/baseball/04cnd-yankees.html.

All of the statistics used for rankings and reported within this book were obtained from the Baseball Reference website (baseball-reference.com). The in-depth descriptions found there of the advanced metrics referenced in this book are highly recommended reading.